"OTHER PEOPLE'S DIASPORAS"

Irish Studies

James MacKillop, *Series Editor*

"OTHER PEOPLE'S DIASPORAS"

Negotiating Race in Contemporary
Irish and Irish American Culture

SINÉAD MOYNIHAN

Syracuse University Press

∞ The paper used in this publication meets the minimum requirements
of the American National Standard for Information Sciences—Permanence
of Paper for Printed Library Materials, ANSI Z39.48-1992.

For a listing of books published and distributed by Syracuse University Press,
visit our website at SyracuseUniversityPress.syr.edu.

ISBN: 978-0-8156-3310-5

Library of Congress Cataloging-in-Publication Data

Moynihan, Sinéad.

    "Other people's diasporas" : negotiating race in contemporary Irish
and Irish American culture / Sinéad Moynihan. — First edition.

        pages cm. — (Irish studies)

    Includes bibliographical references and index.

    ISBN 978-0-8156-3310-5 (cloth : alkaline paper) 1. Ireland—Intellectual life.
2. Irish Americans—Intellectual life.   3. Race in literature.   4. Race in motion
pictures.   5. Immigrants in literature.   6. Immigrants in motion pictures.
7. Whites—Race identity—Ireland.   8. Blacks—Race identity—Ireland.   9. Irish
Americans—Race identity.   10. African Americans—Race identity.   I. Title.

    DA926.R22M68 2013

    820.9'35509415—dc23   2013003859

Contents

Acknowledgments

I wish to express my gratitude to the Leverhulme Trust for awarding me the Early Career Fellowship that enabled me to research and write this book. In July 2007, when the project was still in its nascent stage, I took part in the Clinton Institute for American Studies Summer School at University College Dublin. I am grateful to Professor Werner Sollors and my fellow participants for their helpful comments and questions.

As a Leverhulme Fellow, I was attached to the School of American and Canadian Studies at the University of Nottingham, where I was supported by both academic and administrative members of staff. In particular, I would like to thank Sharon Monteith, Dave Murray, Ruth Maxey, John Fagg, Vivien Miller, Gillian Roberts, Judie Newman, Celeste-Marie Bernier, Ann McQueen, and Jean Darnbrough for their help. Thanks also to Jim Moran in the Department of English at Nottingham and Deirdre O'Byrne at the University of Loughborough.

The meetings of the Irish Association for American Studies and the American Conference for Irish Studies were important forums for testing the Irish/American parameters of the project. Conversations with Claire Bracken, Philip Coleman, Adam Kelly, Liam Kennedy, Pádraig Kirwan, Piaras Mac Éinrí, Aoileann Ní Éigeartaigh, Tina O'Toole, and Aaron Thornburg at these meetings were invaluable.

Writing a book about contemporary Ireland while residing outside Ireland presents certain challenges. I was assisted greatly in this process by Bairbre Moynihan, who recorded relevant television programs on my behalf, and Jennifer O'Sullivan, who was always alert to newspaper articles that would be of interest to me.

I am grateful to Des Bishop for granting permission to reproduce material from *Des Bishop Live, Des Bishop: Live at Vicar St., In the Name of the Fada, The Des Bishop Work Experience, Stop You're Killing Me 2,* and *Tongues.*

Portions of chapter 2 appeared as "Ships in Motion: Crossing the Black and Green Atlantics in Joseph O'Connor's *Star of the Sea,*" *Symbiosis* 12, no. 1 (2008): 41–58; and "'War Is Not a Map': Irish America, Transnationalism, and Joseph O'Connor's *Redemption Falls,*" *Comparative American Studies* 6, no. 4 (2008): 358–73 (http://www.maney.co.uk/journals/cas and www.ingentaconnect.com/content/maney/cas). Portions of chapters 4 and 5 appeared, respectively, as "Stand(ing) Up for the Immigrants: The Work of Comedian Des Bishop," *Irish Studies Review* 16, no. 4 (2008): 403–13; and "Transnational 'Tragic Mulatto': Phil Lynott, *The Nephew,* and Mixed Race Irishness," *International Review of Irish Culture* (2009): 60–77. I thank the anonymous readers for their advice and feedback, and I am grateful to the publishers for granting permission to reproduce this material here.

Also appearing are excerpts from:

Star of the Sea and *Redemption Falls* by Joseph O'Connor, reprinted by permission of Random House.

The Deportees and Other Stories by Roddy Doyle, copyright © by Roddy Doyle, reprinted by permission of Viking Penguin, a division of Penguin Group (USA) Inc.; permission also granted by Random House UK Ltd. and by John Sutton Management.

Landing copyright © by Emma Donaghue, reprinted by permission of Houghton Mifflin Harcourt Publishing Company, all rights reserved, and by permission of CDLA on behalf of Emma Donoghue.

"Other People's Diasporas"

Introduction

Other People's Diasporas

> Yet what happens when *other people's diasporas* converge on
> the homeland of a diasporic people?
> —STEVE GARNER, *Racism in the Irish
> Experience* (2004)

> I'm going to study writing that questions the *we* in *we're
> fuckin' great*.
> —RODDY DOYLE, "Home to Harlem" (2004)

On July 21, 2009, the *Irish Times* editorial was concerned with
two issues: the changing face of migration and the death of Frank
McCourt, who had passed away two days previously. In the first
item, reflecting on a three-part series by migration correspondent
Ruadhán Mac Cormaic, editor Geraldine Kennedy mused on the
global recession and whether "this period will mark a reversal of
these large-scale migrations and see a return movement by most
workers," including those living in Ireland (2009a, 17). In the second, she noted McCourt's contribution to "the literature of emigration" (2009b, 17). For me, the juxtaposition of these two news
items begged connections that were not made. What of the fact that
McCourt's best-known work, *Angela's Ashes* (1996), was itself a
narrative of return migration, the story of a family obliged to leave
the United States during the Great Depression and return to Ireland?
Like the migrants of the first piece, the McCourts were "stranded
between unemployment in their new homes or their old ones." What

1

of the fact that, in the first piece, the "poorer" parts of the world to which Kennedy refers are Latin America, central and eastern Europe, and southern Asia, whereas in the second, it is McCourt's Limerick of the 1930s and 1940s? I draw out these connections because the premise of this book is that one of the most palpable trends in Irish culture of the Celtic Tiger years was the juxtaposition, literal or implied, of narratives of Irish *emigration* to the United States with those of *immigration* to Ireland.

In 1996, after exporting its own population for generations, Ireland became a country of net immigration, which peaked at 71,800 in the year ending April 2006 (Garner 2004, 50; "Population and Migration Estimates" 2008, 2). The 2006 census also found that 10 percent of Ireland's population was born outside the state.[1] As Steve Garner notes, "In absolute numbers, returning Irish emigrants outnumber EU migrants, who outnumber non-EU migrants, who in turn outnumber asylum-seekers. When we say 'immigration' in Ireland, only some of these groups are really being problematised" (2007b, 119). This book is particularly concerned with representations, direct or oblique, of white Irish and Irish American interactions with one of those groups deemed problematic: African immigrants. The turnaround in Ireland's migration pattern may be directly linked to the reversal in its economic fortunes: in 1988, according to the *Economist,* Ireland was the "poorest of the rich" countries (Gibbons 2005b, 555); by 1997 it was headlined "The Celtic Tiger: Europe's Shining Light" (O'Hearn 2000, 67). Over this period, then, it became clear that as well as luring back its own diasporic workforce, the Celtic Tiger economy was also attracting "other people's diasporas" to Ireland. Garner asks, "Yet what happens when *other people's diasporas* converge on the homeland of a diasporic people?" (2004,

---

1. The 2006 census found that Ireland's population was 4,239,848, of which 420,000 were born outside the state, an increase of 87 percent on the 224,000 non-Irish nationals recorded in the 2002 census ("Census 2006: Principal Demographic Results" 2007, 25, 37).

159). It is the contention of this book that (re)imagining Irish diasporic experience in the United States in various ways—particularly as it relates to Irish interactions with African Americans—became absolutely central to representations of multicultural Ireland during the Celtic Tiger years.

One of the ways in which this tendency was realized is that Irish and Irish American artists became increasingly interested in representing "key moments" in the history of US racial and ethnic relations as a means of coming to terms with debates on race and immigration in contemporary Ireland: Frederick Douglass's 1845 visit to Ireland and his relationship with Daniel O'Connell (Donal O'Kelly's "*The Cambria*" [2005]), the Great Famine (Joseph O'Connor's *Star of the Sea* [2002]), the American Civil War (O'Connor's *Redemption Falls* [2007]), the civil rights era (Roddy Doyle's story "Guess Who's Coming for the Dinner," which was subsequently adapted into a play [2000–2001] and Sinéad Moriarty's *Whose Life Is It Anyway?* [2008]), and 9/11 (Jim Sheridan's *In America* [2003]). A second way in which such debates became configured was through cultural versions of what Garner terms the "historical duty" argument—in which "Irish people have been (and still are) immigrants elsewhere. Therefore today they should empathise, and treat others in that position with respect and welcome" (2004, 159). In the context of the "historical duty" argument, the trope of the "returned Yank," as a reminder of Ireland's far-flung diaspora, acquired special resonance (Des Bishop's stand-up comedy, Ronan Noone's *The Blowin of Baile Gall* [2002], Hill Harper's character in *The Nephew* [1998]). All of these motifs—key moments, historical duty, returned Yank—became perceptible in much Irish and Irish American popular culture.

This point is not to suggest that "race" never figured in Irish culture, or that the Irish had not encountered people of color in Ireland, prior to the 1990s. In fact, as John Brannigan argues, "racial ideologies and racist practices have not only undergirded the Irish state and its defining cultural institutions and policies, often in muted and insidious forms, but have been central to the ways in which official discourses of 'Irishness' have been negotiated and contested in the cultural sphere" (2009, 5). The corollary to the view that Ireland was homogeneous prior to the 1990s, that racism was not a problem in Ireland before the mid-1990s, is tantamount to declaring that "racism has increased because the number of immigrants has increased," a rationalization, according to Bill Rolston and Michael Shannon, that involves "switching the blame from the behaviour of the host society to the single fact of the emigrants' presence" (2002, 2). Nonetheless, Garner has found, after comparing attitudinal surveys from the 1970s to 2001, that in the 1970s, "the greatest hostility toward a racialised minority was expressed in regard to the Travellers" whereas, by 1997, "blacks" had joined Travellers and Roma people as the most frequent targets of discrimination (2004, 60, 67). Undoubtedly, racial tension began to rise during the Celtic Tiger years, and the cultural examples I have selected that engage with this phenomenon date from 1998 to 2008.[2]

As Ronit Lentin has argued, the category of "non-Irish nationals"—whether they are eastern Europeans from states not in the European Economic Area (EEA), Asians, or Africans—marks "a new racialization of Irishness: whatever these migrants are, they are definitely 'not Irish'" (2007, 436). In other words, in contemporary Ireland, migrants are racialized and, indeed, become victims of racial abuse, regardless of the color of their skin. I do not wish to imply—in the Irish context, or any other—that the term *race* corresponds to "nonwhite." To do so would be to participate in the very process by which whiteness derives its power and privilege: by promoting itself as normative and nonraced. Nonetheless, I focus here on black immigrants to Ireland, although they represent less than 1 percent of the population, because they became the locus of some of the most

2. As Steve Garner observes, "Ireland presents itself as something of a countercase in that increasing hostility towards Others has been identified in the midst of rapid economic growth and political stability." Now that the Irish economy has entered into a downturn, the prospects for race relations are even more worrying (2007b, 110).

potent analogies circulating in liberal discourse in Irish and trans-atlantic culture: contemporary African immigrant and nineteenth-century Irish Famine refugee, contemporary African immigrant and nineteenth-century African American slave, contemporary African immigrant and contemporary "undocumented" Irish worker in the United States.[3] Put another way, white Irish-black encounters have a great deal of currency in historical and contemporary culture and society on both sides of the Atlantic.

Before the 1990s, Declan Kiberd suggests, Irish liberal intellectuals "viewed Irish racism as a largely North American phenomenon" by which the Irish in Ireland were unaffected. After all, "Bob Geldof invoked a communal memory of famine in helping to make his own people the largest per capita contributors to Third World relief in Live Aid," and in *Dancing at Lughnasa* (1990), Brian Friel "explored analogies between Ugandan culture and the harvest festivals of Donegal" (Longley and Kiberd 2001, 48). However, recent developments in Ireland raise unsettling questions about this comfortable narrative of Irish-black relations in the past and, of course, in the present. Indeed, Garner titles a chapter of his book *Racism in the Irish Experience* "The 'Filthy Aristocracy of Skin': Becoming White in the USA" because "it emphasizes the Janus-faced nature of the relationship between Irish racialisation and the racialisation of Others by the Irish" (2004, 91).

Crucial to this project, then, is the history of African American and Irish relations in the United States, a topic that has proven highly contentious among American intellectual and labor historians, on the one hand, and scholars of Irish studies, on the other. Notably, the

---

3. Representations of eastern European immigrants to Ireland—for example, in John Carney's film *Once* (2007) or Paul Meade's play *Mushroom* (2007)—will therefore not feature, except anecdotally. The 2006 census figures show that 1 percent of the Irish population is black, but, of course, this number comprises Irish-born black people whose presence is not deemed so problematic—though they still report being victims of racial abuse—as the presence of African immigrants to Ireland ("Census 2006: Principal Demographic Results" 2007, 27).

thesis of Noel Ignatiev's *How the Irish Became White* (1995)—that the Famine Irish generation, who were competing with free African Americans for jobs in northern cities in the mid-nineteenth century and were considered, at best, ambiguous in terms of their racial identity, distanced themselves from African Americans in order to pursue their own claims to whiteness—occasioned heated academic debate regarding the degree of agency that may be attributed to Irish emigrants to the United States in the mid-nineteenth century. For Lauren Onkey, the controversy over Ignatiev's book indicates the high stakes involved in the study of African American and Irish relations because "both conservative 'Hibernophiles,' who want to celebrate Irishness and who in some ways cherish the definition of the Irish Americans as oppressed, and nationalists, who value and romanticize Irish-black connections because of what such connections suggest about Northern Ireland, can be hostile to the argument that the Irish contributed to anyone else's oppression in America" (1999, n.p.). If, in the mid-1990s, the whitening Irish and their treatment of African Americans a century and a half previously became a fraught topic in American academe, in Ireland at the same historical moment, ordinary people were on the threshold of demographic shifts that many had probably never imagined possible and would test supposed Irish-black solidarity to its limits.

I should state from the outset that I am only indirectly concerned with the artistic output of recent immigrants to Ireland, of which there are increasing and varied examples. Bisi Adigun's theater company, Arambe Productions, is a vibrant initiative committed to providing "members of Ireland's African communities the unique opportunity to express themselves through the art of theatre" ("About Arambe"). Most notably, Arambe commissioned a reworked version of J. M. Synge's *Playboy of the Western World*—coadapted by Adigun and Roddy Doyle—for the 2007 Dublin Theatre Festival.[4] At University

---

4. This adaptation has not been without controversy, however. Reviews of its original production in September 2007 were mixed, and when it returned to the

College Dublin, meanwhile, the Women Writers in the New Ireland Network circulates information, organizes seminars, and provides a forum dialogue for and between women writers from migrant and new communities. *Metro Éireann,* a newspaper founded by Nigerian journalists Abel Ugba and Chinedu Onyejelem in April 2000, to which Roddy Doyle has contributed several short stories to be discussed in chapter 2, offers an annual writing award for those born outside Ireland or come from immigrant backgrounds. Polish-born painter Marta Wakula Mac and Nigerian sculptor Mike Ogaga Owairu have had their work exhibited at the National Gallery of Ireland and the Crow Gallery, respectively (Mac Cormaic 2007a, 15). I expect that all this work—and more, of which I am doubtless unaware—is providing and will provide fruitful avenues for current and future scholarly inquiry.[5]

I am more interested in the ways in which questions of race, immigration, and citizenship have figured in mainstream—which inevitably means the work of those from white, Irish, or Irish diasporic, settled backgrounds—Irish and Irish American culture. White people, after all, make up 95 percent of Ireland's population, and they set the agenda for what is represented, discussed, and circulated in literature, the media, and popular culture (Lentin 2007, 436). Joseph O'Connor and Roddy Doyle are best-selling, award-winning international authors. American-born Des Bishop is a popular stand-up comedian who also regularly appears on RTÉ television in current affairs shows (*Questions and Answers*), chat shows (*Tubridy Tonight, The Late Late Show*) and in his own documentaries, *The Des Bishop Work Experience* (2003), *Joy in the Hood* (2006), and *In the Name of the Fada* (2008). He has also performed to (predominantly white Irish emigrant) audiences in the United States.

Abbey for a second run in December 2008, the *Evening Herald* reported that Arambe was suing both Doyle and the Abbey for breach of contract (Phelan 2008, n.p.).

5. Jason King has made some initial observations on what he terms "Irish multicultural fiction" (2009, 159–77). On Arambe, see Weitz 2009, 225–36.

Donal O'Kelly is probably best known for his screen-acting roles in the adaptation of Roddy Doyle's *The Van* (Stephen Frears, 1996) and in *Kings* (Tom Collins, 2007), the award-winning screen version of Jimmy Murphy's play *The Kings of the Kilburn High Road* (2001). However, he is also a prolific playwright in his own right whose work has always been politically grounded, and he is particularly concerned with the challenges faced by asylum seekers and refugees. Ronan Noone, on the other hand, is familiar to theatergoers in the United States but virtually unknown in Ireland. Jim Sheridan, along with Neil Jordan, is probably one of Ireland's two most recognizable directors, both nationally and internationally. His films have consistently been nominated for Academy Awards, and, apart from his two most recent films as director, *Get Rich or Die Tryin'* (2005) and *Brothers* (2009), all have foregrounded Irish themes. Irish-born Pierce Brosnan, whose production company, Irish Dreamtime, is responsible for *The Nephew,* is also recognizable to global audiences, especially for his role as James Bond. In each of the five chapters that follow, then, I am concerned with cultural production that foregrounds white Irish interaction with black subjects, cultural production that either refers directly to contemporary African immigration to Ireland (Roddy Doyle's short stories, Des Bishop's comedy, the plays of Ronan Noone and Donal O'Kelly) or, I maintain, *allegorizes* or comments obliquely on African immigration to Ireland (Joseph O'Connor's two novels, the films *In America* and *The Nephew*), in all three cases by thematizing migration between Ireland and the United States.

Ireland's changing demographics are the subject of a great deal of scholarly inquiry in the fields of sociology, geography, economics, and law (Chan; Fanning; Loyal; Mac Éinrí; McVeigh), at the forefront of which is the work of the aforementioned Garner and Lentin. Both scholars have identified the 2004 referendum on Irish citizenship, in particular, as a turning point in the racialization of the Irish State, and the referendum also forms an important backdrop for this project. However, no existing study investigates Irish and Irish American *literature and culture* in the light of Ireland's changing demographics. One of the likely reasons for this is the historical reluctance of Irish studies scholars to engage with issues of race. A number of the annual conferences of the major international Irish studies organizations have, in recent years, taken race and immigration either explicitly or implicitly as their theme. For instance, the theme for the 2008 American Conference for Irish Studies (ACIS) was "Ireland: Arrivals and Departures." The theme of the 2007 conference of the British Association for Irish Studies was "New Irelands," while the Irish Association for the Study of Irish Literatures (IASIL) took "Varieties of Irishness" as its theme. Despite these prompts, few papers in the conferences I attended—New England ACIS in 2007, Southern Regional ACIS in 2008, IASIL in 2008, and ACIS in 2009—addressed what are clearly some of the most pressing issues in Irish studies today. Only the most recent of these—ACIS 2009's "New Irish, Old Ireland: 'The Same People Living in the Same Place,'" a reference to Leopold Bloom's famous definition of the nation in *Ulysses* (1922)—acknowledged the significance of immigration in contemporary Irish society and culture (Joyce 1922, 329). Its program, featuring two panels devoted to Roddy Doyle's multicultural writings and a roundtable discussion on immigration, suggests that scholars are finally showing a willingness to consider contemporary Irish literature and culture in the context of demographic shifts that have taken place over the past fifteen years.

Terminology

Ireland

In my opening remarks, I deployed several terms that need to be unpacked. The first, and most contentious of these is, of course, *Ireland* itself. The sociohistorical phenomena I discuss here—that 10 percent of the population is foreign born, the Celtic Tiger, the Citizenship Referendum—all refer to the Republic of Ireland. This study, therefore, centers upon literature and culture that has emerged from the *Republic* of Ireland (and the United States). However, I use the shorthand *Ireland* throughout because it is less unwieldy.

Non-

I have already deployed this suffix several times—nonwhite; non-Irish; non-EU; non-EEA—and it is a problematic one, as Richard Dyer points out, "because of its negativity" (1999, 11). It suggests that white, Irish, and EU are a standard that those nonwhite, non-Irish, and non-EEA nationals consistently and inevitably fail to meet. However, following Dyer, the two alternatives to nonwhite are "black" and "people of color," the first of which I use when appropriate. After all, this is a study that tests the limits of Irish and Irish diasporic proclamations of affinities with black diasporic subjects, whether these subjects come from Africa, the Americas, or elsewhere. When referring to those immigrants to Ireland who are not white or black, I prefer "nonwhite" to "people of color" because, as Dyer puts it, "we need to recognise white as a colour too" (1999, 11).

Multiculturalism

According to the 2006 census, there are 420,000 non-Irish nationals living in Ireland, representing 188 different countries ("Census 2006: Non-Irish Nationals Living in Ireland" 2008). Lacking a better turn of phrase, I appeal to *contemporary multicultural Ireland* to denote the nation's ethnic diversity. However, I do so very tentatively, taking on board Debbie Ging and Jackie Malcolm's point that the terms *multicultural, antiracist,* and *intercultural* tend to be "employed as descriptive terms in ways that fix and disguise their prescriptive import, the assumptions upon which they are based and which continue to operate in public discourse" (2004, 127). Although I opt for *multicultural,* as this term seems most appropriate for describing Ireland's ethnic diversity, it ought to be noted that from a policy standpoint, the Irish government prefers the term *interculturalism.*

Celtic Tiger

Although the exact parameters of the moment are contested, the *Celtic Tiger,* or the "economic miracle," is a crucial sociohistorical marker for this project because it is generally agreed that Ireland would never have witnessed such a significant influx of immigrants from eastern Europe, Asia, and Africa if it had not undergone, from the mid-1990s on, a period of unprecedented economic prosperity. According to Colin Coulter, the first recorded use of the expression occurred when Kevin Gardiner of the investment bank Morgan Stanley in London "sought to draw a comparison between the performance of the Irish Republic and that of the 'tiger' economies of south-east Asia" (2003, 3). For this reason, the term *Celtic Tiger* will be employed in this book to indicate the twelve or thirteen years of Ireland's economic boom, 1994 to 2006–7.

Transnationalism and Diaspora

As the title of this book—borrowed from Garner—indicates, the concept of "diaspora" is absolutely central to this project. In the inaugural issue of *Diaspora: A Journal of Transnational Studies,* Khachig Tölölyan famously proclaimed diasporas the "exemplary communities of the transnational moment" (1991, 5). The new journal consolidated an academic trend toward "new diaspora theory" or "diaspora studies" that emerged in the early 1990s that also became evident in the popular domain. In her inaugural address as president of Ireland in 1990, Mary Robinson made reference to the Irish diaspora and vowed to keep a candle burning in the window of the Áras an Uachtarán (the presidential residence) to assure them that they were not forgotten. She followed this statement up in her 1995 address to the Joint Houses of the Oireachtas, "Cherishing the Irish Diaspora," in which Robinson drew attention to the "70 million people worldwide who can claim Irish descent." She went on to say that "the men and women of our diaspora represent not simply a series of departures and losses. They remain, even while absent, a precious reflection of our own growth and change, a precious reminder of the many strands of identity which compose our story" (1995, n.p.). As Breda Gray summarizes, "Like many other emigrant nations in the 1990s (e.g. India, Mexico, El Salvador and Haiti), the Republic of Ireland was reclaiming its diaspora as a means of refiguring the national as global" (2003, 157).

However, Irish studies scholars—in disciplines as diverse as cultural studies and sociology—have questioned the usefulness of the concept of "diaspora" in contemporary Ireland. For David Lloyd, the term is connotative of Irish Americans' "sentimental and fetishizing desire to establish their genealogy in the old country" and, as such, thoroughly depoliticizes the social and historical reality of emigration (1999, 102). I agree with Lloyd that we must be wary of appeals to "diaspora" because for all its apparently apolitical emptiness, the term can mask a diaspora's—in this case, the Irish diaspora's—implication in deeply politicized issues and debates. Ronit Lentin contends, for example, that the promotion of Ireland as a "diaspora nation" from the 1990s on enabled the constitutional amendment on Irish citizenship that was passed by 79 percent of the Irish electorate in June 2004. In other words, it was the diaspora nation's insistence upon a deterritorialized notion of belonging that facilitated the shift from *jus soli* (whereupon citizenship is automatically granted to those born on Irish soil) to *jus sanguinis* (whereupon the right to Irish citizenship is determined based upon blood ties) that was effected by the 2004 referendum (Lentin 2007, 135). However, as Garner demonstrates, the claims of the diaspora to Irish citizenship still apply: as long as you have one Irish grandparent, you qualify for Irish citizenship. Thus, "someone whose grandparent emigrated, and who may never have set foot in Ireland, is unproblematically granted citizenship, whereas a child whose parents may live, work and pay taxes in Ireland has citizenship withheld" (2007b, 126).

Tölölyan qualifies his comment about diasporas being the "exemplary communities of the transnational moment" by noting that it is "not to write the premature obituary of the nation-state, which remains a privileged form of polity" (1991, 5). The Irish Republic is no exception, and, in fact, several scholars suggest that Ireland is defining itself more and more as a nation-state since the arrival of significant numbers of immigrants. As Lentin argues (after David Theo Goldberg), through "constitutions, border controls, the law, policymaking, bureaucracy and governmental technologies such as census categorizations, invented histories and traditions, ceremonies and cultural imaginings, the modern state is defined by its power to exclude (and include) in racially ordered terms, to categorize hierarchically and to set aside" (2003, 306). In a similar vein, Eithne Luibhéid concludes that, in the Irish case, far from troubling the boundaries of the nation-state, "refugees/asylum seekers occasion policies, discourses, and practices that provide opportunities for nation-states to reinvent themselves in particular ways" (2004, 337).

The supernational structure of the European Union adds another layer of complexity to the notion of Irish nation or transnation. Needing to align Irish citizenship procedures with the ones employed in the rest of the EU was one of the (erroneous) reasons cited by then minister for justice Michael McDowell for holding a referendum on the subject in June 2004 (Garner 2007a, 441). Though historically positive about the EU, Ireland has, in recent years, seemed less inclined to accept its proposals, as the initial rejection of the Nice (2002) and Lisbon (2008) Treaties indicates. In these contexts, how "transnational" *is* Ireland in its outlook and policies? How are we to interpret, for instance, Tánaiste Mary Harney's famous remarks in 2000 that Ireland is "geographically" closer to Berlin but "spiritually" closer to Boston? (Harney 2000). The concepts of "transnationalism" and "diaspora" are useful to this study, in other words, precisely because of the contradictions they contain and the challenges they pose. If, over the past ten years, "a particular set of cultural and economic pressures"—successive Irish governments' commitment to strategies of globalization and attracting foreign investment to rejuvenate the domestic economy—has "rapidly transnationalized Irishness," immigration to Ireland, one of the consequences of the economic benefits reaped through globalization, has been met with attempts to "renationalize" the nation (Negra 2006b, 1; Luibhéid 2004, 336). Or, as Loyal puts it, "the free movement of people has not matched the free and accelerating movement of goods and capital across national borders" (2003, 89). Equally, if Ireland boasts a global diaspora of some seventy-five million people, how does this diaspora figure in debates about "other people's diasporas" in Ireland?

Theoretical Underpinnings

If the subject matter that I treat here is explicitly transnational, then so too is my theoretical framework, which pits favored positions from Irish studies (postcolonialism) and American studies (critical race studies) against one another. To state my position baldly, this book exists where postcolonialism and whiteness studies collide. What is at stake in this project, in other words, is the status of postcolonialism as the dominant theoretical framework in Irish studies and the growing unease of scholars of whiteness—especially the ones based in or writing about Irishness in the United States—with the comparative impulse that this framework encourages. As such, I add my voice to an expanding group of scholars who are beginning to challenge the extent to which postcolonial Irish studies has marginalized discussions of race. As Gerardine Meaney puts it, "The dominance of the postcolonial-revisionist debate in the formation of Irish Studies and the analyses it produced of Irish nationalism have not only long outlived their usefulness. Both sides of the debate have obscured the role of whiteness in the construction of Irish identity" (2007, 47). Similarly, Brannigan observes that because "racism is routinely understood within post-colonial theories as an instrument of colonial discourses," racial ideologies and racist expressions "within modern Irish culture (that is, since 1922) are merely overlooked as the secondary, or belated, signifiers of an effectively redundant colonial interpretative regime" (2009, 6).

In *Ireland's Others: Gender and Ethnicity in Irish Literature and Popular Culture* (2001), Elizabeth Butler Cullingford argues that "the position of Ireland in postcolonial theory depends on the use of analogy as a comparative historical tool. Is Ireland more 'like' or more 'different from' other former colonies?" (2001, 2). Whereas two of the most prominent Irish studies scholars, Luke Gibbons and David Lloyd, claim that Irish history "is full of reasons to seek out both international and inter-ethnic connections" (Lloyd 1999, 105–6), critics such as Diane Negra and Catherine Eagan are increasingly concerned that appealing to parallels between the experiences of Irish and oppressed peoples of color offers white subjects the opportunity to lay claim to a history of colonial and racial oppression while retaining the privileges of whiteness. In such scenarios, Irishness emerges as a benign, nonthreatening form of whiteness.

Whiteness studies has existed in various forms for many years. However, as an academic field of inquiry, it really began to blossom in the 1980s and 1990s, partly, some would argue, "as a product of debates in America about increasing conservatism, racial politics and the idea of whites as a declining majority" (Garner 2006, 263). Illuminating studies have appeared in literary, film, and cultural studies (Morrison; Dyer; Babb; Lott), sociology (Frankenberg), and social and labor history (Jacobson; Roediger; Ignatiev), many of which devote substantial space to a consideration of the place of the Irish within, and their role in perpetuating, American racial hierarchies. In 2006 two edited collections appeared that were implicitly or explicitly preoccupied with the relationship between Irishness, postcolonialism, and whiteness and, as such, rehearse some of my concerns here.

In *Re-imagining Ireland,* an anthology that arose from the proceedings of a conference and festival on Irish identity in a global context held at the University of Virginia in 2003, several contributors confront this issue, though this is certainly not the overarching impetus for the book, and the contributors do not interact with one another. Fintan O'Toole's introduction sets the tone for the collection, in which he expresses his discomfort, on one hand, with "outrageous comparisons [of Ireland] with Africa or the old Eastern Europe," analogies that are "misleading, especially in the scale of horror that they imply," but finds, on the other, that words like *torture, slavery,* and *apartheid* can "usefully be applied" to certain "aspects of the Irish experience in the twentieth century" (2006, 3). He stipulates, finally, that such analogies "should be placed in the context of an island that avoided the worst of what even the history of privileged Europe had to offer in the twentieth century" (3). Meanwhile, Luke Gibbons's parenthetical observation in his essay that the Irish role in the New York City Draft Riots of 1863 is "(strangely underplayed in Martin Scorsese's *Gangs of New York*)" (2006a, 58) contrasts with Noel Ignatiev's sense that "the film distorts the meaning of the events, turning them into a conflict between native and Irish and reducing the problem of race to a footnote" (2006, 79).

Gibbons's essay engages with the (earlier) work of Diane Negra but finds, ultimately, that Negra's insistence on the whiteness of Irishness risks "reifying pigmentation, as if there is no possibility at all, in Jacobson's phrase, of 'whiteness of a different color,' thus retrieving emancipatory projects for alternative political futures" (2006a, 60). Of course, the reverse claim could be made regarding Gibbons's essay, that he *underplays* the role of pigmentation in racial oppression. In critiquing positions that seem to construe Irish "decolonization itself as a form of racism," Gibbons argues that "on this reading, campaigns by the Aboriginal peoples of Australia or by Native Americans for land entitlements would be racist," with no consideration given to the fact that the Irish were a *white European* colonized group within a white European empire, while indigenous peoples in Australia and the Americas were *nonwhite, non-European* colonized groups within white European empires (ibid., 56).

While several contributors to *Re-imagining Ireland* identify the increasingly troubled (and troubling) relationship between Irishness, whiteness, and postcolonialism, Negra's edited collection, *The Irish in Us: Irishness, Performativity, and Popular Culture,* tackles the issue head-on. (Interestingly, none of the contributors to Wyndham's volume also appear in Negra's, though Gibbons and O'Toole are cited extensively.) From the deployment of Celtic symbols by white suprem-acist groups to *Riverdance,* from Van Morrison's appropriation of

soul music to Sinéad O'Connor's "Celtic Rastifarianism," most of
the essays pose "questions about the romance of the Irish-black connection" (2006b, 2). The motivation behind the collection is Negra's sense that, in a climate in which the popularity of Irish-themed
books, films, dance shows, merchandising, even weddings is widespread, Irishness in contemporary America now operates as a form
of "enriched whiteness" (1). Claiming an Irish identity has become,
in other words, a means of "speaking a whiteness that would otherwise be taboo" (Negra 2006a, 355). For Eagan, this may be attributed in part to "some Irish Americans' failure to admit their shift
from a past history of oppression to a present history of assimilation
and power." By insisting on a connection with African Americans,
they reveal "their desire to re-become the 'other' and deny their past
and present participation in the white power structure" (2006, 23).

For some readers with strong postcolonial leanings, the white-
ness-studies angle may seem like another way of configuring revisionism. Indeed, Gibbons makes this connection when he interprets
revisionist critiques of "Irish identification with the underdogs of
empire" as presenting "the Irish more as sinners than sinned against"
(2006a, 58). Equally, Kerby Miller configures "revisionist logic" as
follows: "If the Irish Catholic experience abroad can be reinterpreted
as one of enthusiastic participation in British and American imperial
and colonial adventures, and in genocidal assaults on dark-skinned
peoples (as well as in the Catholic Church's offensives against indigenous cultures), then the 'exceptionalist' assumptions that underpin
traditional Irish identity and Nationalism—and the latter's alleged
affinities with Third World suffering and resistance—can be fatally
discredited" (2006, 235). Scholars of whiteness share with revision-
ists a suspicion of seemingly disproportionate and anachronous
attention paid to the Irish colonial legacy, that is, if they (revisionist
historians) even concede that Ireland was ever a colony.

However, as an Irish woman whose scholarly background is in
American studies—specifically, in representations of racial and gender "passing"—I find myself sympathetic to both (postcolonial and
whiteness studies) positions. When I read Cullingford's work, I was

intrigued by her discussion of a critique by African American feminist scholar bell hooks of Neil Jordan's *The Crying Game* (1992), a film that implies affinities between Irish and African-Caribbean subjects based on their status as postcolonial subjects. Cullingford notes that hooks "sees the power differentials between white and black, masculine and feminine, as more important than the power differential between Brits and Paddies" (2001, 133). A film that locates gender transgression on the site of an already ambiguously raced body, I was very familiar with *The Crying Game* and with hooks's interpretation of it and recall feeling quite strongly that she disregards the precise historical and colonial contexts so important to the film. She recognizes "the imperialist racism and colonialism of Britain," but seems to think that it only applies to Britain's Caribbean conquests (1994, 58). In particular, her insistence that Dil is a "tragic mulatto"—in a film unquestioningly grounded in a European art house, rather than Hollywood, cinematic tradition (after all, she juxtaposes her interpretation of *The Crying Game* with an analysis of the Whitney Houston vehicle *The Bodyguard* [1992] and finds the latter "far more radical" than the former!)—is extremely unconvincing (ibid., 56, 61).

Nonetheless, my training in American studies and, specifically, in critical race studies does leave me with questions regarding the degree to which such analogies are appropriate and, more important, how useful they are in generating meaningful solidarity between white Irish and nonwhite postcolonial subjects. As George Lipsitz argues, "Colonized and exploited communities have a long history of cultural expression that uses the protective cover offered by seemingly innocent play with new identities to address and redress their traditional grievances" (1994, 71). However, two important questions arise from white Irish forays into this territory: "Which kinds of cross-cultural identification advance emancipatory ends and which ones reinforce existing structures of power and domination? When does identification with the culture of others serve escapist and irresponsible ends and when does it encourage an enhanced understanding of one's experiences and responsibilities?" (56). Whereas in Lipsitz's book, the vehicle for "cross-cultural identification" is hybridized transnational musical forms, here it is the use of particular analogies.

Slippery Things

Like Cullingford's earlier project, in which she examines the ways in which Irish postcolonial subjects have created ethnic analogies between themselves and other oppressed groups such as Native Americans and African Americans, analogies are central to this book. Cullingford warns that analogies can be "slippery things. What looks from a postcolonial Irish perspective like a sympathetic and intellectually coherent identification with the descendants of slaves may appear to an American Black as shameless appropriation, or strike a revisionist as spurious ethnic chic" (2001, 7). Here, I am concerned with the ways in which analogies operate in contemporary Ireland but, in the contexts of globalization, the Celtic Tiger economy, and the arrival of significant numbers of immigrants, require appendices to Cullingford's argument.

The first is the collision of Cullingford's analogies with Garner's "historical duty" argument. During the Celtic Tiger years, in other words, the Irish and African American analogy was reconfigured to incorporate Garner's terms. If, with Cullingford's ethnic analogies, "a white Other attempts, by invoking analogy (my culture and my colonial predicament resembles yours) or genealogy (my culture originates with yours), to create an alternative and exotic Self," Garner's "historical duty" argument adds the following extra dimension: like you, my ancestors were colonized/oppressed and obliged to emigrate as a result. Now that my country is more prosperous than ever before, I understand *your* need to leave your homeland to settle in mine (ibid., 7). The "historical duty" argument became the most pervasive liberal position on immigration during the boom era. In her foreword to *Multi-culturalism: The View from the Two Irelands,* for example, President Mary McAleese writes that, in reexamining their attitudes to the asylum seeker or economic migrant, the Irish on "the whole island can draw on the deep collective memory of emigration, when men and women from every part of Ireland made their homes around the world, driven abroad by economic or political circumstances" (Longley and Kiberd 2001, ix). In his essay, she is echoed by Declan Kiberd, who argues that immigrants "will invariably pay far more in taxes than they will receive in state hand-outs . . . and the money which they earn in the host country helps, through the subventions which they send home, to reduce poverty in their native countries as well. The Irish, many of whom lived on remittance letters from Britain and the United States, should understand this better than most" (ibid., 60). The "historical duty" argument began to circulate widely in Irish culture and is discussed here in relation to Joseph O'Connor's *Star of the Sea*, Donal O'Kelly's *"The Cambria,"* and Des Bishop's stand-up comedy.

Second, if analogies are indeed "slippery things," then they may be used to opposing ends. A liberally intentioned analogy may be deployed in the most conservative terms possible, while the same liberally intentioned analogy in a local (Irish) context may also assume much more problematic undertones when considered transnationally. Take, for instance, the analogy that Jason King describes as follows: "The many heated *Oireachtas* debates and much of the press coverage surrounding Ireland's so-called 'refugee crisis,' influx of illegal immigrants, and then the speedy passage of the Immigration Act, 1999, Illegal Immigrants (Trafficking) Act, 2000, as well as policy directives that have emanated from the Department of Justice . . . tended to be framed against the backdrop of the Famine exodus of 1847, and the calamities of Ireland's colonial history" (2003, 203). The analogy between Famine Irish and African asylum seekers and refugees in contemporary Ireland is a "moral injunction" to the Irish to recall their ancestors' status as colonized subjects (ibid.). However, by tweaking it only slightly and repositioning the Irish in a "backs-to-the-wall, blood-and-soil narrative in which invaders are repeatedly repelled," this analogy "lends itself easily to . . . racist *dérive*," thus achieving the direct opposite effect (Garner 2007b, 129). As Luibhéid notes, in 2002, the Immigration Control Platform dropped leaflets in mailboxes "urging people to 'stop the invasion and colonization of Ireland'" (2004, 339). In the chapters that follow, I discuss many transatlantic analogies, some explicit, some implicit in the material under analysis. Roddy Doyle alone generates several: contemporary immigrants to Ireland and Dust Bowl migrants in the United States in the 1930s; Jimmy Rabbitte, the white Irish impresario obsessed with African American music and Eminem; contemporary Irish racists and the Ku Klux Klan—and these all occur in one story! However, below I unpack the two that recur most frequently throughout the study—the Green Atlantic and the New Irish—and a third that, though not strictly an analogy, was imported at will from US literature and culture: the mixed-race subject.

The Green Atlantic?

One of the most complex analogies to emerge in recent years is that between the Black and Green Atlantics, usefully configured by Hazel Carby as "the ways in which . . . black routes and roots, passages and origins, are constantly interwoven with the migratory histories and cultures of other peoples whose own 'routes and roots' are sometimes carried by and sometimes expressed through political and cultural vessels marked as black" (2001, 326). The extent to which this analogy is problematic depends, in my view, on whether Paul Gilroy's theories are taken on board in a quite general or overly specific manner for the Black-Green Atlantic analogy inevitably leads back to Gilroy. Luke Gibbons, for example, quotes Gilroy to argue that "due to a similar uprooting of Irish experience after the atrocities of the 1798 rebellion and the devastation of the Great Famine, Irish literature in the nineteenth century (especially in its romantic or gothic register) often evinced a 'proto-modernist' outlook" (1996, 6). In his groundbreaking work *The Black Atlantic: Modernity and Double Consciousness* (1993), Gilroy proposed that "cultural historians could take the Atlantic as one single, complex unit of analysis in their discussions of the modern world and use it to produce an explicitly transnational and intercultural perspective" (1993, 15).

Thus, when the Green Atlantic is invoked to suggest, in the broadest possible terms, the degree to which Ireland and the Americas were engaged, and continue to engage, in various social and cultural processes of transatlantic exchange, it is not a problematic proposition.

On the other hand, when scholars draw upon the chronotope of the ship—for Gilroy, "the central organising symbol" of the Black Atlantic (Gilroy 1993, 4)—in order to create an analogy between *the experiences* of enslaved Africans who were packed into slave ships and transported across the Atlantic in the Middle Passage and *the experiences* of the Irish who crossed the Atlantic in coffin ships during the Great Famine, the analogy becomes deeply troubling. As Ian Baucom puts it, "Emigration, however forced, dangerous, and punishing is clearly not at all the same thing as enslavement" (2000, 134). As Nini Rodgers notes, "Elderly vessels, some of which had originally been used to carry timber across the Atlantic and bring back passengers as ballast, were brought out of rotting retirement to transport the desperate numbers clambering out of Ireland" (2007, 290). This characterization is, however, where the similarity ends. One of the preoccupations of this book is whether the analogies that began to circulate in profoundly *liberal* contexts are, to paraphrase Negra, "inevitably *conservative* formulations" (2006b, 3). In other words, if nineteenth-century Famine Irish are analogous to enslaved African Americans and African immigrants to contemporary Ireland are analogous to enslaved African Americans, is this not a circuitous way of, yet again, expressing a spurious and problematic equivalence between the Irish and African Americans? In other words, do such analogies unavoidably operate to reassure contemporary Irish, in *both* Ireland *and* the United States, of their own or their ancestors' claims to victimhood?

Who Are the New Irish?

In a *Questions and Answers* show broadcast on RTÉ1 on November 12, 2007, two consecutive and related questions received the attention of the panelists. The first was: when is Bertie Ahern going to make the undocumented Irish in the United States a priority? The second was: should the Irish government not offer amnesty to illegals? The yoking together of debates on "undocumented Irish" in the United States versus "illegal immigrants" to Ireland has become increasingly apparent across Irish and Irish American public discourse. In a 2001 article for the magazine *Irish America,* Kelly Fincham writes that "many refugees [in Ireland] are afraid of anything that is linked to the government, much in the same way that the Irish in America historically avoided reporting crime to the police for fear of being revealed as undocumented and thus deported" (2001, 23). Interestingly, Fincham is now executive director of the Irish Lobby for Immigration Reform. In his April 2008 address to a joint meeting of the United States Congress, former Taoiseach Bertie Ahern also made the connection. The assumed parallel between the two groups is even evident in the coincidence of their nomenclature. Between 1981 and 1991, almost 360,000 Irish citizens left their homeland, most in the second half of the decade. About 10 percent of these went to the United States and proclaimed themselves the "New Irish" (Almeida 2001, 61). According to Helena Mulkerns, "The New Irish was a term coined to describe this new wave of emigration from Ireland, which really started sometime in the early eighties and escalated into a flood tide from the middle to the end of the decade. Since the education system advanced significantly in Ireland from the sixties and seventies on, the emigrants were a more varied bunch than previous generations, I think, a lot of the time highly qualified" (quoted in Wall 1999, 59). Immigrants to Ireland, from eastern Europe, Africa, and elsewhere, who have been arriving in relatively large numbers since the mid-1990s are now also commonly known as the "New Irish."

The importance of the relationship between the 1980s generation of emigrants (whether they went to the United States or elsewhere) and current debates on Irish multiculturalism cannot be overstated because, as Joe Cleary observes, the postcolonial impulse in Irish studies emerged in the 1980s in a climate of mass unemployment and emigration. He points to a number of scholarly works that appeared during these years that argued that "while the history of Irish economic development appeared anomalous by Western European standards, there were suggestive parallels between Ireland's situation and that of other formerly colonized regions in the 'Third World.'" At a very fundamental level, then, the emergence of postcolonial Irish studies and the 1980s generation of emigrants are profoundly linked (2003, 18–19).

The reason for which so many Irish found themselves living in the United States illegally from the 1980s has its roots in 1965 legislation passed by the US Congress. The goal of the Immigration and Nationality Act was "to eliminate racial and ethnic preferences and grant access to migrants who had previously been denied entry because of the national origins system" inaugurated in the 1924 Johnson-Reed Act (Almeida 2001, 9). One of the changes introduced in the 1965 act was a family unification program: immigrants could gain entry based on their familial relationship with somebody already living in the United States. However, by the 1960s and 1970s, the Irish ethnic community in New York "was shrinking, and it was aging," so by the 1980s, fewer and fewer would-be Irish immigrants could claim direct family ties to legal residents of the United States. Because it was conceived "to correct what was considered preferential treatment of traditional European migrating nationalities," the 1980s generation of Irish emigrants to the United States thus came to see themselves as "adversely affected" by the 1965 legislation (ibid., 55–56, 7). Legislation was again revised in 1986 with the Immigration Reform and Control Act. Although the New Irish benefited greatly from the Donnelly and Morrison visa programs that were introduced under this legislation, the amnesty provision for illegal immigrants who had entered the country prior to January 1, 1982, did not favor them, as the majority of Irish illegals had come to the United States after this date (O'Hanlon 1998, 29). In May 1987, the Irish Immigration Reform Movement was founded by Sean Minihane and Patrick Hurley, and lobbying has persisted in one form or another ever since.

The campaign acquired a new impetus, however, in the wake of 9/11, when the United States became increasingly concerned about the integrity of its borders. In May 2005, Congress passed the REAL ID Act, which advocated a clampdown on the issuing of driving licenses to undocumented workers. In December of that year, Congressman James Sensenbrenner, who had also introduced the REAL ID Act, was the main sponsor of the Border Protection, Anti-terrorism, and Illegal Immigration Control (or Sensenbrenner) Bill, which would have made it a federal crime to live in the United States illegally. Faced with this prospect, the Irish began to mobilize. In December 2005, with the support of Republican senator John McCain and Democratic senator Ted Kennedy, the Irish Lobby for Immigration Reform (ILIR) was formed to oppose the bill and to promote, instead, the much less severe Secure America and Orderly Immigration, or McCain-Kennedy, Bill. In chapters 3 and 4, in relation to the work of Des Bishop and Ronan Noone, I argue that the ILIR participates in and reinforces the discourse of Irish victimhood identified by Negra and others, a discourse that ultimately serves to consolidate whiteness. As such, the "undocumented" Irish in the United States and "illegal" immigrant to Ireland analogy, even if it is well intentioned, must be approached with caution in order to acknowledge the privileges that white Irish and Irish diasporic subjects now enjoy.

Mixed Race

At the end of August of every year since 1959, women of Irish ancestry—predominantly from cities in Britain, Ireland, Australia, New Zealand, the United States, and Canada—have, along with their family, friends, and other visitors, gathered in Tralee, County Kerry, for an annual festival, the culmination of which is the crowning of the Rose of Tralee. Inspired by the nineteenth-century song of the same title, the competition aspires not simply to be a beauty pageant but an acknowledgment that the winner possesses the same admirable qualities as Mary from the song:

> She was lovely and fair as the rose of the summer
> Yet 'twas not her beauty alone that won me

Oh no, 'twas the truth in her eyes ever dawning
That made me love Mary, the Rose of Tralee.

In June 2008, when Belinda Brown, of Irish Jamaican parentage, was selected as the Rose who would represent London in Tralee, she became the victim of sustained racist abuse through online postings on the white supremacist website Stormfront.org. According to the *Sunday Times,* sample posts included "The London entrant for this year's Rose of Tralee is a half-caste mongrel. What the hell are the organisers thinking of?" and "Last time I checked our women were pale-skinned maidens from our Emerald Isle, not some mud from London" (Shortall 2008, n.p.).

The reaction to Brown's participation in the competition—though admittedly, from a tiny, very extreme minority—sounds a warning bell to those writers and scholars who might seize upon the mixed-race subject, or interracial relationships, as heralding the glorious future of a multiracial, multicolored Ireland or, at the very least, of unsettling the correspondence between white and Irish. Angeline Morrison contends, for example, that the mixed-race Irish subject "could, potentially, force whiteness to become visible in a new and previously unimaginable way; in a raw way that could irritate Irish-whiteness into a reconsideration of its prior understandings of both whiteness *and* blackness" (2004, 391). As I argue in chapter 1, the frequency with which ambiguously raced characters surface in *Star of the Sea* and *Redemption Falls* suggests that Joseph O'Connor shares this view. Roddy Doyle's short story "Home to Harlem" is a far more nuanced treatment of mixed-race Irishness, and Eugene Brady's film *The Nephew,* adapted from his own original story, also foregrounds the experiences of a mixed-race Irish American. If Ireland has modeled many of its questionable policies on race and immigration on those of the United States (Lentin 2007, 448), the embracing of the mixed-race subject, as a literary and cultural device, is yet another troubling development. As David Theo Goldberg reminds us, "'Mixed race' may seem to offer exciting proof positive that a deep social taboo has been transgressed, that racial discipline and order have been violated, that liberty's lure once again has undermined the condition of homogeneity by delimiting the constraints of the hegemonic. Yet it at once, and necessarily, reimposes the racial duality between blackness and whiteness as the standard, the measure of mixed-ness" (1997, 63). In the United States, representations of mixed-race subjects have ranged from the pathological to the tragic. They are figures, as Suzanne Bost notes, of both "fear" and "fascination" (2005, 185). In chapters 1, 2, and 5, I examine the implications of importing this trope to Irish culture.

As should be clear by now, while each chapter centers upon the work of one or two figures, the material in each chapter will not be mutually exclusive, linked via the motifs of mixed-race identity, the Green Atlantic, and the New Irish. Indeed, many of the figures treated here work in two or more artistic or cultural forms. Joseph O'Connor is a playwright and short-story writer as well as a novelist. Roddy Doyle writes for the stage and screen as well as fiction. Des Bishop is a stand-up comedian, playwright, and television personality. Chapter 1 examines the work of one of Ireland's most prominent contemporary novelists, Joseph O'Connor. I focus specifically on the first two installments of what is now a trilogy, questioning why he has turned to "key moments" in Irish and Irish American history—the Great Famine and the American Civil War—for his subject matter and arguing that doing so enables him to comment obliquely on contemporary *immigration* to Ireland. Chapter 2 foregrounds short stories by Roddy Doyle that have appeared serialized in *Metro Éireann,* a weekly publication that markets itself as "Ireland's first and only multicultural newspaper," reprinted in American literary magazines, *McSweeney's Quarterly Concern,* and the *New Yorker* and collected in *The Deportees* (2007). As such, the transatlantic resonances of the analogies Doyle draws *within* the stories are reflected in the transatlantic migration of the stories themselves.

Chapter 3 is devoted to the subject of contemporary Irish and Irish American drama. It analyzes Donal O'Kelly's play *"The Cambria,"* first staged in Dublin's Liberty Theatre in 2005, which frames the story of Frederick Douglass's journey to Ireland aboard the eponymous ship 160 years previously with the story of a Nigerian student recently deported from Ireland. On the other side of the Atlantic, Irish-born Ronan Noone's play *The Blowin of Baile Gall* (2002) dramatizes the conflicts that ensue after an African immigrant called Laurence joins a team of white laborers, including a "returned Yank," on a construction site in the West of Ireland. Noone's play is one of the few examples of Irish American cultural responses to demographic changes taking place in Ireland.

Chapter 4 questions the ethics and efficacy of the work of stand-up comedian Des Bishop, a white Irish American from Queens, New York. Expelled from school at age fourteen in 1990, his parents sent him as a boarder to St. Peter's College in Wexford, and he has lived in Ireland ever since. Bishop's stand-up revolves around his outsider status and, more specifically, his construction of a "returned Yank" comic persona. Bishop's marginal status derives from the fact that he is an immigrant—a white Irish American immigrant, but an immigrant nonetheless. By implying that he—a white member of the Irish diaspora—has suffered bigotry in Ireland, he encourages white Irish audiences to question their attitudes toward "other people's diasporas" in Ireland. Bishop is simultaneously one of "us" (white Irish) *and* "them" (foreign-born immigrant).

Finally, chapter 5 interrogates the ways in which race and immigration figure in two films by, respectively, actor-producer Pierce Brosnan and writer-director Jim Sheridan, both Irish born but having spent periods of their professional lives—in Brosnan's case, most of his career—in the United States. While neither *The Nephew* (1998) nor *In America* (2003) is "about" African immigrants to Ireland, the fact that the first features the arrival of a mixed-race Irish American in Ireland and the second juxtaposes Irish and African immigrants to the United States enables the films to be interpreted as "parables," as Kathleen Vejvoda puts it, of race and immigration in contemporary Ireland.

1

Crossing the Black and Green Atlantics

Joseph O'Connor's Fictions of Irish America

> That sergeant understood something very important. He under-
> stood the idea of America, the sheer historical importance of
> America to the young people of Ireland.
>
> —JOSEPH O'CONNOR, *Sweet Liberty: Travels in
> Irish America* (1996)

> Yes, people are commuting long distances now. . . . But not
> nearly so long as the commute to, say, Australia which is where
> many people had to go to find jobs a generation ago.
>
> —JOSEPH O'CONNOR, quoted in "Suddenly
> Rich, Poor Old Ireland Seems Bewildered,"
> by Lizette Alvarez (2005)

In the above epigraphs, Joseph O'Connor identifies the key reversal that took place in Ireland's migration pattern between the 1980s and the early years of the twenty-first century. The first quotation refers to an anecdote that O'Connor recounts from his university days in the mid-1980s. Fuming at the minister for health's proposal to withdraw free health care from those in full-time education, he and a group of fellow students staged a protest in the minister's office, refusing to leave even after the police arrived and issued all sorts of ultimatums. Only one of these threats held any sway: "If any of you get arrested today," the sergeant warns, "you will never be able to get into America" (1996, 16). The 1980s was a decade during which unemployment reached a high of 17 percent in Ireland. To the assembled university students, facing the distinct possibility of emigration, the sergeant's words were thus "the ultimate threat" (17).

The second epigraph is excerpted from a *New York Times* article by Lizette Alvarez in which she suggests that Ireland's newfound prosperity from the mid-1990s on was accompanied by a crisis of national identity. Alvarez asks, "How, for example, should a country once known for sending legions of people abroad deal with its own crop of immigrants?" (2005, A4). The pertinence of Alvarez's and O'Connor's observations is borne out in statistics taken since Irish independence in 1922: emigration from Ireland peaked at around seventy thousand in the twelve months to April 1989; in 2002 immigration into Ireland peaked at around seventy thousand ("Population and Migration Estimates" 2004). In fewer than fifteen years, then, a remarkable shift took place in Ireland. From its status as a country *from* which thousands emigrated out of economic necessity, it became a place that was attractive to thousands of immigrants because of unprecedented economic prosperity.

It is perhaps unsurprising that, even in these brief anecdotes, O'Connor articulates very effectively the reversal in Ireland's migration pattern, for, like thousands of others, he experienced it firsthand. Having emigrated to London in the 1980s and having lived there for about a decade, he returned to settle in Ireland in the mid-1990s just as the country was on the threshold of its "economic miracle." As he recalls:

> So it was the beginning of the boom and the beginning of people starting to come here from other countries. And what a strange thing that was and how new it was to us. And if anybody had ever told me as a child that this remarkable thing would happen and Ireland would become a kind of America to which people from Africa and Asia and Eastern Europe would want to come, I would have thought that they would all be welcomed with open arms, precisely because of that history that we sing about and we make statues about and we tell stories about. And that didn't quite happen, so I was interested in why. (O'Connor 2007b)

Here, O'Connor sums up Steve Garner's "historical duty" argument, and his configuration of contemporary Ireland as "a kind of America" confirms his concern with analogies in the first two installments of his now completed trilogy: between contemporary Ireland and nineteenth-century America as host nations for immigrants, between Famine Irish emigrants and contemporary refugees and asylum seekers in Ireland, and between Famine Irish and African American slaves. This chapter examines *Star of the Sea* (2002) and *Redemption Falls* (2007) in the context of this turnaround in Ireland's migration pattern, arguing that the appearance of *Star of the Sea* in 2002, in particular, is significant because it depicts the defining era in Irish *emigration* history at the exact moment when *immigration* into Ireland was at its peak.[1]

Set aboard the eponymous coffin ship, *Star of the Sea* charts a Famine-era transatlantic crossing, a twenty-six-day journey from Cobh to New York in November 1847 during which the ship carries some 450 passengers and crew. Primarily set in the aftermath of the American Civil War, *Redemption Falls* resumes the story of the Irish in the United States from the 1850s on as they come to participate in military and civic life. In the first two installments of the trilogy, then, O'Connor confronts the Grand Narrative of Irish emigration to the United States, according to which "the Famine provides Irish Americans with a 'charter myth'—a creation story that both explains [their] presence in the new land and connects [them] to the

---

1. The third in the trilogy, *Ghost Light* (2010), moves into the twentieth century, focuses on the romance between the playwright J. M. Synge, and actress Maire O'Neill and is less directly concerned with the United States. Nonetheless, echoes of the previous novels are perceptible in the character names Duane and Mulvey, and numerous references to the Famine and emigration, Irish casualties in the American Civil War and, most notably, in the mysterious and aged Mary Moody who dresses Maire when she is on tour in the United States. Originally from Galway, but having also lived in Louisiana, it is likely the dresser is Mary Duane Mooney.

old via a powerful sense of grievance," while "the Civil War provided an opportunity to transform both their role in American society and their self-image in positive ways" (K. O'Neill 2001, 118). In so doing, he takes on what is, essentially, a narrative of Irish victimhood—or "grievance," as Kevin O'Neill puts it—in which those Irish who left their homeland on coffin ships and survived the transatlantic voyage went from the frying pan into the fire. Having faced discrimination when seeking employment and housing, they subsequently became cannon fodder for the Union army during the Civil War.[2] Indeed, Robin Cohen categorizes the Irish as a "victim diaspora"—along with Jews, Armenians, Palestinians, and Africans—based on the "catastrophic event" that was the Great Famine (1997, x). In tackling this period of Irish and Irish American history, then, O'Connor is faced with two challenges: how to do justice to the "grievances" of Irish colonial history without appropriating the sufferings of other, especially nonwhite, peoples and how to do justice to the "grievances" of Irish colonial history without reinforcing a narrative of Irish victimhood in the present.

This challenge is complicated by the fact that O'Connor expressly wishes that his novels make a comment on the contemporary moment. He describes *Star* as a story about "four or five characters who are trying to live with love and dignity in a world where there is war and terrorism and racism and an enormous movement of refugees— in other words, a world very like the one we live in now" (Lynch 2005, 3–4). Elsewhere, he insists that the historical novel, as a genre, "should have some little echo of stuff going on in the world now." Without it, "there's a kind of deadness about it" (2007c). If so, then what *are* the contemporary "echoes" with which O'Connor is concerned? In this chapter, I argue that the novels represent O'Connor's

2. See, for example, the scene in Martin Scorsese's epic film *Gangs of New York* (2002) in which fresh-off-the-boat Irish immigrants are met by government officials: "That document makes you a citizen. . . . [T]his one makes you a private in the Union army. Now go fight for your country."

meditation upon issues of race and immigration in contemporary Ireland. This concern manifests itself in three ways: in his interest in the respective situations of Irish emigrants to America and African Americans in the nineteenth century in order to (re)awaken in his Celtic Tiger readers a sense of solidarity with those seeking a home in Ireland in the present day, in peopling both novels with mixed-race subjects, and in his deconstruction of (Irish) national identity—which has, after all, conventionally been conceived as white, Catholic, and settled—in favor of *transnational* identity.

Born in Dublin in 1963, O'Connor is the author of fourteen books, including seven novels, four collections of comic journalism, a travelogue, and a collection of short stories. Although he was, from early in his career, a best-selling author in Ireland—notably with his three *Irish Male* nonfiction books—it was not until the appearance of *Star of the Sea* in 2002 that he achieved international recognition and acclaim including, in 2004, endorsement in the book club launched by British chat show hosts Richard Madeley and Judy Finnigan. While the historical and geographical displacement of *Star of the Sea* and *Redemption Falls* may, on the surface, appear to be evidence of a change of direction for the author, whose dabbling in historical settings prior to *Star* was limited to 1985 (in *Desperadoes* [1994]) and 1994 (in *The Salesman* [1998] and *Inishowen* [2000]), it in fact represents the culmination of two distinct thematic concerns of his previous work: Irish emigration (albeit of his own generation, and to Britain) and the place of the United States within the Irish imagination.

The protagonist of O'Connor's first published story, "Last of the Mohicans" (1989), and his first novel, *Cowboys and Indians* (1991), is Dubliner Eddie Virago. A middle-class, university-educated aspiring musician who emigrates to London circa 1989, Virago is "one of the great unwashed migrants of the Ryanair generation" (O'Connor 1991a, 71). Like *Star of the Sea*, *Cowboys and Indians* opens on a ship carrying Irish emigrants, but in this case, it is a Sealink car ferry traveling from Dublin to Holyhead in the late 1980s. In his 1995 play, *Red Roses and Petrol*, two of the three Doyle children are emigrants who return to Ireland, from Britain and the United States, to attend their father's funeral. Although the title perhaps refers to the Sean O'Casey play *Red Roses for Me* (1943)—and O'Connor evokes O'Casey's better-known *Juno and the Paycock* (1924) several times in the play (1995, 3–4, 6, 23, 54)—it is also an allusion to the identically titled 1984 album by traditional punk band the Pogues, who, like O'Connor, capture very eloquently the particular disposition of the 1980s generation of Irish emigrants: painfully aware of their difference from, but also their continuities with, previous generations of emigrating Irish. If Eddie Virago is not "the rough navvy of popular myth," he is still latter-day evidence of Ireland's ongoing inability to provide for its children (Smyth 1997, 151). As Colum McCann puts it, writing in 1993, "Of course the nature of emigration has changed for all of us—when London is a one-hour flight away from Knock it's hard to say that we've actually emigrated. Not in same way as people did before—flocks of wild geese, coffin ships, American wakes" (Bolger 1993, 7). Yet, as the narrator of O'Connor's "Mothers Were All the Same" recalls of his departure for London, there were nonetheless "tears and scribbled addresses and folded-up tenners in the suit pocket. The whole emigrant bit. You'd have sworn I was going to the moon the way they went on. The whole thing was like some bloody Christy Moore song come to life in our front room" (1991b, 19). The narrator's glibness cannot quite dispel the poignancy of his emigrant's farewell. Similarly, as Martin McLoone observes, the Pogues may "rant about the absurdity of nostalgia for Ireland," but they also "twist and bend sentimental ballads to rearticulate feelings of alienation in London or New York, capturing the pain and hurt of the emigrant's experience as well as the exhilaration of escape" (2008, 154).

Moreover, O'Connor's fascination with the transatlantic connections between Ireland and the United States did not begin with *Star of the Sea* but is perceptible in *Inishowen* (2000), his first novel to feature embedded documentation as a narrative device (newspaper reports, letters, songs) and as early as 1994 in his nonfiction. O'Connor's preference for unveiling, in the final pages, the "true" identity of Lord Merridith's murderer (in *Star*) and the narrator

Jeremiah McLelland (in *Redemption Falls*) is also anticipated in *Inishowen*, in which an Irish-born woman adopted by American parents discovers that her birth mother is none other than the nun to whom she applied seeking information on her past.

In a weekly column for Ireland's *Sunday Tribune*, O'Connor described his three-week sojourn in the United States during the 1994 World Cup in the company of a group of Irish soccer fans. His infamous "World Cup Diary" was subsequently reprinted as the final chapter of *The Secret World of the Irish Male* (1994), a collection of O'Connor's journalistic writings. One particular episode in the "World Cup Diary" bears reproducing here because it foreshadows some of the issues that arise in *Star of the Sea* and *Redemption Falls*. After Ireland loses to Holland in the round of sixteen, disappointed Irish soccer fans take to the streets of Orlando for an after-match party that happens to coincide with Fourth of July celebrations. For O'Connor, "a wonderful moment" that is "unforgettably moving" and "lifts the whole night" occurs when Thin Lizzy's "Dancing in the Moonlight" is played from a PA system, and thousands of Irish fans spill from the bars onto the street in order to join in: "The laughing voice of Phil Lynott, reminding us in some weird intangible way that being Irish always has its consolations" (1994b, 254). For O'Connor, Lynott becomes a convenient avatar for multiple crossings and identities—transatlantic, racial, musical—that is still, perhaps paradoxically, distinctly *Irish*. Furthermore, to the soundtrack of Lynott, an Irishman from Derry embraces a black woman from Wisconsin. Lynott, a man of mixed racial ancestry who was born in Britain to an Irish mother and Brazilian father but brought up in Ireland, thus both embodies and authorizes this interracial, transatlantic romantic encounter. O'Connor's interest in Lynott in 1994 prefigures both his own preoccupation with mixed-race Irishness in his most recent novels and more general cultural appeals to Lynott as the embodiment of the possibilities for contemporary multicultural Ireland, a trend that I unpack more fully in chapter 5.

In his flirtation with travel writing, *Sweet Liberty: Travels in Irish America* (1996), O'Connor's journey is structured around the visits he pays to nine of the thirteen Dublins in the United States. *Sweet Liberty* is a key precursor to *Star of the Sea* and *Redemption Falls* for a number of reasons. First, in *Sweet Liberty*, O'Connor insists upon the Great Famine as the privileged moment in Irish emigration history.[3] Like in *Star of the Sea*, O'Connor's chapter epigraphs in *Sweet Liberty* are excerpted letters from Irish emigrants to the United States to their loved ones back home, most of which are from the Famine generation of the 1840s and 1850s. Furthermore, *Sweet Liberty* offers early evidence of O'Connor's attempt to negotiate perceived affinities between Irish Americans and African Americans. Indeed, O'Connor opens and closes the book with anecdotes that speak to these supposed ties. In his introduction, O'Connor dates the moment he became "captivated by America" from a night during his childhood in a Connemara pub listening to the reminiscences of a returned emigrant woman (1996, 9). The woman tells him in one breath that "black people in America . . . had it very hard over there" (8) and in the next that "America was a great country" (9). O'Connor does not comment on this contradiction, but the ambivalence of the woman's comments is reflected in the way O'Connor subsequently structures his chapter epigraphs on the Irish experience in the United States. There are usually two, one of which extols the virtues of America, the other describing its limitations. By implication, then, the Irish—like "black people in America"—experienced both hardship in the United States and the country's greatness.

During his time in Pennsylvania, O'Connor discusses the experiences of Irish indentured servants and claims that "next up" to the blacks on the social scale "were the indentured white servants— very many of them Irish men and women—who were bought and sold like chattels by their Christian masters" (199). Subsequently,

---

3. Incidentally, some historians have taken issue with this privileging of the Famine moment in Irish emigration history. For Kevin Kenny, "What tends to be overlooked is that the great famine was but one especially tragic and dramatic episode in a much larger story. Two million people fled Ireland as a result of the famine, but almost four times that number left the country during other periods" (2003, 144–45).

however, O'Connor phraseology slips from "indentured servants" to "Irish slaves" (202, 204). Like *The Secret World of the Irish Male*, O'Connor closes *Sweet Liberty* by recounting a musical anecdote that speaks to perceived Irish-black connections. On his last night in San Francisco before returning to Ireland, a black woman performs "A Stór mo Chroí"—a "slow and desperate ballad of emigrant longing"—in an Irish pub, bringing, according to O'Connor, "a new level of meaning to the song which was both humbling and moving" (363). The song, which O'Connor quotes in full, reinforces the effect of the juxtaposed positive-negative chapter epigraphs. It foregrounds the contradictions of the migrant's destination: "rich in its treasures golden," but where there are also "faces with hunger paling" (363). The fact that a black woman performs the song in California implies that it is an experience *shared* by both the Irish and the African Americans in the New World.

Smoked Irish?

In *Star of the Sea*, O'Connor's interest in possible connections between Irish and African diasporic subjects takes two interrelated forms: first, the novel provides an example of what Jason King identifies as the "implicit analogy to be drawn between the historical plight of Irish Famine migrants and asylum-seekers and refugees coming to Ireland today" (2003, 202); second, it explores affinities between Famine Irish and their African American contemporaries. As King demonstrates, the Famine Irish and contemporary asylum seeker analogy is prevalent in Irish political discourse and is also perceptible in Jim Minogue's play *Flight to Gross Ile* (1999). In Minogue's play, a French Canadian priest—played, in the Mountjoy Prison production King discusses, by black inmate Tola Mohmoh—welcomes Famine refugees who disembark at Grosse Ile.[4] The actor-character layering

4. Minogue's play was also performed in Skibbereen, County Cork, in May 2009. Skibbereen was chosen to host a week of events organized to coincide with

thus challenges audiences—which, on one occasion, included then minister for justice, equality, and law reform John O'Donoghue— to consider connections between past emigration *from* Ireland and contemporary immigration *to* Ireland. Furthermore, in Gerry Stembridge's TV movie *Black Day at Blackrock* (2001), inhabitants of a small rural Irish town react with hostility to the government's decision to house asylum seekers in the area. At a tense town-hall meeting, the symbolically named history teacher Brian Cross "reads out a letter home from a Famine emigrant whose anxieties and fears in a strange land could equally have been expressed by a contemporary refugee in Ireland" (Gibbons 2005a, 221–22).

Luke Gibbons has argued that "the ability to look outward, and particularly to identify with the plight of refugees and asylum-seekers, may be best served by reclaiming those lost narratives of the past which generate new solidarities in the present" (2002, 105). For some, one such "lost narrative" is the connections between Irish and African diasporic subjects in nineteenth-century America based on the "catastrophic events" of their respective histories: the Great Famine and chattel slavery. However, in Ronan Noone's plays *The Lepers of Baile Baiste* (2001) and *The Blowin of Baile Gall* (2002), which I discuss in more detail in chapter 3, the Famine emerges as a kind of shorthand for Irish victimhood, which, in *Baile Gall*, ultimately absolves its white Irish postcolonial subjects of racial violence. In considering *Star of the Sea*, then, I am concerned, along with Diane Negra, about "the cultural reservoir of associations between Irishness and innocence" in the contemporary moment (2006a, 363).

Does identifying as a postcolonial Irish subject insulate that subject from charges of racism? Do that subject's claims to postcolonial status trump his or her whiteness? How effective are such analogies in generating meaningful understanding by Celtic Tiger Irish subjects of the struggles faced by contemporary asylum seekers and

---

the inaugural National Famine Memorial Day, marked annually since 2009 on May 17.

refugees? Is the potential of such analogies, if they hold any potential, undermined by the fact that parallels drawn between Irishness and blackness also serve to bolster a sense of enduring Irish victimhood—and, by extension, white innocence—in the contemporary moment? In other words, are such analogies too deeply implicated in structures of white power to be effective in generating cross-racial solidarity? Gibbons continues that "to reclaim the memory of those who have been forgotten or who have been written out of history . . . is not to indulge in the self-absorption of victim culture but the opposite: to engage in an act of ethical imagination in which one's own uneven development becomes not just a way in, but a way out, a means of empathising with other peoples and societies in similar situations today" (2002, 104). What is at stake in O'Connor's novel is precisely this question: how effectively does he negotiate his "act of ethical imagination" so that it does not simply collapse into "the self-absorption of victim culture"?

One useful way of configuring proclamations of affinities between Famine Irish and African American slaves is by adapting bell hooks's notion of "eating the other." For hooks, offering examples from popular culture such as "crossover" popular music and interracial buddy movies, "eating the other" signifies the attempt by whites to embody the "spirit or special characteristics" of a perceived "primitive" nonwhite Other (1999, 31). Where such cross-racial transgressions by whites would, historically, have been taboo, their present-day acceptability is not evidence of a radical social transformation or of political advancement for nonwhite peoples, but rather of whites' continued investment in a fantasy of white supremacy and dominance. However, even hooks concedes that there are some (or, at least, one: she cites John Waters's film *Hairspray* [1988]) instances in which white cross-racial transgression translates into solidarity, where blackness "is not vital because it represents the 'primitive' but because it invites engagement in a revolutionary ethos that dares to challenge the *status quo*" (37). Such a dilemma—whether cross-racial sympathy is always an impulse to recolonize and appropriate, or whether it might sometimes be "revolutionary"—has been articulated before and since hooks's "eating the other." Indeed, I return to these ideas in chapter 3's discussion of "*The Cambria.*" What makes the formulation particularly helpful in this context is the concept of "eating," for it is through their own victimhood (literally, their starvation) that the Famine Irish can lay claim to a particular affinity with ("eat") African American slaves. Hooks's formulation conveys powerfully the dangers of overemphasizing this narrative of Irish victimhood in the contemporary moment: that it may act to consume or, as Negra puts it, "displace and/or neutralize the identity claims" of African Americans and other non-white peoples (2006b, 3).

The contemporary resonances of *Star of the Sea* and the implications of the Irish and African American affinities that O'Connor creates can be examined fruitfully by unpacking the novel's central motif, the ship. In "Writing the Boom," Fintan O'Toole claims that "the emergence of a frantic, globalized, dislocated Ireland has deprived fiction writers of some of their traditional tools." For O'Toole, one of these tools is "a distinctive sense of place. To write honestly of where most of us live now is to describe everywhere and nowhere" (2001, 12). The "everywhere and nowhere" quality of the space of contemporary Ireland recalls Michel Foucault's definition of heterotopias as places that are "outside of all places, even though it may be possible to indicate their location in reality" (1986, 24). Distinguishing between "utopia" and "heterotopia," Foucault defines the heterotopia as "counter-sites [*sic*]," a kind of "effectively enacted utopia in which the real sites, all the other real sites that can be found within the culture, are simultaneously represented, contested, and inverted" (24). For Foucault, the ship is "the heterotopia *par excellence*" (27). It could be argued, therefore, that O'Connor's *Star of the Sea* represents contemporary Ireland, displaced in both time (back to the mid-nineteenth century) and the "everywhere and nowhere" space of the ship. Indeed, in his review of *Redemption Falls*, Declan Kiberd identifies the (perhaps overliteralized) significance of O'Connor's ship in the context of contemporary Ireland. Kiberd claims that "*Star of the Sea* used the reports of dead bodies arriving on coffin-ships in 1840s America to cast an angular light upon a contemporary Ireland in which refugees from Eastern Europe arrived asphyxiated in container-trucks in Rosslare" (2007, 12).

The novel's ship setting is important for an additional reason, that is, the importance of the ship chronotope to Paul Gilroy's conceptualization of the Black Atlantic. Gilroy theorizes "the image of ships in motion across the spaces between Europe, America, Africa, and the Caribbean" as "a central organising symbol" of the Black Atlantic (1993, 4). Following Gilroy, to a greater or lesser degree, Atlantic history has, according to David Armitage, "recently become much more multicoloured. The black Atlantic of the African diaspora has been joined by the green Atlantic of the Irish dispersal." There is also the red Atlantic "of expropriation and capitalism, proletarianization and resistance" (2001, 479). Indebted to Gilroy, though he does not cite him, Kevin Whelan also emphasizes the importance of "the 'wooden world' of the ship" to both trajectories of the transatlantic community that he terms the "Green Atlantic" (2004, 231). *Green Atlantic* is a useful term for the purposes of this argument because it foregrounds the central issue that is troubling in relation to *Star of the Sea*, namely, the nature of its assumed relationship with the Black Atlantic. For Gilroy, the history of the Black Atlantic, "continually crisscrossed by the movements of black people . . . provides a means to re-examine the problems of nationality, location, identity, and historical memory" (1993, 16). As I understand it, historians of the "Green Atlantic" do not so much promote it as a culture created by the crisscrossings of the Irish diaspora, but see it as a culture that *always already* intersects with the Black Atlantic. Whelan claims, for example, that "the constant motion of the ships tied and untied connections across and between disparate worlds and a commonality emerged in these Atlantic port cities. Here was the most complex blending of peoples and cultures, where the 'green' and 'black' merged into an incipiently 'red' Atlantic of a newly internationalized proletariat" (2004, 234). A recent edited collection is another case in point. Although Peter O'Neill and David Lloyd acknowledge that the experiences of "racialization and citizenship" of African and Irish diasporic subjects "not only differed utterly but were constituted differentially," their emphasis remains on "'points of contact, overlap and cooperation'—as well as competition and exploitation—across the Atlantic" (2009, xvi). We must be aware, in other words, that the term *Green Atlantic* authenticates itself by its assumed relationship to the Black Atlantic. In *Star of the Sea*, O'Connor invokes the Black and Green Atlantics by drawing parallels, both explicit and tacit, between the institution of American slavery and the Great Famine, most obviously by deploying the motif of the ship itself.

One of the reasons for which ships are important, according to Gilroy, is because they "refer us back to the middle passage, to the half-remembered micro-politics of the slave trade" (1993, 17). Significantly, "in her eighty-year span," the *Star* "had borne many cargoes: wheat from Carolina for the hungry of Europe, Afghanistan opium, 'blackpowder' explosive, Norwegian timber, sugar from the Mississippi, African slaves for the sugar plantations" (O'Connor 2002, xvii). In a former role, then, the aging ship carrying starving Irish peasants to the United States was also responsible for transporting African slaves to the New World. Moreover, Gilroy's formulation of the ship as "a living, micro-cultural, micro-political system in motion" can be applied quite effectively to the *Star of the Sea* (1993, 4). With more than four hundred passengers in steerage and only fifteen in superior accommodation, with its British, Irish, American, and Indian passengers, with its multicultural crew, and with its Catholic, Anglican, Quaker, and Jewish passengers and crew, the *Star* is a space in which issues of class, race, religion, and nationality can and do collide.

From the outset, then, O'Connor establishes a fundamental connection between the Great Famine and American slavery. This link is reinforced through the antagonistic relationship that exists between the American Grantley Dixon and fellow passenger Lord David Merridith. Dixon is a journalist for the *New York Tribune* and an aspiring novelist who, having spent some months in Britain and Ireland, reporting on various matters including the Famine, is traveling back to the United States aboard the *Star of the Sea*. The text of *Star of the Sea* is presented as Dixon's memoirs. Merridith is a Connemara landowner of the Ascendancy class who has been bankrupted by the Famine and is emigrating to the United States with his wife and two children. Their hostility toward each other has its roots in their irreconcilable views on the Famine and, for the reader, is intensified by the fact that, unbeknownst to Merridith, Dixon is having an affair with Merridith's wife. In the first of several bitter exchanges between the two men aboard the ship, Dixon demands of Merridith: "How many of [the tenants his father evicted] are in Clifden Workhouse tonight . . . ? Spouses kept apart as a condition of entry. Children younger than your own torn from their parents to *slave*" (O'Connor 2002, 14; emphasis added). The lexical comparison Dixon draws between slavery and the plantation system in Ireland is turned against him in a subsequent exchange, in which Merridith accuses Dixon of hypocrisy because he himself comes from a slaveholding Louisiana family. Indeed, Dixon suffers from profound guilt for continuing to accept an allowance from his grandfather, although his grandfather is an opponent of slavery and has purchased the freedom of several slaves. Nevertheless, Dixon feels himself "in hock to dirty money" and berates himself for his "duplicitous compromise" (329).

The analogies O'Connor draws between the Great Famine and American slavery are also imaginative. O'Connor's depiction of the Great Famine in *Star of the Sea* resonates with representations of American slavery, notably in Toni Morrison's *Beloved* (1987).[5] In a letter written to his wife, Mary Duane, in 1845, Nicholas Mulvey describes his attempt to prevail upon their landlord to have their eviction overturned. In desperation at his failure, he kills both himself and their daughter. Much like Sethe in *Beloved*, the trauma of the Great Famine was so great, O'Connor implies, that a parent would commit infanticide rather than subject his child to further horrors. Throughout the suicide note, Mulvey describes bearing witness to "unspeakable sights," finally admitting that "I cannot write

---

5. Interestingly, Kiberd calls *Redemption Falls* "a superb artistic achievement, worthy of comparison with Morrison's own book, *Beloved*" (2007, 12).

it. It can never be written, Mary" (39). G. Grantley Dixon, though a wordsmith, is forced to conclude, "The Famine could not be turned into a simile. The best word for death was death" (129). Equally, the ship's captain, Josiah Lockwood, keeps a diary in which he records the shocking discovery of a young man and woman lying dead in each other's embrace aboard the *Star of the Sea*. He concludes by noting: "I can write no more. There is no more to be written" (279). In a radio interview with Tom McGurk, O'Connor reinforces this sense of the Famine as an unspeakable trauma: "People have noted the fact that Dickens, for example, the great storyteller of the poor and his fantastic commitment to the powerless in society, wrote nothing about the Famine. Even the great Irish writers . . . it's a very spectral presence in Yeats, Joyce doesn't mention the Famine much" (O'Connor 2007b). In so doing, he is echoing Terry Eagleton, whose *Heathcliff and the Great Hunger* O'Connor cites in *Star of the Sea* (409), wherein Eagleton claims that the Great Famine was "the threatened death of the signifier" (1996, 11). According to Eagleton, "There is a handful of novels and a body of poems [about the Famine], but few truly distinguished works. Where is the Famine in the literature of the Revival? Where is it in Joyce?" (13). In a 2005 interview, O'Connor cites precisely this passage (Estevez-Saá 2005, 161). Despite Margaret Kelleher's counterassertion that "the extent to which Irish literature contains references to the famine depends, very simply, on where one looks" (1997, 4), O'Connor insists on the unspeakability or unrepresentability of the Famine, just as others— such as Morrison—have claimed that the institution of American slavery "was not a story to pass on" (1987, 274–75).

In the parallels drawn between the Great Famine and American slavery, *Star of the Sea* can be compared with other means by which the Famine is remembered, imagined, and taught.[6] Writing

6. Indeed, there is every indication that *Star of the Sea* is already affecting the ways in which the Irish Famine is remembered and imagined. In June 2007, Irish president Mary McAleese opened Ireland Park in Toronto, a patch of land

on the incorporation of the study of the Irish Famine into American public school curricula in New York and New Jersey from the late 1990s onward, Catherine Eagan contends that "at times, this commemoration and education converged with Irish Americans' romanticized notions of Irish-black solidarity in unhealthy ways" (2006, 40). In other words, focusing on or creating correspondences between the experiences of the Irish during the Famine, Jews during the Holocaust, and enslaved African Americans may have the effect of enabling white Irish Americans "to link 'Irishness' to a heritage of oppression that is in many ways very distant from their present-day lives" (21). Critiquing, in particular, the New Jersey Famine Curriculum, designed by James Mullin, Eagan argues that it "so stacks the deck in favor of concluding that the Irish were victims of racism and genocide that it ultimately fails to encourage the freedom of thinking and complex levels of questioning necessary for such a curriculum to be relevant in a multicultural, multinational world" (44).

Intriguingly, Eagan expressly objects to the curriculum's facile deployment of "racially explosive quotations and cartoon caricatures" (47). O'Connor intersperses his narrative with exactly these kinds of quotations and cartoons. Placed prominently on the title page of *Star of the Sea*, for example, is a cartoon from *Harper's Weekly*, showing the apparent physical similarities between the "Irish-Iberian" subject and the "Negro" subject. Equally, on the page that immediately precedes the opening of the novel proper, O'Connor includes a series of quotations from 1847 right through 1916. This device is a quite a neat, structural decision because the novel ends with ninety-six-year-old Grantley Dixon's final reflections on the *Star of the Sea* voyage on Easter Saturday, 1916, the day before the Rising in Dublin. The

---

commemorating the thirty-eight thousand Irish who arrived in the city between May and October 1847. The centerpiece for the park is a collection of five sculptures by Rowan Gillespie, who was also responsible for creating the Famine figures on Dublin's north quays. One of the five sculptures in Toronto is explicitly based on Pius Mulvey, the fictional character from *Star of the Sea*.

first and the third quotations are of particular interest in the context of Eagan's essay. The first is from British Treasury secretary Charles Trevelyan, claiming in 1846 that the Famine was "a punishment from God for an idle, ungrateful and rebellious country." The third, from an 1862 issue of *Punch,* describes the "missing link" between the Negro and the gorilla: the Irish Yahoo. Eagan refers specifically to both these quotations in her critique of Mullin's New Jersey curriculum, finding that the *Punch* quotation, in particular, is "uncritically used" (62).

By including the "Irish-Iberian" cartoon on the title page, and the *Punch* quotation subsequently, O'Connor is clearly telegraphing the notion that the Irish were racialized, first, under British colonial rule and, subsequently, when they emigrated, in the United States. It is probably no coincidence that George Wellesley, the sole Briton aboard the ship apart from Captain Lockwood, is the mouthpiece for some of the most racist statements in the novel. Interestingly, Wellesley's use of the racial slur "nig-nog" speaks as much to usage in contemporary British culture as it does to application to African Americans in the nineteenth century, as O'Connor is well aware. (In *The Secret World of the Irish Male,* O'Connor recounts how a London florist refers to Pakistanis as "nig nogs" in his presence [1994b, 50]). In a letter written to Grantley Dixon in 1852, Wellesley describes the Irishman Pius Mulvey as "rather like a Caucasian nigger, if such a horrid centaur exists. Not evil as such but more childlike and stupid" (O'Connor 2002, 294). Through Wellesley, O'Connor implies that the process of categorizing the Irish as racially inferior—a procedure undergone when the Irish migrated to the United States—was introduced under British colonial rule.

Is O'Connor's insistence on the fact that the Irish were racialized by first the British and then by native white Americans an "inevitably conservative formulation" (Negra 2006b, 3)? Or does it mean something completely different in the specific context of the Irish nation-state? As Terry Eagleton observes in his review of *Star,* "Brooding on the one million dead and the one million who fled the famine is hardly much in vogue in an Ireland keen to play down its colonial past and flaunt its new-found modernity" (2003, n.p.). O'Connor's decision to revisit the Famine in his fiction could thus be interpreted as a reminder to Celtic Tiger Irish of the status of their ancestors as colonized subjects. This reminder is particularly timely, given that the novel was published at a moment during which there was increasing opposition to immigration to Ireland, especially by that "national bogeyman—the bogus asylum-seeker" (Garner 2007b, 118–19). A comment made by the ship's captain, Josiah Lockwood, seems especially up to date in this regard. Lockwood observes that "if the world were somehow turned downside-up; if Ireland were a richer land and other nations now mighty were distressed; as certain as I know that the dawn must come, the people of Ireland would welcome the frightened stranger with that gentleness and friendship which so ennobles their character" (O'Connor 2002, 279). There is every indication that, in this passage, Lockwood's consciousness is very close to O'Connor's: Ireland has quite clearly *not* welcomed the frightened stranger despite the reversal in its fortunes.[7] The novel might thus be interpreted as an indictment of contemporary complacency and historical amnesia.

Ultimately, I believe that Joseph O'Connor avoids "eating the other" by revealing the complexities of the relationship that existed between the Irish and African Americans. First, while I emphasized the first and third quotations above, it would be entirely misleading not to mention that the third quotation is Young Irelander John Mitchel's 1856 words: "England is truly a great public criminal. England! All England! . . . She must be punished; that punishment will, as I believe, come upon her by and through Ireland; and so Ireland will be avenged. . . . The Atlantic ocean be never so deep as the hell which shall belch down on the oppressors of my race." However,

---

7. It is also significant that Lockwood is a Quaker, known for their antislavery efforts in both Britain and the United States. After the disastrous *Star of the Sea* voyage, Lockwood moves to Ireland with his wife and dedicates the rest of his life to alleviating the sufferings of the starving. Through Lockwood, then, O'Connor implies that Irish Famine relief and abolition are comparable causes.

O'Connor's awareness that Mitchel was "a passionate advocate of freedom in Ireland" *and* "of slavery and white supremacy in the states [*sic*]" mitigates any simplistic correspondence between Irish and African American victimhood that the other quotations, and the novel, might otherwise seem to endorse (O'Connor 2006, n.p.).

Second, O'Connor establishes a structural link between the peasants in steerage and the passengers in first-class accommodation through those individuals who wait upon the first-class passengers. In other words, they inhabit the same space as the first-class passengers, at least for a time, but as mere servants of the upper classes, they have closer socioeconomic ties to the people in steerage. They thus mediate between the class positions of both groups. Significantly, many of these servants are black. Chapter 2 opens with a "Negro" steward stumbling and letting slip an overloaded salver of charged champagne flutes (O'Connor 2002, 5). In a subsequent exchange between the captain and some of the first-class passengers on the appalling conditions in steerage, Surgeon Mangan points out that "those people down in steerage aren't Africans, after all," to which the agent of the Royal Mail, George Wellesley, responds, "Nig-nogs are cleaner" (13). This discussion is important because it references the Middle Passage, and the ship's own role in the slave trade, immediately after the reader has encountered a nonslave black waiter.

In *Black Jacks: African American Seamen in the Age of Sail*, Jeffrey Bolster laments the fact that "an image of manacled ancestors crammed together aboard slave ships has triumphed as the association of African Americans with the sea," and recovers the contribution of African American sailors to maritime history (1997, 2). Although, as Bolster points out, whites expected African American maritime workers to sail as cooks or stewards—jobs "not defined by nautical skill and physical courage"—because it reinforced their associations of African Americans with femininity, many black men "paradoxically assumed the most 'feminine' roles aboard white-dominated ships to maintain their masculine roles as respectable providers in the black community" (167–68). The characters of color—Chinese, Jamaican, Haitian, African American—present in *Star of the Sea* are not slaves, but free, working men. Under the plantation system in Ireland at the time, the passengers in steerage would have been servants of the passengers in first-class. In the "countersite" that is the *Star of the Sea*, O'Connor substitutes the Irish servants for black stewards. Rather than making them symbolically interchangeable, however, I interpret this move as O'Connor's gesturing toward the competition of Irish and free blacks for domestic service positions in the New World. Once the *Star* docks in New York Harbour, those passengers in steerage who have survived the journey will jostle with free African Americans for employment. O'Connor thus recognizes that the relationship between the emigrant Irish and African Americans was often one of antagonism rather than solidarity.

Last, and to return finally to the chronotope of the ship, it is significant that when the *Star* first embarks upon its voyage, it encounters another famous ship, *The Duchess of Kent*, which is carrying the remains of Daniel O'Connell "from his death-place in Genoa in August of that year, to be laid to rest in his motherland" (O'Connor 2002, xv). Only six years prior to the setting of this novel, of course, Daniel O'Connell had led the signatories of an address by sixty thousand Irish to their compatriots in the United States calling upon them to unite in support of the abolitionist cause. For O'Connell, slavery represented "the worst of all aristocracies—that of human skin" (Ignatiev 1995, 16). The encounter between the two ships, the crisscrossing of *The Duchess of Kent* and the *Star of the Sea*, reminds readers of the short-lived coalition between the leaders of the Irish national struggle and prominent American abolitionists. Established through the figure of Daniel O'Connell, the alliance disintegrated completely after O'Connell's arrest on charges of conspiracy and inciting sedition in October 1843. The encounter between the two ships thus symbolizes the transatlantic transition undergone by countless Irish of the period: from oppressed race in the Old Country to oppressing race in the New World. In so doing, O'Connor's novel ultimately resists facile equations of Irish and black solidarity, refusing to romanticize the relationship while reminding his readers of both the presence and the prescience of the past.

In *Redemption Falls*, O'Connor is also attentive to the relationship between the Famine Irish generation and their African American contemporaries, though he is even less equivocal about the nature of this relationship. The novel's opening sentence, which situates Eliza Duane Mooney—the daughter of Mary Duane from *Star of the Sea*—hurrying out from Baton Rouge "through the criminal districts of the town, then the black section, then the Irish," immediately signals O'Connor's interest in the relative places of Irish and African Americans within the socioracial hierarchy of 1860s America and provokes readers to consider whether such physical proximity always or ever translated into solidarity (O'Connor 2007d, 3). The novel follows the last years in the life of Irish-born former Union general James C. O'Keeffe, who is appointed acting governor of the Mountain Territory (likely Montana) after the Civil War. Also known as Con O'Keeffe or "O'Keeffe of the Blade," "elements of [his] curriculum vitae have echoes in that of Irish nationalist Thomas F. Meagher," as O'Connor acknowledges (458). Meagher, known as "Meagher of the Sword," participated in the ill-fated Irish uprising against Britain in 1848 and, having had his sentence to hanging commuted, was transported to Van Diemen's Land. After escaping in 1852 and settling in the United States, he subsequently became brigadier general of the 69th Regiment of the New York Militia during the American Civil War. Like Meagher, O'Keeffe participated in the failed 1848 Young Ireland rebellion against Britain, had his sentence to hanging commuted, was transported to Van Diemen's Land, escaped to the United States, and becomes a Civil War general and subsequently governor of newly organized western territory.

While living in the Mountain Territory town of Redemption Falls, O'Keeffe takes in a displaced, apparently mute Confederate drummer boy called Jeddo Mooney, against the wishes of O'Keeffe's progressively estranged wife, aspiring poet Lucia-Cruz McLelland. The novel opens in January 1865 with Jeddo's sister, eighteen-year-old Eliza Duane Mooney, setting off from her home in Baton Rouge, Louisiana, to search for her lost brother. Two years later, in a bloody dénouement, a series of misunderstandings between Eliza's people (led by the man she marries on her travels, the bandit Johnny Thunders) and O'Keeffe's posse results in the deaths of twenty-nine people, including Eliza and O'Keeffe, whose body is never recovered. Like *Star of the Sea*, *Redemption Falls* is a compilation of documents—songs, excerpts, evidence, letters, interview transcripts, poster bills—collected in scrapbooks belonging to Jeremiah McLelland, the professor of folklore who narrates the McLelland-O'Keeffes' story from the vantage point of 1937.

In Will Kaufman's study *The Civil War in American Culture*, he finds that "progressively antagonistic relations between the Irish and African-Americans before and during the Civil War" are "central to the war's transnational dimension" (2006, 135). Drawing on Ignatiev's *How the Irish Became White*—a work with which O'Connor is also familiar (Spain 2007, 11)—Kaufman focuses on Daniel O'Connell's involvement with the cause of abolition, representations of the New York City Draft Riots of 1863, and Steve Earle's song "Dixieland," which Kaufman describes as "a significant attempt to depict an alternative history of the Irish in Civil War–era America—an attempt to wrest that history from Bill the Butcher, the rioters of New York and Margaret Mitchell's Irish slaveholder, Gerald O'Hara" (2006, 139). Like Kaufman, O'Connor sees encounters and interactions between Irish and African Americans as key to the legacy of the American Civil War and recognizes both the Draft Riots and Mitchell's novel as important to cultural reimaginings of this period. Reflecting on the material contained in his scrapbooks in 1937, Jeremiah McLelland notes that the New York riot, "one of the most shameful atrocities in the history of Irish-America," does not feature "in Irish balladry" (O'Connor 2007d, 444). In his introduction to *Ireland in Exile: Irish Writers Abroad*, O'Connor observes that Ireland's "emigrant culture has traditionally been described in songs rather than novels, plays or poems" and announces his suspicion that "all those sententiously vile ballads about dear little shamrocks, grey-haired macushlas and shagging shillelaghs were written by people who had never been out of *Leitrim*, never mind Ireland, in their lives" (1993, 16). For O'Connor, then, Irish balladry is as selective and problematic as any other form of narrative, occluding and omitting as much as it reveals and uncovers about the Irish emigrant experience.

O'Connor also engages self-consciously with Mitchell's notorious tale of an Irish American southern family in the period 1861 to 1875. In fact, in his review of the novel, Brian Lynch writes that *Redemption Falls* is "*Gone With the Wind* rewritten by a Dublin-born apprentice to Charles Dickens" (2007, 18). Through Elizabeth Longstreet, the former slave who keeps house for O'Keeffe and his wife, O'Connor systematically deconstructs the mythology of *Gone with the Wind*. In Mitchell's novel, Gerald O'Hara's "natural aptitude for cards and amber liquor . . . brought [him] two of his three most prized possessions, his valet and his plantation" (Mitchell 1936, 46). Pork, the valet whom O'Hara wins at cards, admires his master so much that he even attempts an Irish brogue (48). Reversing Mitchell's insistence on the benevolence of O'Hara and the contentment of Pork, O'Connor reveals the inhumanity of southern slaveholders, bartering in human flesh and carelessly separating entire families. Elizabeth recounts how "my mastuh lost my father playin cards in Marianna. My father got took away for his debt. Some say he ended in Texarkana but no way to know it. Missippi. Georgia. Any place" (O'Connor 2002, 45). That this statement is an allusion to *Gone with the Wind* is confirmed when Elizabeth continues: "Mastuh a Irishman. O'Hora his name . . . Wolf got more nature than O'Hora . . . Do ever thing but kill you . . . Cause he paid for you, see. You a dollar to O'Hora. You was livestock" (45).

However, O'Connor's vision of Irish–African American relations before and during the American Civil War is far more expansive than his reference to the Draft Riots and his brief, but clever, reworking of Mitchell's novel. If, for Kaufman, Earle's song represents an "alternative history," O'Connor's novel offers more substantial and wide-ranging "alternative histories." In a 2007 interview, O'Connor observes that "the real story of Irish America is not the Statue of Liberty myth. It's the fact that Irish people were assimilated into all aspects of American life—both the progressive and the reactionary, the anti-slavery side and the absolutely racist side. So we like to pretend that our story in America is a lot simpler than it is. And one of the things I've tried to do in *Redemption Falls* is reflect that it's a lot more complicated" (2007a). For some characters, the Irish–African American relationship is emphatically *not* one of solidarity. For instance, Jeddo Mooney recounts how an Irish Confederate soldier told him, "Pat nothin but a coolieman prayin the beads. Nothin but a slave in a scapular. When they trenched that canal down the hell of New Orleans, it was Irish they put to the gullies. Wouldn't put no slave in. Cause a slave cost him money. But a Irish cost him nothin but pennies a day" (O'Connor 2007d, 53). The Irishman's "powerful sense of grievance" in this case relates to the perceived "worth" of the slave compared with the value of the Irishman. Similarly, Patrick Vinson, one of O'Keeffe's lawmen in the Mountain Territory, claims that there "aint a darkey of this country hungry this mornin, forty acres an a mule to ever last one of these majesties, they are laughin at us, laughin, an why wouldn they laugh itself, for the Irishman as fought like the gawms for the so-call union got a fresh air sandwich for his pains an his trouble and a empty pocket for to put it in" (108).

At the conclusion of *Star of the Sea*, the journalist Grantley Dixon writes, "No doubt some [of *Star*'s survivors] were among the 80,000 native Irishmen who would fight for the Union in the Civil War. And others were among the 20,000 of their countrymen who would take up arms for the cause of the Confederacy; for the legal right of a freedom-loving white man to regard a black man as a commodity" (O'Connor 2002, 387). As O'Connor demonstrates in *Redemption Falls*, however, even the soldiers who fought on the Union side were not necessarily motivated by opposition to slavery. O'Keeffe's attitudes toward the impending war and toward African Americans are profoundly ambivalent. According to Kieran Quinlan, several of the Young Irelanders in the United States had Southern sympathies, "the general opinion [being] that supporting the South seemed to be the right thing to do because its struggle for self-determinacy was very much like Ireland's" (2005, 79). Consistent with the historical figure of Meagher, O'Connor writes O'Keeffe as a man who loves the "sultry, stately cities" of Savannah and Charleston (O'Connor 2007d, 152).[8] When the South secedes, however, O'Keeffe chooses to stand with the Union states (153).[9] O'Keeffe's views of African Americans are also deeply conflicted. Though his beloved nursemaid in Wexford, Beatrice, was a former African slave, "he permitted himself to be attended by her stolen siblings in America . . . and at no time raised his oratory in support of their emancipation" (153). In fact, in a passage deeply reminiscent of fellow US-exiled Young Irelander John Mitchel's racist diatribes in his *Citizen* newspapers of the 1850s, O'Keeffe describes Southern slaves as "well-cared-for and fed, merrier in Mississippi than in the Paganlands of Ethiop" (153). In the *Southern Citizen* in 1857, Mitchel wrote: "I consider Negro slavery here the best state of existence for the Negro and the best for his master; and I consider that taking Negroes out of their brutal slavery in Africa and promoting them to a human and reasonable slavery here is good" (Rolston and Shannon 2002, 8).[10]

---

8. David Gleeson notes that when Meagher came out for the Union, the Charleston Hibernian Society unanimously withdrew the honorary membership it had given him (2010, 143).

9. Citing the following passage from Meagher's writings, Quinlan argues that the federal government's sympathy for the Irish nationalist cause and the prediction that Britain would support the Confederacy likely swayed Meagher in his decision to fight for the Union:

> The identification of the Irish people at home with the Orangemen and Tories of England in their avowed sympathy and active connivance with the rebels . . . will not be forgotten by the jealous exclusionists [the Know Nothings] of this country when the war is over . . . when they remember how, even in the very season when the Loyal States were pouring their grain and gold into Ireland to relieve the starving poor [during the crop failures from 1860 to 1863], the public opinion of Ireland . . . went forth to condemn the action of the national government, and approve the infidelity and usurpation of its enemies. (2005, 79–80)

10. If Meagher inspires the fictional character of O'Keeffe, it is likely that Mitchel appears in *Redemption Falls* in the guise of John Fintan Duggan, a fellow

One of the most pressing challenges in Irish studies today, given that 10 percent of the population of the Republic of Ireland is now foreign born, is the construction (or invention) of an Irish tradition of antiracism (Garner 2004, 214). However, if building an antiracist tradition means appealing endlessly to supposed affinities between Irish and African Americans, white Irish and Irish Americans run the risk of "recalling their oppression while continuing to enjoy the benefits of white privilege, thus appropriating the suffering of people of color for their own psychic ease" (Eagan 2006, 43). This double bind—the desire to acknowledge instances of Irish–African American solidarity without the self-congratulation and self-absolution from charges of racism that such proclamations may encourage—has resulted in the "mixed strategies of self-criticism and historical retrieval" that Michael Malouf has identified in recent attempts to build a tradition of Irish antiracism (2006, 321). In *Redemption Falls*, O'Connor reveals Irish and Irish American attitudes toward African Americans and slavery to be multifarious and ambivalent across and even within the individual psyches of his diverse cast of characters. O'Connor's novel is thus capacious enough to do justice to "the complex and ambivalent legacy of encounters between Irish people and people of colour both inside and outside Ireland" (Rolston and Shannon 2002, 6).

The Future of This Republic?

O'Connor's preoccupation with issues of race and immigration in contemporary Ireland is also evident in the proliferation of mixed-race subjects in *Star* and *Redemption Falls*. Indeed, one of the arguments of this study, as I indicate in the introduction, is the adoption, if you will, of mixed-race subjects from American culture into contemporary Irish literature and culture. This burgeoning fascination

---

Van Diemen's Land escapee who ends up supporting the Confederacy and loses two sons in the war (O'Connor 2007d, 241).

with mixed-race subjects, which I unpack in greater detail in chapter 5, must surely be a consequence of the increasingly visible presence of nonwhite individuals in Irish society. In her introduction to the only (to my knowledge) collection of testimony by mixed-race Irish subjects, Margaret McCarthy recounts her own experiences as a mother of a mixed-race child born in 1978. From a trip to South Africa in 1981, where McCarthy faced abuse by Afrikaner men disgusted that she could "lower [herself] to give birth to something like *that*," to Dublin in 1995, where her teenage daughter is subjected to Nazi-style salutes, slogans and shouts of "Niggers out. Keep Ireland white," McCarthy suggests that attitudes toward mixed-race subjects in contemporary Ireland are not all that different from the ones prevalent in apartheid-era South Africa (2001, 9). At "the start of this new Millennium, it is not easy for a non-white person living in Ireland," writes McCarthy. It is "difficult to predict the future beyond speculation and careful optimism," she continues, "Some things are different today. Others are not" (10).

McCarthy's "careful optimism" contrasts with O'Connor's (rhetorical) championing of ambiguously raced subjects in both *Star of the Sea* and *Redemption Falls*. Although it is clear that his motivation is to endeavor, first, to interrogate whiteness as a racial category (in other words, to challenge the process by which "race" becomes synonymous with "nonwhite" or "person of color") and, second, to dismantle the notion of "race" altogether, the mixed-race subject has, as several critics have shown, proven to be a dubious device in attempts to contest the tenacity of racial categories. As Habiba Ibrahim observes, although whiteness studies and mixed-race studies share "a similar commitment to disrupting the assumptions on which racial hierarchies are based," they may also serve "to particularize mixed racialism, so that it becomes a distinct mode of subjecthood, neither inauthentically or tragically black nor not quite white" (2007, 157). Ibrahim's concerns echo Amy Robinson's with regard to racial "passing"—usually undertaken by a light-skinned, possibly mixed-race African American subject—which, as Robinson puts it, is "thoroughly invested in the logic of the system it attempts to subvert" (1996, 237). In other words, by "crossing the color line," the passer *simultaneously* subverts and reinforces the racial binary. She or he subverts it by exposing its constructedness, its permeability, its instability. But in the very act of passing, she or he also reinforces it by granting authority and credibility to the mythical "color line" as a real and true boundary to be transgressed.

In this context, it is worth considering the multiple ambiguities of *Star*'s author-protagonist, Grantley Dixon. Asserting his own claim to native Irishness, Lord Merridith tells Dixon that his family has been in Ireland since 1650, "a while before the white man stole America from the Indians" (O'Connor 2002, 131). This statement is intended as a jibe at Dixon, because he subsequently excoriates the American's grandfather for not having rid himself of the lands that slavery purchased for his ancestors and for not giving back his inheritance to the children of those slaves who made it (134). He thus implicates Dixon in a double act of dispossession: dispossession of Native Americans and of African Americans. However, in a final twist, it emerges that Dixon is himself one-eighth Choctaw on his father's side, a fact that precludes him from adopting a child when he returns to the United States (his "negritude" the reason for his "unsuitability" [403]). In the year or two preceding Ireland's sesquicentennial commemoration of the Famine, it was discovered that the Choctaw Nation donated $170 toward Irish Famine relief in 1847, which was reasonably widely reported in the Irish and Irish American press from the mid-1990s on (Cullingford 2001, 173). The revelation of Dixon's Choctaw ancestry may represent O'Connor's desire to convey the very fine ("blood")line separating whites from nonwhites, dispossessing from dispossessed. However, the fact remains that *despite* Dixon's ancestry, he "looks" white—as white, indeed, as President Wilson (O'Connor 2002, 403)—and remains socially and economically privileged, thus reinforcing, rather than challenging, the socioracial hierarchy.

In *Redemption Falls*, ambiguously raced subjects surface with some frequency. Jeddo Mooney, like Joe Christmas in William Faulkner's *Light in August* (1932), believes his father to have been "a mexicano" (O'Connor 2007d, 131), but his half-sister, Eliza, appears to confirm that his parents were *"Darkey and Irish"* (197). When Jeddo first sees Lucia, he wonders if *she* is a mulatta (57). Moreover, Lucia's pet name for her sister is "Malinche" (O'Connor 2007d, 261), a reminder that the Americas were built upon what Sharon Monteith terms "interracial foundational relationships" such as Pocahontas and John Smith, La Malinche and Hernán Cortés, and Thomas Jefferson and Sally Hemings (1993, 33). By becoming lovers of conquering men, according to Suzanne Bost, Pocahontas and La Malinche "have thus assumed symbolic responsibility for fusing the cultures of the colonizer and the colonized" (2005, 59). O'Keeffe's son, Robert Emmet O'Keeffe, his child with his Aboriginal wife, is of nonwhite ancestry, not only on his mother's side but also, O'Keeffe reveals, on his own: "I myself have Caribbean blood, from an ancestor who was once established at Jamaica. So you see, dearest Robert, I am myself of 'the Negro race,' whatever those words might signify" (O'Connor 2007d, 411). Writing to his son in Australia, O'Keeffe assures him that "any person that uses the term 'half-breed' about his fellow human being requires our prayers and our pity" (411). He further claims that "the bravest heroes in this country are of African ancestry, indeed are, in my estimation, the future of this Republic" (412). Like Josiah Lockwood's "downside-up" remarks in *Star of the Sea*, O'Keeffe's reference to "this Republic" could equally pertain to contemporary Ireland as to nineteenth-century America.

To what end, then, does O'Connor include these racially mixed characters? Undoubtedly, he seeks to contest the notion of whiteness as the normative standard from which nonwhite people, by virtue of their "color," deviate. As Elizabeth Longstreet puts it: "see ignorant people dont got no ken of the world: Nigger ain no color, it the place you put to stand. I seen slaves white as milk. Masters darker than me. Ever black they call a nigger, not ever nigger black" (105), effectively paraphrasing whiteness studies scholar Valerie Babb, who writes that "whiteness can be better comprehended if thought of not solely as a biological category of pigmentation or hair texture, but rather a means through which certain individuals are granted greater degrees of social acceptance and access than other individuals" (1998, 3). Similarly, Eliza Duane Mooney reflects on the word "Colored. What does it mean? Does anyone not have a color?" (O'Connor 2007d, 199). As Richard Dyer argues, "As long as race is something only applied to non-white people, as long as white people are not racially seen and named, they/we function as a human norm" (1999, 1).

However, O'Connor reinforces some of the most problematic aspects of "tragic mulatto" narratives, which often position the mixed-race protagonist as a passive victim, the object of an inquisitive white gaze. This point is certainly true of Jeddo, as various characters attempt to determine his racial ancestry. O'Keeffe writes on first encountering the boy that he is "maybe mulatto" (O'Connor 2007d, 37). One of O'Keeffe's deputies, Calhoun, believes him to be a "Melungeon," an "Appalachian whose ancestry is white, black and Indian, for his coloring is unusual, and he is fast on his feet, more nimble than most white children are" (178). A Civil War memoirist speculates that "his mother might have been a fine-countenanced Portugee or what the Cubanos call 'a moro,' meaning a moor" (123). Lucia remarks on his "Mediterranean appearance" (237) and Allen Winterton on his "dark complectedness" and a physiognomy similar to that of "southern Italians, also cockneys" (297). Jeddo's objectification is reinforced by his apparent muteness: not only is he "looked at" obsessively, but he cannot (or does not) talk back to those individuals who attempt to define and circumscribe him. Ultimately, as is borne out in my analysis of *The Nephew* (1998), appeals to the mixed-race subject as embodying the possibilities of a multiracial Ireland invite as many representational problems as they appear to resolve.

"The Prison of National Tribal Vanity"

In negotiating issues of race and immigration in contemporary Ireland in his historical novels of Irish America, O'Connor is arguably most effective where the connection is least obvious: that is, in his privileging of transnational over national identity. As Steve Loyal contends, the nation-building project that characterized the

postindependence years of the Irish Free State relied upon the assertion of an Irish identity that was uncompromisingly white and Catholic (2003, 75). Meanwhile, O'Connor himself writes that Ireland
had always conceived of itself as "greater than its borders" until it
became a "disconnected island . . . in the early years of its semi-
independence" (1993, 17). If, for O'Connor, Irish independence is
associated with a very narrow, territorial sense of Irish identity, for
Loyal, postindependence Irish identity also purports to be racially
and religiously homogeneous. O'Connor's favoring of transnational
over national identity in *Redemption Falls* thus perhaps represents
an attempt to insist upon a kind of Irishness that is more diverse than
many would previously have been prepared to acknowledge.

O'Connor's interest in the tensions between "nation" and "trans-
nation" is evident in several ways. In the first issue of the *Global
South*, Diane Roberts asks, "Where is the South? Nobody's sure.
Is it the eleven states of the old Confederacy? Does Texas count?
Does Florida? It was the third state to secede after South Carolina
and Alabama. Why does the boundary surveyed by Charles Mason
and Jeremiah Dixon in the 1760s still have such symbolic importance? What about Missouri, Maryland and Kentucky, slave states
that didn't secede?" (2007, 127). Roberts explicitly invokes the Civil
War as a reference point for the problem of defining "the American South." However, the Civil War era and its aftermath also presented problems in terms of delineating the rest of the United States.
After all, the immediate concern of *Redemption Falls* is not with the
Civil War years per se, but with western expansion, with the frontier, with newly organized Montana Territory acquired by the United
States during the Louisiana Purchase in 1803. Moreover, the town of
Redemption Falls is situated on the border with Canada. The novel
thus emphasizes the arbitrariness of the United States' self-defini-
tion—to the south, to the west, and to the north.

Another way in which O'Connor explores the conflict between
nation and transnation is by highlighting the extent to which the "nation" cannot contain apparently domestic conflicts. At the beginning

of *Star of the Sea*, the eponymous ship encounters *The Duchess of Kent* returning from Genoa and carrying the remains of Daniel O'Connell. For P. J. Mathews, this encounter represents "the passing of O'Connellite Ireland." According to Mathews, "If O'Connell represented a non-violent democratic tradition within Irish nationalism that strand was eclipsed by more revolutionary tendencies as the nineteenth century progressed. . . . Significantly, the novel's epilogue is dated 'Easter Saturday, 1916'" (2005, 259). *Redemption Falls* could be interpreted as filling in the gap suggested by the shift from the main action of *Star* (set in 1847) to its epilogue (set in 1916), a meditation on the "more revolutionary tendencies" of the Young Irelanders and, indeed, the Fenians who succeeded O'Connell. I read the episode differently, but, in fact, the two analyses are complementary, as Frederick Douglass recognized at the time:

> It was not long after my seeing Mr. O'Connell that his health broke down, and his career ended in death. I felt that a great champion of freedom had fallen, and that the cause of the American slave, not less than the cause of his country, had met with a great loss. All the more was this felt when I saw the kind of men who came to the front when the voice of O'Connell's was no longer heard in Ireland. He was succeeded by the Duffys, Mitchells [*sic*], Meaghers, and others,--men who loved liberty for themselves and for their country, but were utterly destitute of sympathy with the cause of liberty in countries other than their own. (1994, 683)

Coleman Hutchison shows that at any number of moments, "the American Civil War threatened to become an international conflict, one into which Mexico, Germany, France, Britain, and others might well have been drawn" (2007, 435). In *Redemption Falls*, O'Keeffe drifts between the Irish national conflict, the American Civil War, and back to the Irish national conflict. In a (final) letter to his mother in 1862, one of O'Keeffe's soldiers writes, "*general okeef says when this war is over we wll get in boats & go over to ireland & put out the englishmen which som of the boys reckons a mighty plan but i think i will have my belly ful of sogerin by then & will go no more to it"* (O'Connor 2007d, 101–2). Indeed, as Kieran Quinlan notes, some moves were made by the Fenians in the aftermath of the American Civil War to "use the military experience gained by Irishmen in both the Union and Confederate armies, as well as by those in Britain's army, to free their homeland from British rule" (2005, 98).[11]

Equally, O'Connor effectively rejuvenates the by now familiar metaphor of the Civil War as a broken marriage in order to contest the boundaries of "nation."[12] According to David Blight, the "popular literary ritual of intersectional marriage" became common in the three decades following the Civil War (2002, 205). It is not unreasonable, therefore, for O'Connor to present the years leading up to the Civil War as "an unwieldy marriage" edging toward "a brutal divorce" (2007d, 152). By the end of the war, as O'Keeffe sees it, "the shamed continent has been stripped of its name, disowned by the warring parents" (10). Alongside the rift between the states, the marriage between O'Keeffe and Lucia is rapidly deteriorating. As she writes to her sister in 1866, "Con and I have not lived as husband and wife for nine years, since even before the War, since he started

11. Quinlan continues: "Although some of them entertained the quite fantastic hope the Irish-born Union general Phil Sheridan might lead them on such a campaign, the only outcome of all their plotting were several abortive raids into British Canada" (2005, 98).

12. The juxtaposition of war or military conflict with domestic or marital strife is a familiar O'Connor trope. In *Desperadoes* (1994), estranged husband and wife Frank and Eleanor Little travel from Dublin to Nicaragua to identify their dead son, Johnny, and to bring his body back to Ireland to be buried. Like in *Redemption Falls*, then, Irish subjects find themselves caught up in "someone else's civil war," and like in *Redemption Falls*, the "war at home"— flashbacks of the Littles' marital breakdown—is juxtaposed against both their contemporary predicament in war-torn Nicaragua and the conflict in Northern Ireland. In *The Salesman* (1998), Billy and Grace marry on October 20, 1968, the same day that a protest march about Northern Ireland is held in Dublin, thus foreshadowing the domestic conflicts that will tear their family apart: "'Neutral territory?' I remember saying, at one point. 'What Grace, it's a fuckin' war now, is it?'" (O'Connor 1994a, 169).

traveling away from me" (265). In a subsequent letter to O'Keeffe, she writes, "If you wish to fight a war, I will give you one" (310).

If the O'Keeffes' marital problems ostensibly reflect the discord within the nation, a closer look at the marriage metaphor reveals that their problems have distinctly transnational dimensions. Both Lucia and O'Keeffe are transnational subjects: O'Keeffe was born in Ireland, imprisoned in Australia, and now lives in the United States. Though we never learn her precise national or ethnic origin, Lucia is the child of an Anglo-American father, Peter McLelland, and a Latin American mother. When Lucia claims that her husband is "traveling away" from her, she is referring to both physical and psychic removal. He travels to Panama, Nicaragua, Cuba, and Mexico, "where he claims to have associates" (268). One of the recurring issues in their relationship is O'Keeffe's past life in Australia and his marriage to an Aboriginal woman there, of which Lucia is privy to only some of the details. In her attempt at a literary rendering of O'Keeffe's time in Australia, she puns upon the physical space of "Van Diemen's Land" and "Demonland," the psychic space that O'Keeffe occupies, as she perceives it (86). Consistent with her claim that O'Keeffe is "traveling away" from her, marriage is configured as a country, "the Republic of Matrimony": "As with many an exciting destination, once finally reached, you wonder was it worth setting out" (149).

O'Connor's interest in the tensions between nation and trans-nation is reflected in the characters' extreme suspicion of maps. In *Imagined Communities,* a work that paved the way for subsequent theories of transnationalism, Benedict Anderson argues that three institutions in particular—census, map, and museum—"profoundly shaped the way in which the colonial state imagined its dominion— the nature of the human beings it ruled, the geography of its domain, and the legitimacy of its ancestry" (1991, 163–64). Mapping, in an Irish context, has thus historically been associated with British imperial might. The Ordnance Survey Office, established in Dublin in 1824 to map Ireland for land-taxation purposes, came "to be linked in popular memory with the loss of the Irish language and the defeat of the culture" (Connolly 2003, 29). For Catherine Nash, this "mapping of the Irish landscape did not function merely to ease colonial administration, but fixed the 'other' and neutralized the threat of difference by the apparent stability of the map's coherence" (1994, 234). It is significant that *Redemption Falls*'s cartographer, Allen Winterton, leaves the United States to work on the Great Trigonometric Survey of India, testifying to Britain's insistence on mapping its colonies (O'Connor 2007d, 59). However, as Claire Connolly observes, even in an Irish colonial context, the role of mapping is more equivocal than it may first seem. The same detailed maps produced by the Ordnance Survey Office were also a tool used by nationalist groups—of Daniel O'Connell and his successors—"for democratic organization" (2003, 29). Maps may be the instrument of an oppressive colonial administration, but they are also useful in bolstering the emerging postcolonial nation-state. In one of the earliest articulations of Irish transnationalism, Fintan O'Toole contends that a map "is a convenient fiction, a more or less confident representation of the shape a place might take if only you could see it. While the place itself persists, the map, the visual and ideological convention that allows us to call that place 'Ireland' has been slipping away. Its co-ordinates, its longitudes and latitudes, refuse to hold their shape" (1994, 16). O'Toole further argues that "any accurate map of [modern Ireland] must be a map, not of an island, but of a shoreline seen from the water, a set of contours shaped, not by geography, but by voyages. The shape of the island is the shape of all the journeys around it that a history of emigration has set in motion" (17–18).

O'Connor's two novels appear to confirm O'Toole's observations, the ship the overarching symbol in *Star of the Sea*, the map the omnipresent "fiction" in *Redemption Falls*. O'Keeffe finds, in his post as acting governor of the Mountain Territory, that "the maps are all wrong: immense regions uncharted. What maps we possess are copies of older ones, so that they replicate the old faults, &, invariably, multiply them" (O'Connor 2007d, 68). For O'Keeffe, maps tell you "nothing"; compasses are "untrue" (21). Meanwhile, Lucia, describing her husband's "Demonland," echoes O'Keeffe when she writes that "the world has corners that can never be imagined. Maps tell you little worth knowing" (84). War and maps are complicit in their dehumanization of individuals: "Marker moved on a map and ten thousand die, and the map won't remember they ever existed" (56). In his confrontation with Winterton, O'Keeffe shouts: "Men do not *fall* in war, sir. They die! Do you mind me? *War is not a map. It is real*" (299). It is significant, of course, that Winterton is revealed to be untrustworthy and duplicitous, a fortune hunter, and a bigamist. Winterton has a profound faith in maps, claiming that they do not instigate difficulties, "they solve them, or at least make solutions the clearer" (341). In *Redemption Falls*, cartography ultimately emerges as "a euphemism for conquest and thievery; how the burglar inventoried his pickings" (342).

At the end of the novel, O'Connor draws together the transnational, transhistorical aspects of the American Civil War, confirming Kaufman's contention that, "as a cultural event, [it] has transcended time just as it has transcended national boundaries" (2006, 129). McLelland describes the annual Fourth of July gathering of surviving veterans of O'Keeffe's brigade: "They process down the Broadway to Battery Park, a tortuous walk in a Manhattan July. . . . Past those vertebrate turrets that are the glory of our architects—and of all of us, for they speak of indomitable New York. . . . By the walls of the Battery, a silent prayer is offered. . . . A wreath of lilies is blessed and thrown into the harbor, from where so many of their hungry forefathers first set foot on America" (O'Connor 2007d, 452). Although ostensibly a description of a specific geographical location in 1937, O'Connor draws in diverse national contexts, conflicts, and historical moments. July 4 marks the declaration of American independence from Britain in 1776 and conjures the specter of the subsequent Revolutionary War. In 2002 the *Irish Hunger Memorial*, located at Battery Park in the shadow of the decimated Twin Towers, was dedicated. American independence from Britain, the Great Famine, Irish American migration, Irish participation in the American Civil War, the terrorist attacks on the Twin Towers at Manhattan's southern tip on September 11, 2001, subsequent US intervention in the Middle East, and the War on Terror thus converge upon this site as O'Connor configures it. In her analysis of American constructions of Irishness post–September 11, Diane Negra discusses this very site, arguing that it "invites us to perceive the sense of injustice many Americans associate with the famine as equally applicable to Ground Zero. In this respect, the famine cottage [of the *Irish Hunger Memorial*] functions as U.S. constructions of Irishness so often do, as a flattering prism for American national identity" (2006a, 266). Although O'Connor has himself described the Irish Famine as "Ground Zero . . . the absolute disaster zone of Victorian Europe" (2007b), *Star of the Sea* and *Redemption Falls* ultimately reveal the complexity of Irish and Irish Americans' relationship to notions of whiteness and (racial) innocence and challenge readers to consider how Ireland will conduct its future relations with the global community both within and beyond its borders.

2

"Maybe It Was *Riverdance*"
Roddy Doyle's Fictions of Multicultural Ireland

> "We are the blacks of Europe," observes a character in Roddy
> Doyle's novel *The Commitments*. But that isn't really true any
> more. . . . An Irish passport gives you what people in advertising
> call a reachier punch, I don't know why. . . . The whole world
> longs to be oppressed and post-colonial and tragically hip and
> petulantly Paddy, and we Irish just want to be *anything* else.
> —JOSEPH O'CONNOR, introduction to *Ireland in
> Exile* (1993)

> And it's as bad since the country went sexy . . . *Riverdance* and
> that. The same ol' shite with shorter dresses. Compulsory sexi-
> ness. You know, like, we used to be miserable but now we're
> fuckin' great.
> —RODDY DOYLE, "Home to Harlem" (2004), in
> *The Deportees*

In his introduction to *Ireland in Exile*, Joseph O'Connor looks back
to 1987, the year in which Roddy Doyle's *The Commitments* was
first published, just as he anticipates the views of Doyle's Declan
O'Connor in 2004. As Diane Negra and others contend, the promotion of Irish identity as "oppressed and post-colonial" is precisely
what has rendered Irishness "sexy" in the contemporary moment.
Asserting a kind of "miserable" Irishness in the past is what enables
it to be considered "fuckin' great" in the present. Although, for
O'Connor, Doyle's "blacks of Europe" analogy is no longer true
(and many would argue that Doyle delivered it with tongue firmly in
cheek), in fact, black-Irish analogies have helped to bolster Irishness

67

as a "tragically hip" identity. The persistence of such analogies is confirmed in Declan's invocation of *Riverdance* as shorthand for the seductiveness of Irishness in the contemporary moment. This point is significant, on the one hand, because the global success of the Irish-themed dance show became a widely cited analogy for the economic success that accompanied Ireland's commitment to globalization in the 1990s and, on the other, because the appeal of the show is derived, in part, from its "romanticized narrative of shared [Irish and African American] oppression" (Eagan 2006, 29).[1] The inclusion of this narrative in the dance show, according to Natasha Casey, "consoled Irish-American audiences by assuring them of their egalitarian past" (2002, 17). In other words, the marketability of Irishness in the contemporary moment relies on the affirmation of both Irish victimhood *and* solidarity with other oppressed peoples (notably African Americans) in the past. This chapter examines the work of Roddy Doyle, who, throughout a career bridging the "bad old days" of the 1980s and the Celtic Tiger years, has retained a profound interest in the possibilities and limitations of ethnic analogies and takes on, in a more literal way than O'Connor, the issues of race and immigration in contemporary Ireland.

If O'Connor's major literary endeavors in the Celtic Tiger years were his two historical Irish American novels, this point is not to suggest that he has not published works that are more obviously related to events occurring in contemporary Ireland. In one fascinating venture, O'Connor revisits the signature character of his early work. Irish emigrant to London Eddie Virago is the protagonist of O'Connor's first published short story, "Last of the Mohicans" (1989); his first novel, *Cowboys and Indians* (1991); a further story, "Four Green Fields" (1993); and resurfaces, twelve years on, in "Two Little Clouds" (2005). An homage, of sorts, to James Joyce's

---

1. According to Belinda McKeon, "Some believe Whelan himself, with *Riverdance* in 1994, wrote the official soundtrack [to a particular era in Irish history]: the Celtic Tiger" (2009, 7).

"A Little Cloud," the story appears in *New Dubliners*, a collection celebrating the centenary of the composition of Joyce's *Dubliners* in 1904–5 (eventually published in 1914). In Joyce's story, Dublin law clerk Little Chandler is reunited with his old friend Ignatius Gallaher, who made good after emigrating to London eight years previously. The encounter provokes Little Chandler to question somewhat regretfully his own decision to stay in Dublin, get married and start a family, and achieve comparatively modest success.

In "Two Little Clouds," the unnamed narrator is a London-based Irishman visiting his hometown of Dublin who bumps into returned emigrant Eddie Virago on Fownes Street "a decade or more" after he last saw him (O'Connor 2005, 1). The story is thus a cleverly worked sequel not only to O'Connor's own Eddie Virago stories but also to Joyce's "A Little Cloud," a sequel predicated on a set of reversals. If Virago was an Irish emigrant in London in the early stories, he is a returned emigrant in 2005. Notable for his dramatic Mohican hairstyle in the late 1980s, he is now "just about bald" (1). If Ignatius Gallaher becomes a "vulgar" and "gaudy" newspaperman upon emigrating to London in "A Little Cloud," in O'Connor's story the narrator, a journalist for the *Guardian,* is the Little Chandler figure to Virago's brash Dublin estate agent (Joyce 1914, 83, 84). Just as Gallaher tells Chandler he "feels a ton better since I landed again in dear, dirty Dublin," Virago asks the narrator what he thinks of "dear auld durty Dubbalin, wha'" (Joyce 1914, 82; O'Connor 2005, 9). Whereas in 1905, Little Chandler's soul revolts "against the dull inelegance of Capel Street" (Joyce 1914, 79), for the 2005 narrator, it is "one of those Dublin summer evenings that smells of fresh linen," an evening on which "you could almost fall for Dublin" (O'Connor 2005, 4). In "Two Little Clouds," in other words, O'Connor deploys the sequel form to reflect on changes that have taken place in Dublin not only in the sixteen years that have elapsed between Eddie's first and latest appearances in 1989 and 2005, respectively, but also in the century since Joyce penned "A Little Cloud." O'Connor is decidedly equivocal regarding these changes. Although they have ensured that Dublin is no longer a place that you are obliged to leave "if you want to succeed" (Joyce 1914, 79), it is also a city in which refugee mothers must beg, a city "turning into Disneyland with superpubs," where rush hour gets "longer and meaner every day" (O'Connor 2005, 15, 13, 17).

Through his roles as newspaper columnist (formerly in the *Sunday Tribune,* later in the *Sunday Independent*), book reviewer (for the *Irish Times* and the *Guardian,* among others), and radio presenter (a weekly slot on RTÉ Radio 1's *Drivetime*) as well as novelist, playwright, and short-story writer, O'Connor has emerged as something of a ubiquitous figure in contemporary Irish culture. As such, he has gained upon his near contemporary Roddy Doyle, five years his senior but for whom success came much sooner, with the adaptation of his acclaimed first novel into a hit film, *The Commitments* (Alan Parker, 1991), the short-listing of *The Van* for the Booker Prize in 1991, and the award of it for *Paddy Clarke Ha Ha Ha* (1993) two years later. Like O'Connor, Doyle's oeuvre is extremely diverse. He is a novelist, playwright, short-story writer, and screenwriter. He has also published five children's books and a memoir of his parents, *Rory & Ita* (2002). In the past ten years, Doyle, like O'Connor, has been occupied in the writing of a trilogy. Entitled "The Last Roundup," *A Star Called Henry* (1999), *Oh, Play That Thing* (2004), and *The Dead Republic* (2010) represent Doyle's panoramic view of twentieth-century Ireland (sometimes by way of America) as perceived through the eyes of Henry Smart. Born in a Dublin slum, Henry bears witness to and participates in two of the defining events of twentieth-century Irish history, the Easter Rising of 1916 and the War of Independence (1919–21), before emigrating to the United States, returning in the 1950s, and becoming a publicly recognizable republican figure through the 1980s Troubles and the 1990s peace process.

Like O'Connor, moreover, Doyle has also been writing stories that are more visibly rooted in contemporary Ireland, and these works will form the nucleus of this chapter. In September 2007, Doyle published his first collection of short stories, *The Deportees.* All eight stories in the collection had previously been serialized in

Metro Éireann—"Ireland's first and only weekly multicultural newspaper"—and five had also appeared subsequently in the American literary quarterly *McSweeney's*. Founded in April 2000 by Nigerian journalists Abel Ugba and Chinedu Onyejelem, *Metro Éireann* describes its mission "to be a channel through which the diverse peoples of Ireland will inform, challenge, understand and learn to respect each other" ("About Us"). In the inaugural issue, the editors claim that the majority of immigrants to Ireland "want to contribute to the development of Ireland, the country they now regard as their new home." The "main job" of the newspaper is "to articulate this desire and help it become a reality" (Reddy 2007, 15). The goals of the newspaper are thus expressly political, though not "radical or revolutionary" (16). In his foreword to *The Deportees*, Doyle maintains that he decided to write for *Metro Éireann* in reaction to scaremongering stories he had heard from taxi drivers about new immigrants to Ireland: "An African woman got a brand new buggy from the Social Welfare and left it at the bus stop because she couldn't be bothered carrying it onto the bus, and she knew she could get a new one. A man looked over his garden wall and found a gang of Muslims next door on the patio, slaughtering an Irish sheep. A Polish woman rented a flat and, before the landlord had time to bank the deposit, she'd turned it into a brothel, herself and her seven sisters and their cousin, the pimp" (Doyle 2007, xii). With his *Metro Éireann* contributions, Doyle aimed to offer alternative narratives to the myths circulating about Ireland's multicultural population. Indeed, there is no disputing Doyle's commitment to the cause of fostering understanding between native born and so-called New Irish. As part of the 2007 Dublin Writers' Festival, he participated in a roundtable debate called "Ireland of the Welcomes." Fellow participants included prominent sociologist Ronit Lentin, director of the master's program in racial and ethnic studies at Trinity College Dublin and frequent contributor to *Metro Éireann,* and British writer, researcher, and policy adviser Naseen Khan.

Each of the stories deals with characters and scenarios that emphasize the struggles faced by immigrants and nonwhite people in contemporary Ireland—a Polish nanny, a mixed-race student, a Rwandan schoolboy—as well as the reactions of white, Irish-born people to their arrival. In his foreword to the collection, Doyle opens with a typically glib observation: "Maybe it was *Riverdance*. A bootleg video did the rounds of the rooms and the shanties of Lagos and, moved to froth by the sight of that long, straight line of Irish and Irish-American legs—*tap-tap-tap, tappy-tap*—thousands of Nigerians packed the bags and came to Ireland. *Please. Teach us how to do that*" (2007, xi). In the remainder of the foreword, however, Doyle punctures his own irony and assumes a more serious tone: "I suspect it was more complicated. It was about jobs and the E.U., and infrastructure and wise decisions, and accident" (xi). The issue here, as in much of Doyle's early work, is to establish the extent to which he positions himself, or his narrator-surrogate, at a distance from the main character or characters in his fiction and, consequently, the degree to which even apparently serious statements collapse under the weight of his irony. Excepting *Paula Spencer* (2006), from *Paddy Clarke Ha Ha Ha* on, Doyle's novels are narrated in the first person. However, the proximity of his third-person narrator's consciousness to the main character's in the Barrytown Trilogy (comprising *The Commitments* [1987], *The Snapper* [1990], and *The Van* [1991]) was a deliberate aesthetic strategy, as Doyle indicates: "I've always wanted to bring the books down closer and closer to the characters—to get myself, the narrator, out of it as much as I can" (White 2001, 181). If he removes himself from the narrative completely, readers risk eliding his views and his characters'. On the other hand, if he asserts his distance, no matter how subtly, from his characters, he risks establishing a kind of hierarchy between a knowing Doyle and more naive characters, for, as Linda Hutcheon observes, irony "manages to provoke emotional responses in those who 'get' it and those who don't, as well in its targets and in what some people call its 'victims'" (Hutcheon 1994, 2). In fact, the difficulties that Doyle reports encountering in reading Jane Austen's work—"I always wondered what if she weren't being ironic at all but being literal?"—could equally apply to his own work (White 2001, 174).

It is perhaps for these reasons—the difficulty of separating author from character, ostensibly politicized messages delivered with heavy irony—that Doyle's work has always been controversial among literary critics, some of whom object to what they perceive as the author's condescending attitude toward his working-class subjects. As Ian O'Doherty puts it, "It's hard not to get the impression that if Doyle and not George Orwell had studied grinding poverty in the north of England in the 1930s, we wouldn't have seen *The Road to Wigan Pier*, but a quirky slice of life celebration of those cheeky Northern types" (2007, 18). *The Deportees* has proven no exception in this regard, and reviews of the collection were very mixed. Roger Perkins finds that *The Deportees* "highlights how the notion of Irishness being diminished, as scare stories in the press would have it, is at odds with the culture's reputation for ease, civility and humour. But there's no whiff of worthiness or preaching here—just honest, quality writing" (2007, 56). On the other hand, O'Doherty notes "the remarkable diversity of quality" in *The Deportees* and concludes that the collection "reads like it is a selection of stories from an amateur writers [*sic*] workshop, with the competent strewn amongst the worth, the patronising and the plain dull" (2007, 18). Most critical of all, Margaret Spillane objects to the fact that "the immigrant characters almost never exist in their own dense, sharp, complicated terms. Most are colorful wisps blowing past the far more substantial native Dubliners" and identifies only "New Boy" and "I Understand" as two "jewels" amid otherwise "problematic tales" (2008, 146, 150).

Consistent with this book's claim that issues of race and immigration in contemporary Ireland are increasingly being mediated through an American lens or displaced to an American context, this chapter focuses on two of three stories from the collection that resonate with this assertion in useful ways: the title story and "Home to Harlem." (In the epilogue, I revisit *The Deportees* in a discussion of the *Guess Who's Coming to Dinner* scenario in contemporary Irish writing.) "The Deportees" is set in Ireland, whereas "Home to Harlem" is the only story in the collection that features a non-Irish location, New York. In "The Deportees," Doyle forces readers to unravel a dizzying array of (American) musical analogies, while in "Home to Harlem," he presents the reader with a number of (African American) literary references. The musical and literary allusions testify to Doyle's ongoing preoccupation with an "Irish culture that is a complex processor of exogenous (largely America) influences and indigenous tastes and needs" and his sense that the politics of American popular and literary culture may be instructive in the context of a globalized, multicultural Ireland (D. McCarthy 2003, 236).

From *The Commitments* to "The Deportees"

If O'Connor's Eddie Virago is transplanted to contemporary multicultural Dublin in "Two Little Clouds," what of Doyle's Jimmy Rabbitte, the memorable band manager immortalized in his first novel, *The Commitments* (1987)? How will the mouthpiece for those famous words—"The Irish are the niggers of Europe"—react when "real" African diasporic subjects arrive in Ireland? (Doyle 1987, 9). In "Two Little Clouds," O'Connor emphasizes that the experiences undergone by Virago's generation of Irish emigrants do not necessarily translate into empathy for contemporary immigrants to Ireland. Virago, for example, claims not to be "a racist or anything. No bleedin way. Hadn't he picketed the South African embassy in the bad old days? . . . It was just—you know—these immigrant fellas. They were *different* somehow. Not like us bog-gallopers. Their *culture* was different, their music, their food. Nothing *wrong* with it, of course. All very colourful. But these Nigerians, for example—what could he say?" (O'Connor 2005, 9). Similarly, the changed context from 1987 to 2001 will test Rabbitte's (always uneasy) proclamation to its limits.

Doyle's groundbreaking first novel, which he self-published in 1987 before it was picked up by Heinemann the following year, is set in the (fictional) working-class community of Barrytown on Dublin's Northside, a demographic ravaged by chronic unemployment, poverty, and drug addiction that had rarely, if ever, been represented in Irish fiction before. Local aspiring music impresario Jimmy Rabbitte forms a band, telling prospective members that soul will be the most appropriate musical form for them because:

> —The Irish are the niggers of Europe, lads.
> They nearly gasped: it was so true.
> —An' Dubliners are the niggers of Ireland. The culchies have fuckin' everythin'. An' the northside Dubliners are the niggers o' Dublin.
> —Say it loud, I'm black an' I'm proud. (Doyle 1987, 189)

Along with a guitarist, bassist, drummer, saxophonist, and pianist (all men), the band boasts a powerful lead vocalist (Deco), whom Rabbitte heard singing drunkenly at a Christmas party, a trumpeter (Joey "The Lips" Fagan), who claims to have played with all the greats, and a triumvirate of female backing vocalists. The band enjoys some degree of local success, not least because they adapt the lyrics of their soul covers to make them "more Dubliny" (20). However, after sustained infighting—largely owing to Fagan's affairs with the backing singers and Deco's increasing arrogance—the band members go their separate ways, and Rabbitte's dreams of musical success are thwarted.

In "The Deportees," which was serialized in *Metro Éireann* between March 2001 and May 2002, Doyle resurrects Rabbitte, now settled into a comfortable life of job, marriage, and children. Nostalgic for his past life as a manager, Rabbitte decides to form a band, which he calls the Deportees, composed entirely of nonwhite and non-Irish-born musicians. In "The Deportees," the soul music of James Brown, Otis Redding, Marvin Gaye, and Smokey Robinson that animated *The Commitments* yields to the Dust Bowl ballads of Woody Guthrie. Notwithstanding three threatening phone calls that Rabbitte receives from an anonymous caller who labels him a "nigger lover," the Deportees proves a triumph for manager and band members alike. This discussion of *The Commitments* and its sequel emphasizes the apparent incongruity of Doyle's postmodern techniques and his political commitment through an analysis of musical analogies and Bakhtinian carnivalesque in a Dublin that has been thoroughly transformed, economically and demographically, between 1987 and 2001.

In his foreword to *The Deportees*, Doyle writes, in understated fashion, that the "I'm black an' I'm proud" passage from *The Commitments* "became quite famous" (Doyle 2007, xii). Indeed, several scholars have noted the "ubiquity in Irish cultural discourse" or the "near-canonical status" of this passage, debates about which have centered upon whether Doyle—through the novel's narrative voice—affirms or undermines Rabbitte's claim that northside Dubliners, disenfranchised because of their class and regional positioning, share an affinity with oppressed African Americans (McGonigle 2005, 163; Cullingford 2001, 158). Declan Kiberd, for example, claims that with this passage, Doyle "was one of the first artists to register the ways in which the relationship between 'First' and 'Third' Worlds was enacted daily in the streets" (1996, 611). Equally, after an extended comparative discussion of the Irish Literary Revival and the Harlem Renaissance, Timothy Taylor asserts that "Jimmy's weapon against his postcolonial condition—and the weapon with which attempts to arm his musicians—is soul music" (1998, 294). With "The Deportees," it is tempting to suggest that Doyle has written the story that some postcolonial critics insisted *The Commitments* was: in other words, a story about cross-racial solidarity.

However, the most convincing interpretations of *The Commitments* demonstrate that "the plethora of meanings bestowed upon soul" (drugs "aren't soul" [Doyle 1987, 74]; soul is "democratic" [124]; Guinness is "soul food" [74]; "the feuding Brothers in Northern Ireland . . . needed some soul" [26]; the novel's epigraph, "Parents are soul") along with the unreliability of its most devoted promoters, Rabbitte and Fagan, ultimately conveys Doyle's suspicion that "the analogy between the Irish and the African Americans is well meaning but inappropriate: it reinscribes both ethnicities within the suspect rubrics of 'timeless' primitivism, emotionalism and rhythm" (McGonigle 2005, 168; Cullingford 2001, 159). After making some initial claims for *The Commitments* as a text about postcolonial solidarity, even Taylor is forced to concede that the last scene of the novel "ends up heavily ironising its argument: the band's desire to articulate a political vision is now rendered insincere. They look like they want to cash in on the exoticism of a Dublin working-class band making old American pop music. Even the band's name becomes ironic: Commitment to what?" (1998, 297).

That Doyle positions himself at an ironic distance from Rabbitte, and thus communicates that Rabbitte is "a dubious harbinger of postcolonial solidarity," is evident in his chosen mode of narration (McGonigle 2005, 163). Mary McGlynn argues that the narrative voice in *The Commitments* ensures "the most neutral, nonjudgmental tone available" (2004, 240). In fact, the narrator occasionally intervenes in the story in order to undermine Jimmy's more extravagant claims. Because of the narrator's intrusions, according to Dermot McCarthy, Jimmy's "niggers of Europe" analogy emerges as "a 'con'—a 'pitch'; and the narrator's deflation of Jimmy's rhetorical balloon should prevent anyone from ascending into the ideological ozone" (2003, 39). There are at least two significant examples of Doyle's narratorial intrusions: having dismissed Depeche Mode's music as "fuckin' art school stuff," Jimmy is challenged by Derek, who counterargues that "the Beatles went to art school." "Struggling" to justify his statement, Jimmy "fight[s] back a redner," and once he manages to claw his way back into the argument, the narrator observes in parentheses that "he had something" (Doyle 1987, 4–5). Similarly, Jimmy is at loss to explain his opposition to band members' smoking joints. The narrator tells us that "what had annoyed him at first was the fact that they hadn't got the go-ahead from him before they'd lit up" (73). As he racks his brain to think up a suitable reason to condemn hash, the narrator notes that he is "grateful" for Deco's interruption. With these narratorial interventions, it becomes clear that Doyle does not intend for the reader to take Jimmy's rhetorical authority at face value (McGonigle 2005, 168).

At the beginning of *The Commitments*, Outspan Foster attempts "to work his thumb in under a sticker" that his brother, "an awful hippy," has put on the guitar Outspan has borrowed from him. The sticker reads "This Guitar Kills Fascists" (Doyle 1987, 2). Hippies are, in *The Commitments*, as worthy of derision as "Rednecks," "Southsiders" (11), and "middle-class white kids with little beards and berets" (125), a point that is borne out by Jimmy's judgment on Pete Seeger's "The Bells of Rhymney" as "a piece of hippy shite" (Doyle 1987, 162; T. Taylor 1998, 296). In "The Deportees," however, the music of that "awful hippy" whose guitar sported the sticker "This Machine Kills Fascists" takes center stage. Rabbitte's inconsistent views on folk from *The Commitments* to "The Deportees" are significant because they raise a series of important questions regarding Doyle's treatment of his protagonist in the novel's sequel: can they simply be attributed to changing tastes as he grows older? Or is it just a further example of Jimmy's infamous inconsistency? Has he changed enough from 1987 to 2001 that readers can now take him seriously? Or does he remain a "dubious harbinger," in the case of "The Deportees," of Irish multiculturalism? If his embracing of soul in *The Commitments* reflects his own awareness of musical trends contemporary to the composition of the novel, can his celebration of Woody Guthrie in "The Deportees" equally be attributed to zeitgeist, rather than any political commitment?[2] For Mary Burke, "The Deportees" is disappointing because it is "far too similar to *The Commitments* in arc, humor, dialogue, and white Irish perspective to provide any real sense of the motley collection of immigrants

---

2. The British music scene of the late 1980s and early 1990s was dominated by "Brit-soul." Black and white artists such as Soul II Soul, Lisa Stansfield, Seal, Paul Weller, Sade, Simply Red, and George Michael were, with few exceptions, "critically praised for their innovative appropriation of soul music traditions" (Wald 1998, 141). Meanwhile, the prominence of Woody Guthrie's songs in the Deportees' repertoire is embedded in a vogue identified by Hester Lacey of the London *Independent* in February 2000 when he proclaimed that "folk music is back" some days after the inaugural BBC Folk Awards were held at London's Waldorf Hotel (2000, 3). Legendary American folk singer Joan Baez performed at the ceremony. My thanks to David Hesmondhalgh for pointing this fact out.

who make up the band" (2009, 14). But how *different* does Rabbitte need to be in order for Doyle to make his point?

These questions are crucial because they bespeak a fundamental tension in Doyle's work. In his discussion of *A Star Called Henry* (1999), McCarthy argues that the novel should be read in the context of the "discursive-ideological controversy over the application of postcolonial theory to Irish politics, society and culture" (2003, 191). In other words, in its deflation of Irish nationalist heroism, the novel is deeply indebted to revisionist approaches to Irish history. However, as McCarthy contends, "a work of historiographical metafiction is a double-edged device for a writer with a revisionist agenda, for while it may substantially subvert the historical orthodoxy it wants to challenge, its destabilising methods also prevent its giving credibility to any rival perspective it may seem to propose" (ibid., 203). Historiographic metafiction is, of course, a postmodern literary form, and McCarthy's observation could equally be applied to another of postmodernism's, and Doyle's, signature techniques: irony. It is irony's very "destabilising methods" that "prevent its giving credibility to any rival perspective it may seem to propose." Like Rabbitte in *The Commitments*, Henry's motives are, McCarthy argues, "a combination of self- and class-interest" (ibid., 210). Asked, in *Oh, Play That Thing*, whether he believes in freedom of speech, Henry responds: "It's a good idea. . . . But I don't believe in anything," a statement that could just as easily be attributed to Rabbitte (Doyle 2004, 83). The decision facing Doyle in "The Deportees," then, is whether to maintain his ironic detachment from Rabbitte or to abandon it in order to remain faithful to his own avowedly sincere political motives in writing for *Metro Éireann*: to "make up a few of his own" stories to counter the myths circulating about recent immigrants to Ireland (Doyle 2007, xii).

The issue is even further complicated by the form of "The Deportees": the sequel. In his foreword to the collection, Doyle describes the story as "a sequel, sort of, to *The Commitments*" (xiii). In a 2004 interview, he calls it "a mock sequel to *The Commitments*"

(Monteith, Newman, and Wheeler 2004, 68). Reviewers, too, seem unwilling to name "The Deportees" as a straightforward sequel: Patricia Craig calls it "a kind of offshoot" of Doyle's first novel (2007, 18); O'Doherty regards it as "a sort of follow-up" to *The Commitments* (2007, 18). This reluctance on the part of Doyle and reviewers to characterize "The Deportees" as a sequel perhaps reflects the conflicted nature of the form itself. In her explanation of why "sequels are always disappointing," Terry Castle identifies one of the key tensions that exist in relation to sequels: "A sequel can never fully satisfy its readers' desire for repetition, however; its tragedy is that it cannot literally reconstitute its charismatic original. Readers know this; yet they are disappointed. Unconsciously they persist in demanding the impossible: that the sequel be different, but also *exactly the same*" (1986, 133–34). In "The Deportees," Doyle handles this delicate balancing act by showing how Jimmy is, on the one hand, "different" from his character in *The Commitments* but, on the other, "*exactly the same*" fourteen years on.

Jimmy and his environment have changed dramatically in the period spanning 1987 and 2001. In *The Commitments*, when the band changes the lyrics to "Night Train" to make them "more Dubliny," it is transformed into a song about the DART journey from the city center to the northside, working-class suburbs where the band members live (Doyle 1987, 20). In "The Deportees," when Jimmy walks down Dublin's Parnell Street, a neighborhood that has become conspicuous for the cultural diversity of its inhabitants, on his way to Tara Street Station, it is clear he is taking the DART only because his "car [is] being serviced" (Doyle 2007, 35). When he submits an advertisement to *Hot Press*, he types it on his "laptop" (36). When he gets the band together for the first time, he suggests to his wife that they will "have some finger-food" (45). In other words, Rabbitte has become what was, in *The Commitments*, the very thing he professed to despise: "bourgeois" (Doyle 1987, 7). Similarly, Doyle's Dublin has been transformed between 1987 and 2001. The reader has every reason to believe that Rabbitte still lives on Dublin's northside, but the northside suburbs have become so gentrified, Doyle suggests, that the old northside-southside distinction no longer applies. When Jimmy asks prospective band member Mary whether she is from the northside or southside of Dublin, she tells him to "grow up" (Doyle 2007, 55). Emphasizing the irrelevance of the northside-southside divide in contemporary Dublin, the band's first gig takes place on a raft on the river Liffey, where northside and southside meet (60).

In fact, a closer look at the sequel to *The Commitments* that never was provides further insight to these shifts. The novel ends with Rabbitte's formation of another band, the Brassers, who will play country punk. Rabbitte hopes that a country band will be more successful than the Commitments because, as he tells his followers, "half the country is fuckin' farmers" (Doyle 2007, 164). If Doyle had written a Brassers-focused sequel to *The Commitments*, no doubt it would have been embedded in Ireland's 1990s love affair with New Country and, in particular, with Garth Brooks. As Ireland became increasingly prosperous in the 1990s and the economically depressed Dublin of *The Commitments* began to look more and more remote, it was New Country's "compromise—between upward mobility and working-class roots, between pop and country, between the myth of the West and the lifestyle of the suburbs—which ma[de] Garth Brooks such a comfortable fit for so many Irish fans" (McGlynn 2006, 206). If the Commitments expressed Rabbitte's working-class identity, the Brassers would have reflected his move toward the middle class, a position that has been fully realized by the time "The Deportees" is published in 2001–2.

However, Doyle also infers that—apart from his class and marital status—Jimmy has not really changed at all in the fourteen years that have elapsed since his first appearance in fiction. This point is suggested at the very outset through Doyle's recourse to a musical analogy that confirms Jimmy's fundamental dubiety and insincerity. Chapter 1 is entitled "The Real Slim Shady," an Eminem song. On the level of pure plot, the chapter heading reflects Jimmy's admiration for the artist: his wife, Aoife, even calls him "Slim." However, there are multiple layers to the Eminem allusion. Doyle may be suggesting that the connection between Rabbitte and Eminem is one of appropriation: just as Rabbitte identified soul music as a suitable form of expression for the Commitments, so Eminem has been accused of appropriating an African American art form—hip-hop—in his articulation of a poor, urban, white identity (Watkins 2006, 85–86). Rabbitte's somewhat questionable obsession with African American music even extends to the naming of his children: Mahalia, Marvin, and the new baby, whom he wishes to call Smokey but whom Aoife insists on calling Brian. Peel back the layers of Eminem's own multiple personas—Marshall Mathers, Eminem, Slim Shady—and the particularities of the song "The Real Slim Shady," and the issue becomes even more complicated. The song excoriates the falseness and hypocrisy of contemporary American culture, especially celebrity culture. The chorus, in particular—"So won't the real Slim Shady please stand up, please stand up, please stand up?"—toys with ideas of realness, imitation, and authenticity that could equally apply to Rabbitte. In Rabbitte, readers of *The Commitments* and, so it seems, "The Deportees" are faced with a protagonist whose substance, if indeed there is any, remains thoroughly inaccessible.

Like in *The Commitments*, moreover, Doyle establishes his ironic distance from Rabbitte by deflating his pomposity and flagrant posturing. For instance, when Jimmy recalls the days when he had managed some "great" bands, he reflects on the reviews these bands received from local Dublin publications. Here, in parentheses, Doyle juxtaposes the positively hyperbolic with the negatively pithy, rendering Jimmy's pretensions laughable: "There was The Commitments ('The best Irish band never recorded'—*d'Side*. 'Shite'—*Northside News*). There was The Brassers ('Sex and guitars'—*In Dublin*. 'Shite'—*Northside News*)" (Doyle 2007, 29). Equally, when Jimmy meets a prospective band member in a multicultural café, Doyle ironizes Jimmy's white Irish gaze— "Portuguese-looking barman, Spanish-looking lounge-girl, Chinese-looking girl on the stool beside him"—by drawing attention, finally, to the "good-looking pint settling in front of him" (39). In addition to narratorial distance, the tension between irony and sincerity in "The Deportees" becomes clear in two ways: in Doyle's ironic use of musical analogies (the shift from soul in *The Commitments* to folk in "The Deportees") and in his parody of Bakhtinian carnivalesque.

In *The Commitments,* the jazz-soul dichotomy established by Joey "The Lips" Fagan encouraged some critics to read the novel as promoting a socialist identification between economically disadvantaged subjects the world over, regardless of their racial identity. Certainly, there is evidence in the text to support this interpretation. Soul, in Fagan's configuration, is the musical equivalent of a socialist outlook: "Soul is the people's music. Ordinary people making music for ordinary people. . . . Soul is democratic" (Doyle 1987, 124). On the other hand, jazz is "intellectual music." It's "anti-people music. It's abstract" (125). Fagan implies that the emphasis in jazz on the virtuoso solo performance is the aesthetic equivalent of individualistic capitalism that benefits only the elite, a minority composed of "middle-class white kids with little beards and berets." It is no coincidence that, according to Fagan, the Russians, living embodiments of socialism in practice at this historical moment, banned jazz because it is "decadent" (126).

The destructiveness of individualism is further suggested by the fact that the Commitments begin to fall apart when the lead singer, Deco, decides to go solo. Equally, Fagan's prefixing of fellow band members' names with "Brother" might speak as much to his socialist principles as to his born-again Christian identity. However, the jazz-soul dichotomy ultimately collapses because of the unreliability of its advocate and because soul becomes an empty signifier, connoting everything and nothing (McGonigle 2005, 169). Furthermore, as M. Keith Booker argues, a close look at Rabbitte's politics "shows that they may in fact work very much in the interest of the global hegemony of American (or at least capitalist) values" (1997, 30–31). In other words, Rabbitte's determination to make music that sells implicates him in the very ideology he and Fagan critique, thus undermining the seeming radicalism of their statements on working-class, northside Dublin identity.

In a brief contribution to *Re-imagining Ireland*, Doyle introduces his discussion of contemporary multicultural Ireland by recounting a musical anecdote: "In July 1930, the American country singing legend Jimmie Rodgers, 'The Singing Brakeman,' went into a studio in Los Angeles. With him was Louis Armstrong. Together, they recorded a Rodgers song called "Blue Yodel No. 9." . . . A mix of rural country and urban jazz; the blues sung by a white man, country-and-western played by a black man. Rural meets urban. White meets black" (2006, 69). Here, Doyle seems to hold out hope for the potential of hybridized musical forms to bring about cooperation between groups of people whose relationships have historically been characterized by hostility and asymmetries of power. As George Lipsitz argues of such musical "detours," "especially when carried on my members of aggrieved communities—sexually or racially marginalized 'minorities'—these detours may enable individuals to solve indirectly problems that they could not address directly" (1994, 62).

Similarly, in "The Deportees," Rabbitte forms a band comprising a diverse group of people united by their experience of being outsiders in Ireland. Like the jazz-soul dichotomy in *The Commitments,* Doyle appears initially to uphold an opposition between "good" folk music such as Guthrie's that is politically engaged, "angry and confident, knocking shite out of the enemy" (Doyle 2007, 52) and "bad" folk music such as that enjoyed by his wife. Aoife sings "some shite by The Corrs" in the shower; she owns the soundtrack to *Titanic,* and she even wants to name their (as yet) unborn child Andrea, after Andrea Corr (27, 28, 46). In Aoife's musical tastes, Doyle lampoons the late-1990s and early-2000s popularity of vaguely Celtic-sounding music. At the 1997 Grammy Awards, for example, three Irish recordings were victorious: Enya's *The Memory of Trees* won for "Best New Age Album," the Chieftains for "World Music Album," and *Riverdance* for "Best Musical Show Album." What is interesting about this trend, according to Natasha Casey, is that this kind of music enjoys "critical acclaim and popularity through its conspicuous lack of political relevance" (2002, 24).

By contrast, Doyle seems to insist upon the value of the political messages in Guthrie's songs: Guthrie is "authentic," "true," and politically grounded, while the Corrs are bland, trite, and politically vacuous. The title of the story and the name of the band is a reference to Guthrie's "Deportee (Plane Wreck at Los Gatos)," a song he wrote in 1948 after reading a newspaper account of a plane crash in which a group of migrant workers being deported to Mexico were killed (Garman 2000, 241). The fourth verse of the song, "Some of us are illegal, and some are not wanted / Our work contract's out and we have to move on / Six hundred miles to that Mexican border / They chase us like outlaws, like rustlers, like thieves," becomes an apt analogy for the very real threat of deportation faced by several members of the band in contemporary Ireland ("Plane Wreck" 2008). Indeed, Gilbert, the band's Nigerian drummer, has to take refuge in the Rabbittes' attic to avoid deportation. The songs of Woody Guthrie—including "Do-Re-Mi," "Vigilante Man," "Dust Bowl Refugee," and "Dead or Alive"—feature prominently in the Deportees' repertoire, reflecting the experiences of migration and dispossession faced by many new immigrants to Ireland.

Ultimately, however, even Guthrie is subjected to Doyle's irony. Instead of performing Guthrie songs exclusively, each member of the band is invited to contribute his or her own musical choice to the Deportees' repertoire. Although this may be an indication that the controlling presence of Jimmy Rabbitte as band manager in *The Commitments* (who wants to be consulted when band members smoke joints) has yielded to a more democratic Jimmy in "The Deportees," some of the selections make a mockery of the politically engaged Guthrie songs: "Singin' in the Rain" is Agnes's choice; Ricky Martin's "La Vida Loca" is Young Dan's. Equally, Rabbitte's early admiration for Guthrie's political conscience is undermined when he confesses toward the end of the story that he is "getting a bit bored with Woody Guthrie. All that dust, it got on your wick after a while" (Doyle 2007, 74).

If irony is a postmodern technique par excellence, then several critics have also identified "carnivalized writing"—or writing that enacts the principles of anarchy and subversion that, for Mikhail Bakhtin, characterize medieval carnival—as an exemplary form of postmodern literature (Dentith 1994, 65). As Linda Hutcheon argues, the postmodern period, as treated by Bakhtin in *Rabelais and His World* (1965), "has witnessed a proliferation of parody as one of the modes of positive aesthetic self-reference as well as conservative mockery" (2000, 82). Indeed, Doyle's work has been discussed in relation to Bakhtinian carnivalesque previously. For Dermot McCarthy, "The scatological, sexual, profane, and generally unrelentingly 'vulgar' argot of Doyle's characters represents . . . a contemporary expression of what Bakhtin calls the carnivalesque—the expression of a popular culture that sites itself in difference and opposition to the norms, conventions, and conformism of the 'official' culture" (2003, 27–28). In "The Deportees," rather than deploying stylistic devices that roughly translate into carnivalesque, Doyle includes a *scene* that parodies Bakhtin's vision of carnival-as-parody.

After their disastrous first gig, Jimmy secures another gig for the band, playing at the twenty-first birthday party of the daughter of Fat Gandhi, the owner of a local curry house. The costume sported by an undercover Gilbert ("shades and a silver wig" [Doyle 2007, 64]) and the party's venue (a "circus tent" in Fat Gandhi's enormous garden [65]) announce Doyle's playful engagement with Bakhtinian carnivalesque. If, in medieval culture, carnival represented a "second, joyous, inverted world" existing "in opposition to official, serious, ecclesiastical culture" (Hutcheon 2000, 72), then it is surely significant that a character known only as "John the Baptist" is removed from the scene of the party and sedated "with a mix of Pal and paracetamol" (Doyle 2007, 67). Equally, Fat Gandhi, a born-again Christian, almost immediately abandons his religious principles when he realizes he has fallen in love at first sight with Gilbert. The chaotic scenes that ensue to the soundtrack of the Deportees' performance ("Jimmy was sent flying; a dancing auntie followed and landed on his chest"; "The birthday girl was wearing Gilbert's wig" [73]) testify to the anarchic, and potentially subversive, nature of carnival. If, for Bakhtin, carnival is "an anti-authoritarian force that can be mobilized against the official culture of Church and State" (Dentith 1994, 71), it is unsurprising that when Jimmy receives a third "nigger lover" call to his mobile phone at the party, he dismisses the threat with laughter, as he has not previously been able to do (Doyle 2007, 73).

However, because Doyle is obviously *parodying* Bakhtinian carnivalesque, he undermines its radical potential at the same time that he asserts it. His use of mise en abyme—parody of a parody—ensures that meaning is endlessly deferred and remains ultimately inaccessible. At the same time, because Doyle does not fully commit to celebrating the possibilities of carnival, he equally does not succumb to its limitations, which, as several scholars have shown, are many. John Docker observes that it might "merely be a safety-valve, a temporary release of contrary or dissident feelings and passions that, once humourously spent, actually strengthen the usual social order" (1994, 186). For Simon Dentith, meanwhile, "it is hard to accede to a version of carnival which stresses its capacity to invert hierarchies and undermine boundaries, without at the same time recalling that many carnival and carnival-like degradations clearly functioned to reinforce communal and hierarchical norms" (1994, 72).

In Roger Perkins's review of *The Deportees,* he borrows a line from Woody Guthrie to observe that Doyle's message in the collection is implicit: "this land is your land" (2007, 56). But how can Doyle have a message if he persists in undercutting himself at every opportunity? Perhaps the best way of characterizing *The Commitments* and its sequel is by recourse to Linda Hutcheon's configuration of postmodernism, which, she argues, "takes the form of self-conscious, self-contradictory, self-undermining statement" (1991, 1). Postmodernism "ultimately manages to install and reinforce as much as undermine and subvert the conventions and presuppositions it appears to challenge" (1–2). The political leanings of both *The Commitments* and "The Deportees" as postmodernist texts can thus be described as "complicitous critique" (2). Just when Doyle appears to be on the threshold of endorsing with sincerity a particular position, he explodes his own seriousness. Although this ensures that Doyle finds it impossible to give "credibility to any rival perspective," as McCarthy puts it, he nonetheless forces readers to consider the representation of immigrants in public discourse, by the political and legal establishments, and by the media, as linguistic and rhetorical constructs that can and must be challenged.

Things Like Skunks: Race and Nation in "Home to Harlem"

> Races and nations were things like skunks, whose smells poisoned the air of life. Yet civilized mankind reposed its faith in their ancient, silted channels. Great races and big nations!
> —CLAUDE MCKAY, *Home to Harlem* (1928)

Although Margaret Spillane's critique of "Home to Harlem"—that Doyle does not permit the newcomers to Dublin in his other *Deportees* stories to express the same sophisticated concerns as Declan O'Connor, the story's middle-class Irish protagonist, because "they're too busy being symbols" (2008, 148)—is a point well made, this story is nonetheless very accomplished and an interesting treatment of mixed-race Irish identity that, as I argue throughout this study, has become an increasingly prominent theme in contemporary Irish culture. In "Home to Harlem," serialized in *Metro Éireann* in 2004, Declan O'Connor is a young Irishman of mixed racial ancestry, the grandson of an African American GI and a white Irishwoman, who travels to New York ostensibly to examine the influence of the Harlem Renaissance on Irish writers. A further, more important, reason for his visit is that he thinks of the United States as the "land of his ancestors" on his mother's side and seeks information on his African American grandfather (Doyle 2007, 180). In chapter 5, I examine *The Nephew* (1998), a film in which a mixed-race Irish American returns to his late mother's birthplace in Ireland to scatter her ashes. A roots journey of the opposite trajectory, then, is the subject of "Home to Harlem," in which Doyle refers to, but transforms, at least two standard narratives of Irish transnationalism (the "returned Yank" narrative and the Irish emigrant's arrival in the United States) to convey the complexity, historically and in the contemporary moment, of Irish identities.

The story, as with much of Doyle's work, is highly self-referential. Declan is engaged in two related acts of sleuthing: tracing his genealogy in New York and attempting to come up with a thesis topic by reading (or investigating) African American literature. Declan's project—to find some means of reconciling his Irish and African American ancestry through literary endeavor—is also Doyle's. While Declan tries to read his way into a hybrid Irish-African diasporic identity, Doyle attempts to guide *his* readers into accepting Declan's overlapping, and seemingly incongruous, racial and national subject positions. In Dublin, Declan is Irish but not white. In New York, Declan is black but not African American. The act of reading bears further significant connotations in the sense that Declan's racial identity is legible in a way that his national identity simply is not, at least until he opens his mouth and his Irish accent becomes audible. The story opens with Declan attempting to fill in a registration form at New York University, but finding that there is "nowhere for [him] to tick":

> The woman looks at him. She looks over her glasses.
> —African-American, she says.
> —I'm not American, he says. (179)

Doyle emphasizes the woman's gaze as she tries to reconcile the box on the form with the person she sees: "She takes the form from him. She looks at the categories . . . and she looks at him" (179). It is significant that Doyle opens with this episode, for the story sounds a warning bell regarding the power of reading. It may allow the reader to take intellectual and imaginative journeys, but it may also encourage him or her to define, circumscribe, and delimit.

If Doyle's project mirrors Declan's, the story, like "The Deportees" and much of Doyle's work, presents the reader with the particular challenge of separating author-narrator from protagonist, an issue that has proven perplexing to many critics. For example, in the only extant scholarly discussion of Doyle's *Metro Éireann* stories, Maureen T. Reddy draws attention to a particularly naive claim made by Declan and concedes that she is "not sure whether the fundamental misunderstanding is the character's or Doyle's own" (2007, 24). Similarly, in her review of *The Deportees*, Spillane takes issue with the unrealistic premise for the story (that Declan, who does not even know from where in the United States his grandfather came, locates a potential relative in New York after fewer than a dozen phone calls) and asks drily: "Why not? Don't all African Americans live in Harlem?" as if this assumption is Doyle's rather than Declan's (2008, 148). In discussions with his adviser, Declan confesses that he's "always felt [he] was being pushed out [of Ireland]":

> —Like Joyce?
> —Fuck Joyce. Sorry. Not like Joyce. Well, he said.
> —A little bit. More like Bloom.
> —Created by Joyce.
> —Fair enough. I take it back. Like Joyce. Only, I'm not leaving. (Doyle 2007, 213)

His adviser's view, that there is an inherent connection between James Joyce and Leopold Bloom because Joyce is the author of *Ulysses,* is, perhaps, Doyle's sly way of engaging with his own critics who puzzle over his relationship, as author, to the characters he creates. In fact, Declan's distinction between Joyce and Bloom is crucial: he identifies with Bloom (rather than Joyce) because he has been made to feel less-than-fully-Irish in a country that defines national identity according to very narrow criteria: white ("I'm black and Irish, and that's two fuckin' problems" [185]), Catholic ("He hasn't been to mass since his father's funeral" [186]), rural ("Dublin wasn't really Ireland" [212]), and Gaelic ("And there's the language. The fuckin' *cúpla focail.* You're not fully Irish if you can't fart in Irish" [212]). Just as the author-character distinction between Joyce and Bloom should not be elided, so Doyle's ironic detachment from Declan becomes evident by unpacking the story's many other literary allusions.

Upon arrival in New York, Declan embarks on an intensive sweep of early-twentieth-century African American literature, including Paul Laurence Dunbar's *The Sport of the Gods* (1902),

W. E. B. DuBois's *The Souls of Black Folk* (1903), James Weldon Johnson's *Autobiography of an Ex-Colored Man* (1912), and the poetry of Langston Hughes in order to write a thesis on the influence of African American writers on Irish writers. However, Declan's approach to his thesis material echoes the attitude of the receptionist he encounters at the beginning of the story. While she fixes him with a stare ("reads" his racial identity) and tries to make him "fit" into one of the categories on the form—white, non-Hispanic, African American, Hispanic, the rest (179)—Declan reads Johnson's *Autobiography* and is dismayed to find "there's no way he can *fit* this book into his theory" (201; emphasis added). However, his discovery of the theme of passing in Johnson's novella and Hughes's "Passing" (1934) leads him to believe he is "on to something" (201). Mistaking "passing" for a liberatory ability to evade categories, Declan fails to realize, as I note in chapter 1, that passing is "thoroughly invested in the logic of the system it attempts to subvert" (A. Robinson 1996, 237). Seizing upon the theme of passing, Declan attempts to apply it to Irishness: "That's what being Irish is a lot of the time, passing for something else—the Paddy, the European, the peasant, the rocker, the leprechaun" (Doyle 2007, 201). As if to confirm this point, Declan performs a version of Irishness when he goes on a date with an American woman named Kim:

> He'll give her the whole Irish bit, get in a few grands. They love it. . . .
> He picks up the pint.
> —Sláinte, he says.
> God, he fuckin' hates himself. (195)

Kim's attraction to Declan is undoubtedly based, in part, on her own assumptions regarding Irishness, assumptions that Declan is all too happy to corroborate. Declan's performance of Irishness does not provide a "way out" of essentialized identities, but serves to reinforce them. Like the receptionist— who "writes OTHER beside Hispanic. And a little box" (180)—Declan's approach to reading, and his enactment of practices he reads *about,* does not undermine categories, but merely rehashes old ones, produces new ones, or both.

While Declan is busy reading Dunbar, DuBois, Hughes, and Johnson, he does not once refer to Claude McKay, the author of the 1928 novel from which Doyle derives the title for his story. This fact is even more surprising given Declan's enthusiasm for "passing," an issue that McKay also confronts in his story "Near-White" (1932). That McKay's novel is invoked in "Home to Harlem," but not read by Declan, leads me to suspect that it is a deliberate distancing gesture on the part of Doyle and one that sheds considerable light on the respective positions of author-narrator and character in relation to Declan's mixed-race Irish identity. McKay, like Declan, is an African diasporic subject who is *not* African American, and *Home to Harlem* was written neither in the United States nor in his birthplace of Jamaica, but in Paris. The novel, like McKay's biography, reveals the potential transnationality of African diasporic identities: its protagonist, Jake Brown, is an African American from Petersburg, Virginia, who is working as a longshoreman in Brooklyn when the United States enters World War I in 1917. He enlists, is sent to France, but never sees combat, deserts, and ends up in London. After the Armistice, he returns to the United States, and while working as a chef on the railroad, he befriends another transnational African diasporic subject, Ray, a Haitian student who attends Howard University and has been displaced by US occupation of his homeland in 1915.

For both Jake and Ray, then, World War I is the catalyst for their uprooting, just as, for Declan's grandfather, World War II is the reason for his own. However, for Jake, ostensibly, Germany is the enemy, whereas for Ray, "Uncle Sam" is (McKay 1928, 137). Nonetheless, when Ray recounts the noble history of Haiti's struggle for independence, Jake finds himself wishing he had "been a soldier under sich a man [as Toussaint L'Ouverture]" (132) rather than mixing himself "up in a white folks' war" (8). United by "race," potentially divided by "nation," what Ray and Jake share, more important, is their status as *transnational* subjects. Citizens of the United States and Haiti, respectively, their life experiences are not nation bound.

After all, they make their introductions when they realize that they both speak French, a smattering of which Jake acquired in Brest and Le Havre and which, as a citizen of a former French colony, is Ray's "native language" (131).

Declan's encounter with a fellow African diasporic subject, his African American adviser at the university, is also rendered in linguistic terms. However, unlike Jake and Ray, whose initial communications in a shared language other than English mark the beginning of a deep friendship, the linguistic exchanges between Declan and his adviser are combative rather than mutually compatible. When Declan uses a swear word in her presence, his adviser responds: "The Irish and their famous profanity" (Doyle 2007, 184). Declan takes umbrage at her shameless recourse to stereotypes and counters with one of his own to make this point: "Did you get here on a sporting scholarship?" (184). Unlike Jake in *Home to Harlem*, whose encounter with a fellow African diasporic subject who is a citizen of a country other than his own provides an opportunity to engage in discussions on both Haiti and the United States, Declan, after first meeting his African American adviser, silently mocks her ignorance of Ireland: "If this was Ireland, she'd be putting on the kettle. *The Ulster*. For fuck sake" (183).

In McKay's novel, Ray is so troubled by the "skunks" that are race and nation that he eventually decides to leave the United States, gets a job on a freighter, and takes to the sea. Just as the first part of the novel begins with Jake's arrival on a freighter, the third part concludes with Ray's departure on a freighter, effectively confirming Gilroy's promotion of "the image of ships in motion across the spaces between Europe, America, Africa, and the Caribbean" as "a central organising symbol" for his configuration of transnational African diasporic consciousness (1993, 4). In "Home to Harlem," Doyle overcomes the effect of these "skunks," that Declan has been made to feel that the categories of "black" and "Irish" are mutually exclusive categories, by situating Declan on a historical continuum of transnational Irish identities: returned Yanks and Irish emigrants to the United States.

Declan's is not a typical roots journey because Declan is neither an Irish American returning to the Old Country nor an African American going "back to Africa." Indeed, Declan's odyssey draws attention to the troubling relationship that exists between these two kinds of roots journey, a process by which white ethnic Americans appropriated Alex Haley's attempt to recover the "story of our people" in his best-seller *Roots* (1976) in order to reflect on the grievances of their own pasts. The popular rediscovery of ethnic forebears in the aftermath of *Roots* had, as Matthew Frye Jacobson argues, at least two important effects: it became one way for white ethnic Americans to say, "We're merely newcomers. The nation's crimes are not our own," and it "gave way, in some cases to a politics of white grievance that pitted itself against unfair *black* privilege (as in the ensuing affirmative action debates), often, ironically, couched in a Civil Rights language poached from blacks themselves" (2006, 21, 22). In other words, it insulated white ethnics from charges of racism at the same time that it enabled them to assert their own narrative of victimhood and triumph over adversity to be considered alongside that of African Americans. Although "Home to Harlem" is neither an Irish American nor an African American roots journey, Doyle certainly gestures toward the "returned Yank" version in particular. In such narratives, it is the matrilineal line that is emphasized, the (usually male) subject's relationship with the "motherland" traceable through his mother's side of the family. It is the case in *The Quiet Man* (John Ford, 1952) and the numerous films it has inspired, such as *The Field* (Jim Sheridan, 1990), *The Nephew* (Eugene Brady, 1998), and *This Is My Father* (Paul Quinn, 1998). Similarly, in "Home to Harlem," it is significant that Declan's (presumably white) father is dead and his more meaningful relationships are with his mother and, especially, with his white grandmother. When he muses on what "home" is, he wonders, "Where is it? His granny's house, he thinks" (Doyle 2007, 194).

Equally, Doyle draws attention to Declan's tendency to romanticize his African American "roots" just as Irish Americans' sentimental perception of the homeland has been a key issue in "returned

Yank" narratives at least since *The Quiet Man*. When Franklin Powell, an African American man whom Declan thinks may be his uncle, suggests they meet at the Starbucks in Barnes and Noble, Declan is disappointed: "He'd expected to be heading up to Harlem; it's what he would have chosen. He's not sure why—stupid, really. Sentimental" (204). Just as, for Seán Thornton in *The Quiet Man*, his birthplace of Inisfree in the West of Ireland is "another word for heaven" compared with the "hell" of Pittsburgh, so Declan betrays his own assumptions regarding "authentic" African American space, place, and class. Declan may take issue with his adviser's recourse to national stereotypes, but he succumbs to stereotypes of race and class when he supposes that his "maybe-uncle" is "serving" or "cleaning" at Starbucks in Barnes and Noble when, in fact, Franklin Powell is a white-collar professional who works in human resources (208).

If Declan's story revises the typical roots journeys, he, as an Irishman, can also partake in the white immigrant narrative of arrival at Ellis Island (212). Indeed, though no mention is made of Declan's white ancestors, specifically, emigrating to the United States, his family's involvement in the history of Irish emigration is ensured by the fact that his grandmother was an Irish emigrant in Glasgow, working in a hotel, when she meets Declan's grandfather (181). Upon arrival at Ellis Island, Declan notes that he "feels Irish today" and, like a fresh-off-the-boat immigrant, "feels fresh, and kind of new. It's good; it's grand" (210). On this visit, he stays for hours, staring at old photographs and fighting "back the sentimentality" (211). As Werner Sollors demonstrates, points of arrival are extremely important in ethnic American literature, and early ethnic writers such as Mary Antin attempted to endow the immigrant ship and Ellis Island with the same symbolic significance held by the *Mayflower* and Plymouth Rock in the American national imaginary: "For Antin, any arrival in America after a transatlantic voyage was thus comparable; and her view of Ellis Island as a synonym for Plymouth Rock as well as her self-inclusion as an 'American' were to become central to the expansion of the term 'American' that supported the integration of minorities" (n.d.).

When Declan tells his adviser at the university, somewhat naively, that "you're not any less American . . . because your people didn't come over on the fuckin' *Mayflower*," she responds: "My *people* . . . came over on a *fucking* slave ship" (Doyle 2007, 211–12). As Sollors elucidates further, African American writers have responded with ambivalence to WASP Americans and white ethnic Americans' valorization of the *Mayflower* and the immigrant ship, respectively. Richard Wright, for example, writes in his *12 Million Black Voices* (1941) that "the Mayflower's nameless sister ship, presumably a Dutch vessel, which stole into the harbor of Jamestown in 1619 and unloaded her human cargo of 20 of us, was but the first ship to touch the shores of this New World, and her arrival signalized what was to be our trial for centuries to come" (n.d.).

Whereas Declan is keen to assert himself within the long history of Irish transnational identities, he is much less self-conscious regarding African American transnational identities. For him, Irish identities are mobile, but African American identities are static. African American identity corresponds to Harlem, whereas Irish identity, while narrowly defined in Ireland, can move to Glasgow or New York and back again. Unlike Jake and Ray in *Home to Harlem* and his adviser in "Home to Harlem," Declan fails to realize, along with Gilroy, that ships are equally, if not more, important within African diaspora consciousness as they are for white ethnic Americans. Ships "immediately focus attention on the middle passage, on the various projects for redemptive return to an African homeland, on the circulation of ideas and activists as well as the movement of key cultural and political artefacts" (Gilroy 1993, 4).

In an autobiographical piece written for the *New York Times*, Chinese American author Gish Jen, whose husband is Irish American, considers the identity of their mixed-race son. She writes that "certain ethnicities trump others; Chinese, for example, trumps Irish" (1996, n.p.). Similarly, Declan has found that, in Ireland, his blackness trumps his Irishness. He is "less Irish" because he is of mixed racial heritage (Doyle 2007, 212). Instead of discrediting a national identity that sees some of its citizens as "less Irish" than others on the basis that they are not white and embracing a transnational identity, Declan attempts to accommodate himself to it. Reversing the terms of the Irish dominant culture, instead of exploding them, he tries to have his Irishness trump his blackness. The problematic nature of Declan's conclusions on his Irishness and mixed racial identity is reflected in the evolution of his project: from one of the *influence* of African American writers on Irish writers (he wants to prove that "Yeats had died clutching his copy of *The New Negro*. Beckett never went to the jacks without *The Souls of Black Folk* under his arm" [Doyle 2007, 181]) to one of *parallels* between African American and Irish literature. It is a subtle shift, but one that reinforces the separateness of these identities rather than the possibilities of overlap. Declan does not deconstruct traditional notions of Irishness (white, Catholic, rural, Gaelic); he merely accommodates himself to them. On the other hand, Doyle's assertion of Declan within historical narratives of Irish transnationalism is successful because it adapts the narratives to Declan rather than Declan to the narratives. Reddy is correct in her contention that the story has an "unresolved ending," but it is because Declan's conclusions on his own identity are at odds with Doyle's (2007, 25).

Both "The Deportees" and "Home to Harlem" reflect Doyle's impulse, from early in his career, to revisit both his own work and the work of others. *The Snapper* (1990) and *The Van* (1991) followed *The Commitments* and other members of the Rabbitte family to form the Barrytown Trilogy (1992), although it was not originally conceived as such. The domestic abuse victim from the Doyle-scripted RTÉ/BBC television drama *Family* (1994) became the subject of two subsequent novels, *The Woman Who Walked into Doors* (1996) and *Paula Spencer* (2006). His screenplay for *When Brendan Met Trudy* (2000) is indebted to *A Bout de Souffle* (Jean-Luc Godard, 1960) and *Sunset Blvd.* (Billy Wilder, 1950). While Margaret Spillane claims that "The Deportees" is the story "most likely to be turned into a film," in fact Steph Green's *New Boy* was nominated for an Academy Award for Best Live Action Short Film in 2009 (2008, 149). Doyle transformed the first story of the collection,

"Guess Who's Coming for the Dinner"—which I discuss briefly in the epilogue—into a play, which premiered in September 2001, just one example of several interventions into race and immigration that the Irish stage has witnessed in the past ten years. They provide the focus for chapter 3.

3

Playing the Race Card

*Staging Immigration in Irish
and Irish American Drama*

> But what happens when the fuckers get their human rights?
> Huh? They turn around and grab someone else's. Oh, not right
> away. There's always a decent interval 'til they get on their feet.
> Then they deliver the old drop-kick to the crotch of some other
> miserable poor bugger.
>
> —JANET NOBLE, *Away Alone* (1989)

In Janet Noble's play *Away Alone*, which opened at the Irish Arts
Center in New York in December 1989, young Irish immigrants
struggle with homesickness, low-paid jobs, and, for the ones without
the appropriate work permits, fear of discovery by the authorities.
Desmond, a particularly sensitive young man, grows despondent at
feeling at home neither in the Bronx nor in Ireland, his dejection
eventually leading, it is implied, to his suicide by drowning. Arguing with fellow immigrant Liam over the futility of wars, Desmond
asks: "But what happens when the fuckers get their human rights?"
and answers his own rhetorical question. Desmond's claim is the
direct opposite of what the historical-duty argument would hope to
achieve. For him, a history of subjugation emphatically does not lead
to solidarity with other oppressed peoples but results in the desire to
become an oppressor in turn. This chapter interrogates the validity
of Desmond's statement by examining two interventions in debates
on race and immigration on the Irish and Irish American stage. In
Ronan Noone's *The Blowin of Baile Gall* (2002) and Donal O'Kelly's

"The Cambria" (2005), Ireland's colonial past is invoked in order, in the first case, to explain or even justify the ill-treatment of non-white immigrants to Ireland and, in the second, to appeal to a collective Irish conscience regarding immigrants based on the historical memory of colonialism and emigration.

While issues of globalization have dominated discussions of Irish theater for some time now, only one scholar has devoted himself consistently to unpacking stage representations of one of its chief consequences: immigration.[1] In such representations, Jason King finds that the historical-duty argument is pervasive. He argues that Irish theater, more than any other artistic or cultural form, "has served to provide a vehicle and a venue for . . . the staging of spectacles of intercultural contact, in which the interconnections between immigrant perceptions and Irish historical memory have become dramatized as a recurrent narrative conceit" (2005, 24). While King's work serves to draw attention to the diversity of Irish dramatic treatments of race and immigration, the six productions on which he focuses are not mainstream. As he acknowledges, his readings of them are based on "mainly unpublished scripts" (26). They thus form a counternarrative to the dominant mode of contemporary Irish drama that is still preoccupied with the Irish *emigrant* experience and not, like *The Blowin of Baile Gall*, in a way that juxtaposes "New Irish" with "New Irish." As Margaret Llewellyn-Jones observes, "A key figure in Irish drama is either the individual who decides on exile, or the family member whose return visit from abroad acts as a catalyst, challenging the identities and lifestyles of those who have stayed at home" (2002, 119; Trotter 2008, 184). She goes on to discuss no fewer than thirteen Irish plays, most of them staged in the 1990s and beyond, that dramatize these events. While King's observations on the receptiveness of Irish theater to intercultural interactions are insightful, then, it is also crucial to recognize that plays about Irish emigrant or returned emigrant subjects by high-profile

---

1. For an overview of globalization debates in Irish theater, see Lanters 2005.

and award-winning dramatists such as Brian Friel, Frank McGuinness, Tom Murphy, and Martin McDonagh continue to dominate the mainstream Irish stage.

For Shaun Richards, meanwhile, King's point regarding the receptiveness of Irish theater, in particular, to the dramatization of immigrant experiences is "moot" because except for these six plays, "what the contemporary Irish theatre has certainly done most successfully is capture some of the surface of social change, albeit often in plays whose superficiality accords with, rather than penetrates, the society they purport to examine" (2007, 9). In other words, Richards worries that the majority of plays staged in Ireland during the Celtic Tiger years depict the malaise of "latte-drinking" middle-class (their whiteness is implied, though not stated) Irish subjects and, as such, fail to do justice to Ireland's position as a "now active participant in global economic processes of which it is beneficiary rather than victim" (12, 4). Whereas Richards's discussion is, implicitly, more interested in class than race, Patrick Lonergan devotes a chapter of his book *Theatre and Globalization* (2009) to considering how "globalization can simultaneously inspire and inhibit genuine multiculturalism, both in society generally and in theatre particularly." In concluding his analysis of Brian Friel's *The Home Place* (2005) and Elizabeth Kuti's *The Sugar Wife* (2005), Lonergan is concerned that "contemporary Irish society is again constructing identity as a process of 'becoming white,' but for the first time within its own borders at—ironically and worryingly—a period when for the first time in its history Ireland is also becoming a multiracial society" (2009, 188, 204).

The observations of King, Richards, and Lonergan provide important groundwork for this chapter's sustained examination of race and immigration on the contemporary Irish and Irish American stage. While King remains ambivalent about the deployment of the historical duty argument in the six productions he discusses, he argues that it "can at least serve to lay the groundwork for creating that imaginative space of sympathetic engagement and generating a sense of cross-cultural solidarity" (2007b, 61). I am less convinced of the benefits of the approach than King is. For me, the dangers of the historical-duty argument become evident when *The Blowin of Baile Gall* is examined alongside *"The Cambria,"* for whereas the latter calls upon (Irish) audiences to recall their ancestors' sense of solidarity with other oppressed subjects, the former's preoccupation with Ireland's colonial past emerges as a troubling form of self-absorption that ultimately serves to reinforce its (Irish American) audience's sense of their own (white) victimhood.

Before turning to the plays, it is necessary to elaborate a little on the playwrights themselves and some of the key differences and similarities between their two works. In many ways, Noone is a typical representative of the New Irish generation of the 1980s. Having obtained a bachelor of arts degree and postgraduate qualification in journalism from University College Galway, Noone encountered difficulty finding work in Ireland. After securing a green card in 1994, he emigrated to the United States and worked for six years in the construction and hospitality industries before being admitted to the master's in fine arts program in playwriting at Boston University in 2000, where he studied under Nobel Laureate Derek Walcott.[2] In that same year, Noone became an American citizen. Born in 1970 in Newry, County Down, and raised in Clifden, County Galway, Noone came to prominence in the United States after winning the National Student Playwriting Award in 2002 and subsequently a cluster of other awards, for *The Lepers of Baile Baiste*, the first in his Baile trilogy. Unlike *Riverdance* and Frank McCourt's *Angela's Ashes* (1996), Noone's work is virtually unknown in Ireland. However, its popularity in the United States is undoubtedly embedded in the same "mania for all things Irish" that gave these two Irish and Irish American cultural products such cachet from the mid-1990s on

---

2. It is perhaps unsurprising that Walcott has championed Noone's work since Walcott recalls having felt "a special intimacy with the Irish poets" as "colonials with the same kind of problems that existed in the Caribbean. They were the niggers of Britain," comments that confirm professions of Irish-African diasporic solidarity are not simply one-way traffic (Ramazani 2001, 49).

(Eagan 2006, 20). The trilogy, of which *The Blowin of Baile Gall* is the second installment, bears more than a passing resemblance to Martin McDonagh's Leenane trilogy, if not in mode (they are realist rather than absurdist), then in conception. McDonagh's three plays, like Noone's, feature bleak West of Ireland settings and likely became familiar to Noone when they received awards and accolades upon being staged in the United States from 1998 on. In addition to the trilogy, Noone has written two other full-length plays, *Brendan* (2006) and *The Atheist* (2007), the last of which is his first to focus on a non-Irish or Irish American theme.

Actor and playwright Donal O'Kelly has, throughout his career, been a devotee of a "theatre of conscience" philosophy (Fitz-Simon and Sternlicht 1996, xix). He was a founder of and, until 2003, director of Calypso Productions, which not only tells "dramatic stories and look at people whose lives are shaped by dramatic events" but also publishes and disseminates "educational material on the issues raised in our plays and projects" ("About Calypso"). He is also an associate director of the peace and justice organization Afri, a group of artists that "seek to promote debate and influence policy and practice in Ireland and internationally on human rights, peace and justice issues" ("What is Afri?"). Afri, along with Abhann Productions and the St. Patrick's Festival, cosponsored the staging of *"The Cambria."* O'Kelly's 2005 play can be seen to build explicitly on his earlier work, in particular *Asylum! Asylum!* (1994), a damning indictment of the asylum process in Ireland. Joseph Omara, an asylum seeker from Uganda who witnessed, and was forced to facilitate, the torture of his father and four others, becomes involved with the Gaughran family through his relationships with Leo, an ambitious immigration official; Leo's sister Mary, a recently qualified solicitor who takes his case; and their father, Bill, who offers Joseph a place to stay while his application to remain in the country is being considered. Whereas *"The Cambria"* draws upon the historical memory of Irish emigration, *Asylum! Asylum!* appeals to Irish Christianity in order to elicit audience sympathy for Joseph. When Leo tells him, "There's no room for anyone else. It's obvious and it's simple. We're full up!" O'Kelly calls to mind the turning away of the holy family from places of lodging in Bethlehem (Fitz-Simon and Sternlicht 1996, 120). As Jason King notes, it is also significant that Bill, who offers refuge to Joseph, is a recently retired sacristan (2007a, 162).

Whereas Noone's work has played exclusively to audiences in the United States, O'Kelly's *"The Cambria"* toured throughout Ireland in 2005 and has also been performed at venues in Britain and the United States. Noone's play is staged naturalistically with a full cast of characters and a minutely described set, whereas in O'Kelly's, two actors play eleven characters, and there is not so much a set as a series of props to indicate changes of scene and character. A crucial commonality between the two plays, however, is their deployment of a melodramatic mode. In Patrick Lonergan's review of *"The Cambria,"* he claims, citing Roddy Doyle's *Guess Who's Coming for the Dinner* (2001), Ken Harmon's *Done Up Like a Kipper* (2002), Jim O'Hanlon's *The Buddhist of Castleknock* (2002), and Charlie O'Neill's *Hurl* (2003) as examples, that melodrama "seems to dominate recent Irish dramatic treatments of race" (2005, 63). Some of the reviewers of Noone's play also criticized it for perceived melodramatic excesses. For Jeffrey Gantz of the *Boston Phoenix*, by the second act of *Blowin*, "the many confrontations turn drama into melodrama, and the last scene is as puzzling as that of [*The Lepers of*] *Baile Baiste*, both improbable and overloaded" (2002, n.p.).

Lonergan is clearly uncomfortable with the use of the melodramatic mode in contemporary Irish stagings of racial conflict, finding it "troubling" and asserting, at the end of his review, that "it's time for Irish drama to move beyond melodrama in its treatment of race" (2005, 63). However, this move is unlikely to happen as long as the historical-duty argument is explicitly or implicitly thematized in plays such as O'Kelly's and Noone's. If Jason King is correct in his claim that contemporary Irish intercultural drama presents (predominantly) white Irish audiences with a "moral injunction" to recall their ancestors' status as colonized, diasporic subjects in order to empathize with other people's diasporas in Ireland, then it follows that melodrama will persist as its preferred structuring framework

(2003, 203). Melodrama is, after all, as Linda Williams puts it, a "mode of storytelling crucial to the establishment of moral good" (2001, 12). In other words, melodrama is the ideal formal complement to the thematics of historical duty. In *Playing the Race Card: Melodramas of Black and White from Uncle Tom to O. J. Simpson*, from which I borrow the title to this chapter, Linda Williams contends that the melodramatic mode in all its manifestations (literature, stage, film, and television) has exerted an "almost incalculable influence on American attitudes toward race" (8). If Lonergan is correct regarding the pervasiveness of melodrama in Irish theatrical treatments of race and immigration, and I suspect that he is, then this provides yet another instance of the adoption of American strategies in Irish attempts to negotiate its changing demographics.

Williams, drawing upon Peter Brooks's seminal work *The Melodramatic Imagination: Balzac, Henry James, Melodrama and the Mode of Excess* (1976), identifies five features of the melodramatic mode, several of which are common to *The Blowin of Baile Gall* and *"The Cambria."* First, melodrama *"begins, and wants to end, in a 'space of innocence'"* (Williams 2001, 28; emphasis in original). Williams adds that this "space of innocence" need not be a literal home, but that "the most enduring forms of the [melodramatic] mode are often suffused with nostalgia for a virtuous place that we like to think we once possessed, whether in childhood or the distant past of the nation" (28). For Noone, this "virtuous place" is the house—the childhood home of Eamon—now in need of rehabilitation from a legacy of (post)colonial hatred, nationalist struggles, and small-town bigotry; for O'Kelly, it is the Ireland that once welcomed Frederick Douglass. Second, melodrama *"focuses on victim-heroes and on recognizing their virtue"* (29; emphasis in original). For O'Kelly, it is the nineteenth-century Douglass and the absent Patrick of the present day. However, for Noone, it is slightly more complicated. Ostensibly, it is Laurence, arguably the only "likable" character in the play. In reality, though, all the characters in the play are cast as victims, a situation that detracts from the play's moral power and, as I suggest below, renders it extremely problematic. Third, melodrama's *"recognition of virtue involves a dialectic of pathos and action—a give and take of 'too late' and 'in the nick of time'"* (30; emphasis in original). Both Noone and O'Kelly err on the side of "too late": *Blowin* ends with irrevocable racial violence; in *"The Cambria,"* Patrick has been deported despite Colette's best efforts. Fourth, melodrama *"borrows from realism but realism serves the melodrama of pathos and action"* (30; emphasis in original). Of the two plays, *Blowin* is more invested in the realistic mode than *"The Cambria,"* which, with its surrealistic character "morphing," succeeds in destabilizing essentialized notions of identity, as I argue below. Last, melodrama presents *"characters who embody primary psychic roles organized in Manichaean conflicts between good and evil"* (40; emphasis in original). This character is Laurence/Eamon in *Blowin* and Douglass/Dodd in *"The Cambria."*

As is the case with the book as a whole, this chapter is preoccupied with analogies—implicit (between "New Irish" immigrants to Ireland and "New Irish" emigrants to the United States in *Blowin*) or explicit (between Frederick Douglass and the fictional asylum seeker, Patrick, in *"The Cambria"*)—which rely on the generation of cross-racial sympathy (affect) to achieve political change (effect). As Kimberly Chabot Davis argues in an article on the readers of Oprah's Book Club selections, affect is a controversial area of scholarly inquiry. She summarizes various scholars' objections to one manifestation of affect, cross-racial sympathy, as follows: "While some object to the sympathetic emotions on the grounds that they substitute for political action, other cultural critics and race theorists treat sympathy as an inherently colonizing action, and they reduce empathy to an imperialistic drive to incorporate the other into the self" (2004, 404–5). Meanwhile, Linda Williams demonstrates the fickleness of racial sympathy in her examination of Harriet Beecher Stowe's *Uncle Tom's Cabin* (1852) and D. W. Griffith's film *The Birth of a Nation* (1915). Whereas the former drew previously uninvolved Northerners into the debate over slavery, "making the 'good nigger' into a familiar and friendly icon, for whom whites had sympathy," some sixty years later, the latter "solidified North and South into a new national feeling of racial antipathy, making the black man into an object of white fear and loathing" (2001, 99). Depending on the context, in other words, racial sympathy can frequently translate into appropriation, political paralysis, or antipathy. However, although Davis, like those critics upon whose work she draws, is wary of the potential problems posed by cross-racial sympathy, she distinguishes between different types of sympathy, some of which may, in fact, prove "radically unsettling" for the reader or viewer (2004, 409). This analysis of Noone's and O'Kelly's plays, both of which draw upon the historical-duty argument, teases out such different encodings of cross-racial sympathy.

A Darker Shade of Green:
Ronan Noone's *The Blowin of Baile Gall*

In his introduction to the Methuen edition of Tom Murphy's *The House*, Fintan O'Toole poses the following question: "In a society struggling to cope with immigration, what meaning can a play like *The House*, steeped in the psychic disruptions of emigration, possibly have?" (2000, 6). Murphy's play, first performed on April 12, 2000, at the Abbey Theatre in Dublin, is set in 1950s rural Ireland and dramatizes the tragic determination of returned emigrant, Christy Cavanagh, to buy the bourgeois home of his late mother's employers, the de Burcas. This family, with their "Norman blood" (25) and their ownership of a "Victorian house" (45), represents a long history of Irish occupation and dispossession by successive colonial powers—now domesticated, as indicated by the house's all-female residents. When Christy tells Marie, one of the de Burca daughters, that he would "die" for the house, Murphy evokes Ireland's bloody and destructive national struggle (112). As if to respond to O'Toole's question, Ronit Lentin expresses the relationship between past emigration and contemporary immigration as the return of the repressed, the national repressed being "the pain of emigration, returning to haunt the Irish, through the presence of the immigrant 'other' and in its wake invoking the unseemly presence of the 'less than fully Irish' indigenous and non-indigenous minorities—the Traveller, the Asian, the black, the

Jew" (2002, 233). Equally, in his contribution to *Multi-culturalism: The View from the Two Irelands* pamphlet, Declan Kiberd attempts to unpack this relationship. However, despite stating initially that "it would be too simple to explain the recent racist outbreaks as a legacy of the colonial system," his subsequent, somewhat contradictory claim that "the presence of black Africans in the streets of Dublin is a reminder of a colonial past of shame and shared humiliation which some might prefer to ignore" reflects Kiberd's own investment in the legacy of colonialism within the contemporary Irish psyche (Longley and Kiberd 2001, 47, 72).

This connection becomes explicit in Noone's *The Blowin of Baile Gall* who, for the titles to his plays in the Baile trilogy, is likely indebted to Murphy's earlier work *Bailegangaire* (1985).[3] Like Murphy, Noone utilizes the motif of the house as a powerful symbol of Ireland's colonial occupation, but introduces an African immigrant to further nuance the relationship between the colonial legacy, emigration, and contemporary immigration. Set on a construction site in a small town in the West of Ireland in the present day, the play dramatizes the conflicts that ensue between former lovers, Molly and Eamon, and their coworkers whom Eamon considers outsiders or "blowins" in various ways: Stephen, because he is an orphan and was raised by nuns in a local institution; Sam Carson, the general contractor, because he is a "returned Yank"; and Laurence, because he is a Nigerian immigrant who is working in Ireland illegally. The construction site is actually the childhood home of Eamon, which has been sold and is being renovated by an English couple with the highly evocative surname of "Bull." The fact that the couple remains unseen throughout the play reinforces the notion of the absent presence of the colonial legacy. The name of the town itself translates as "Town of the English" or "Brit Town." The play ends with all three

---

3. Indeed, Noone has written of his admiration for Tom Murphy's *Conversations on a Homecoming* (1987), a play in which he believes that "the true mirror was held up to nature" (Noone 2007, 616).

blowins having been expurgated from the stage and the suggestion that Molly and Eamon will resurrect their dysfunctional relationship. Noone thus implies that this insular community—and, by extension, Irish society—will stop at nothing to preserve the fantasy of its racial and cultural homogeneity.

Noone's play is unique in providing American audiences with an insight into Ireland's changing demographics, for while Irish interest media have reported on immigration to Ireland (Fincham 2001; Shouldice 2005), Irish American *cultural* representations of this phenomenon are virtually nonexistent. The real strength of *Blowin* is that the "returned Yank" figure serves to remind American audiences that immigration, while a relatively recent trend in Ireland, is an issue with which the United States continues to grapple. Just three months after the play had its off-Broadway debut on September 9, 2005, the House of Representatives passed the Border Protection, Anti-terrorism, and Illegal Immigration Control (or Sensenbrenner) Bill by 239 votes to 182. In other words, Noone has a knack—certainly in the first two plays of his trilogy—of choosing themes that are relevant in both Irish and American contexts. *The Lepers of Baile Baiste* confronts the issue of clerical child abuse. By 2001 this issue had emerged in a series of highly publicized scandals in Ireland, the United States, and elsewhere, and, with the resignation of Cardinal Bernard Law as archbishop of Boston in December of the following year, the play was about to become even more topical. (The subject was, arguably, more successfully rendered in a subsequent play by John Patrick Shanley: his Pulitzer Prize–winning *Doubt: A Parable* [2004].)

At first glance, it appears that the moral power of *Blowin* relies on Noone's construction of parallels between the "New Irish" generation of emigrants to the United States in the 1980s and the "New Irish" immigrants to Ireland from the 1990s to present. In other words, by suggesting a connection between these two groups, Noone attempts to elicit sympathy for Laurence from an audience who, likely comprising many of the first group, will identify with the second. Originally staged in Boston in 2002, *The Blowin of Baile Gall* had its off-Broadway debut, as stated, on September 9, 2005, at the Irish Arts Center in New York. The Irish Arts Center, which was established by a group of political activists in 1972 to challenge the shamrock-and-shillelaghs versions of Irish culture that were felt to be prevalent in the United States at the time, had become, by the 1990s, one of the key "groups actively producing Irish drama in New York" (Almeida 2001, 127). It is likely that Noone's play, which was produced by Gabriel Byrne, attracted audiences that were themselves composed of many of the New Irish generation.

In *The New Irish Americans*, Ray O'Hanlon sketches the "alpha immigrant, 1980s style," positing that "he or she probably left Ireland in the summer of 1982 or 1983 with a return ticket on Aer Lingus and a yarn about a long lost aunt in Philadelphia, a family funeral in Boston or a wedding in the Bronx. He or she might have been a university graduate and most certainly would have completed high school" (1998, 21). As Linda Almeida points out, "Older Irish Americans, either immigrants themselves or the children of immigrants, in many instances employed the New Irish on construction sites and in restaurants and bars" (2001, 74). Carson, who emigrated to the United States twenty years before the setting of the play in 2002, and worked in construction, accords almost exactly with O'Hanlon's and Almeida's configuration of the typical New Irish emigrant. When Carson tells Laurence, "If immigration knows I hired you then you won't be the only one in trouble," this statement would almost certainly resonate with any undocumented workers among the play's New Irish audiences (Noone 2006, 25). Admiring Laurence's commitment to work, Carson asks him if he has ever been to America. When Laurence replies that he has not, Carson tells him, "Well I was there and I worked hard. I did well. So I recognise strong hands" (26). Carson and Laurence are similar, as Carson sees it, in that they have the initiative to go abroad and look for work. However, the audience senses the limits of Carson's identification with Laurence when he tells Eamon that Laurence represents "cheap labour" (34).

In contrast to Carson, who worked "all those years" and then returned to Ireland to start a business, Eamon is "still sitting on [his] arse when [he] could have had [his] own company" by now (Noone

2006, 34–35). Carson tells Eamon, "This country is flying, and look at ya. You use your brains to let a grudge eat away at ya instead" (34–35). However, Carson's statement suggests the extent to which Stephen, Molly, and, especially, Eamon are incapable of escaping the demons of their collective traumatic past. Indeed, Eamon admits that Carson raises his ire, forcing "old ghosts" to rise to the surface, as he puts it (28). In this respect, the construction site is an appropriate setting for the play not only because it resonates with Irish emigration history more generally and with the New Irish generation in particular, but also because it is emblematic of the property boom that characterized Celtic Tiger Ireland, which, in turn, fueled the demand for immigrant labor in the building industry. Luke Gibbons, writing in a different context, questions "the naïve optimism according to which the ghosts of the past, even the recent past, are lifted by the cessation of conflict, or the first upswing in the economy" (2002, 94).

In Gibbons's terms, then, the house that the characters are renovating is probably a haunted house. Indeed, what I find worrying about the play becomes evident by unpacking this central metaphor. As one of Noone's early reviewers observes, "The renovated house that Laurence . . . blows in to is an obvious metaphor for Ireland, and it's not in good shape." For the most part, this reviewer finds that Noone's metaphors "serve him well, like the Irish house that can't be rebuilt without 'blowin' help" (Gantz 2002, n.p.). For me, however, the metaphor fails for two reasons, one formal and one thematic, although the two are, of course, linked. First, Noone's play is structured around the "stranger-in-the-house" formula that Nicholas Grene identifies as prevalent in one-act plays of the National Theatre movement by Douglas Hyde, W. B. Yeats, Lady Gregory, and J. M. Synge, among others. Such plays usually unfold as follows: "A room within a house, a family in the room, stand in for normality, for ordinary, familiar life; into the room there enters a stranger, and the incursion of that extrinsic, extraordinary figure alters, potentially transforms the scene" (2000, 52). Lonergan adds that it is often the kitchen of the house, in particular, that symbolizes the nation, and Noone's play is no exception (2009, 146). The stranger-in-the-house plays, like *Blowin*, are characterized by "a simple set of equivalences by which family = house = community = nation" (Grene 2000, 135). For this reason, according to Brian Singleton, strangers in the house "took on the mantle of imperialist forces whose colonial project, practices and values had to be resisted and expelled" (2001, 293). Because the trope of the stranger in the house is so deeply embedded in the assertion of an anticolonial Irish nationalism, Noone's reliance on the strategy bespeaks his investment, conscious or not, in an Irish dramatic tradition with an almost obsessive preoccupation with the colonial legacy.

Singleton argues that the stranger-in-the-house motif has been adopted and adapted by contemporary Irish playwrights (Frank McGuinness, Tom Murphy, Marina Carr, and Gary Mitchell) in such a way that the "house" trope "is no longer the resting place for a secure sense of Irishness" (2001, 303). Even more radical, perhaps, is the antiracist parade, *Féile Fáilte,* produced in December 1997 by Donal O'Kelly and Calypso, featuring "a monster Celtic Tiger breathing flames and an enormous fire-sculpture of a cosy house with an open door [that] pronounced welcome to refugees, asylum-seekers and vulnerable immigrants" (O'Kelly 1998, 13). If McGuinness et al. transform the connotations of the stranger in the house, O'Kelly deconstructs it by taking it outside the potentially hegemonic space of the theater altogether. On the other hand, Noone's play reinforces the politicized nationalist origins of the stranger-in-the-house formula by failing to distinguish adequately between the British colonial invaders who dispossessed Eamon and recent immigrants to Ireland such as Laurence, whom Eamon also perceives as "invading our territories," a form of rhetoric reminiscent of the Immigration Control Platform's attempt to mobilize Irish citizens to "stop the invasion and colonization of Ireland" (Noone 2006, 28). In other words, when Eamon declares, "This is my house," he wishes to protect it from colonial oppressors, returned Yanks, and immigrants alike (27). While Eamon's racist diatribes are certainly discredited by Noone— when he objects to "those feckin fugees walking around our basterin' town? And us accommodating them with our taxes," Molly points out that he does not actually pay tax (14)—his depiction of Eamon as so extreme a racist hypocrite fails to do justice to the more subtle nuances of racial hierarchies.

Rather than showing racial violence as embedded in hierarchies established at a social level, *The Blowin of Baile Gall* not only makes it a function of the pathologies of the play's individual characters, but also maps these pathologies onto the colonial legacy. In *Lepers,* when Father Gannon attempts to suppress revelations of abuse by schoolteacher Brother Angelus, he claims, "That was a long time ago," to which Daithí, one of the victims, replies, "So was the fuckin' famine and we still feel the effects" (Noone 2003, 73). Noone thus deploys a metaphor that was relatively widespread in self-representations of Britain's colonial relationship with Ireland (and, indeed, other countries): the catastrophe that was the Great Famine becomes a symbol for the abuse by a colonial power or adult of a vulnerable colony or child. As Declan Kiberd shows, in British colonial representations, "if John Bull was industrious and reliable, Paddy was held to be indolent and contrary; if the former was mature and rational, the latter must be unstable and emotional; if the English were adult and manly, the Irish must be childish and feminine. In this fashion, the Irish were to read their fate in that of two other out-groups, women and children" (1996, 30). In *The Blowin of Baile Gall,* the colonial legacy is felt most vividly in the infantilization and feminization of its white male postcolonial subjects. Orphaned Stephen, deprived of the care of a mother(land) or father(land), is entrusted to Mother Church instead, where he fails to develop an adequately robust masculinity. Molly accuses him of being "unmanly," "a child," and a "eunuch" (Noone 2006, 30, 43). Eamon calls him a "peacemaking pussy" (41) and tells him he has "no balls" (59). Meanwhile, Eamon's discovery of an Action Man figure he owned as a child in the house they are renovating is emblematic of the vestiges of his own masculinity stripped away by the forces of colonial rule.

For Eamon, the "returned Yank" Sam Carson is also a nefarious presence, complicit with the English in his acquisitiveness. While the trope of the "returned Yank" appears in many guises in Irish and

Irish American culture—and will be discussed in greater detail in chapter 4—for Eamon, Carson corresponds to the version presented in *The Field* (1990), Jim Sheridan's screen adaptation of John B. Keane's play. In what is a very self-conscious revision of Sean Thornton from *The Quiet Man*, Tom Berenger's character is, as Luke Gibbons argues, "a more destructive, intrusive presence, subscribing to the industrial logic and profit motive rejected by Sean: instead of seeking to reconnect with the maternal past, his plan is to bury it forever under the concrete of a hydroelectric station" (2006b, 98). Eamon claims that Carson has "forgotten where he comes from, bosses us around, and we fixin' another Blowin's house. . . . And us livin' in our own little tenements" (Noone 2006, 20). The suggestion of Carson's collusion with English oppressors is reinforced by the fact that Carson is having an affair with Mrs. Bull, whose husband has left her. In *The Blowin of Baile Gall*, ultimately, Noone's emphasis on past colonial traumas enables its white characters to abdicate all culpability in their treatment of Laurence.

Although postcolonial solidarity is, in the end, impossible for these characters, there is a brief glimmer of hope for a shared class consciousness among them. When Stephen defines the "us" in "us against them" as "employ*ees*" rather than "employ*ers*," he reconfigures the battleground as one of class instead of race. Molly remarks that, in that case, "Lionel [Laurence] is one of us," to which Eamon responds, "My white arse he is" (Noone 2006, 42). For Eamon, not surprisingly, race trumps class as a category of identification. However, the intertextual references Noone makes to Eugene O'Neill's play *The Hairy Ape* (1922), from which he derives one of his epigraphs to *The Blowin of Baile Gall*, appear to suggest that Noone sees what his characters do not: that racial identity may be complicated by the notion of class. Depicting the lives of coal handlers who work in the bowels of a ship, the dramatic conflict of *The Hairy Ape* pivots on the moment during which the furnace is visited by a bourgeois white woman called Mildred Douglas, who recoils in horror at the vision of the "filthy beast" that is Yank, one of the workers (E. O'Neill 1960, 157).

Yank's encounter with Mildred Douglas precipitates a crisis of identity whereby he is transformed into a raced and classed "other" through the gaze of an upper-class white woman. In *The Blowin of Baile Gall,* the epigraph from O'Neill's play reproduces the words of the Irish character Paddy, who compares the second engineer's exhibiting of his workers to a tour guide in a museum: "In this case is a queerer kind of baboon than ever you'd find in darkest Africy. We roast them in their own sweat—and be damned if you won't hear some of thim saying they like it!" (E. O'Neill 1960, 161). Like in *The Hairy Ape,* Noone suggests that his characters have been dehumanized by years of physical labor. Stephen, in particular, is repeatedly referred to by himself and others as a "lackey" (Noone 2006, 12, 33, 35, 44, 48, 52, 59, 68) and a "slave" (68). To reinforce the connection with O'Neill's play, the word *ape* is used with some frequency by the characters in *The Blowin of Baile Gall.* In one of Eamon's racist diatribes, he claims that "soon we won't know what colour we are, and we the palest colour in the world after the Eskimos, that no one can ever accuse us of coming from apes" (15). Eamon also goads Molly about his crossword clue "Lead apes in hell," the solution to which is "spinster" (13, 16). Eamon's cousin Bulldog, whom Eamon had lined up for the job Carson gives to Laurence, is, for Molly, not "a man, he's an ape" (43). O'Neill, then, interrogates the way in which a native-born American worker is "undone" by a white, upper-class woman who looks him "out of the ranks of white humanity" (Roediger 2003, 47–48). Despite his invocation of O'Neill, in *The Blowin of Baile Gall,* Noone's characters are unable to reach out across the racial divide to form allegiances along class lines. Although Laurence, like Stephen, is "not local," Stephen is keen to protest that he is not "the same as [Laurence]" (Noone 2006, 41). Despite the fact that they are the two characters who have the most in common in terms of their class positioning (the other characters are skilled; Laurence and Stephen are both laborers), it is Laurence who eventually kills Stephen.

Although it was probably not his intention, Noone's nods to O'Neill's play function to point up his own preoccupation with the colonial legacy. Like the white woman Mildred Douglas in *The Hairy Ape*, the African man Laurence is a mere catalyst in the play, his role subordinated to the Irish characters' individual and collective identity crises. In fact, in so doing, Noone's play exposes the problems at the heart of Kiberd's claim that "the new immigrants are providing a priceless service, reconnecting people with their own buried feelings" (Longley and Kiberd 2001, 72). Noone is, in the end, much more interested in the Irish story than in Laurence's, as becomes evident in one particular scene. When it emerges that Laurence is familiar with the town's Famine memorial, Molly responds, "Well—wish I could tell you I knew something about your place" besides what she sees "on the television" (Noone 2006, 37). After a pause, Laurence absolves Molly of her ignorance and beckons her to continue: "I interrupted your story" (37) and, after telling her something about his life, apologizes for it: "Now I'm sorry—I talk too much" (39). Ultimately, Noone's excessive interest in Ireland's colonial past mitigates his ability to unpack with any real conviction the impact of the characters' racial and class positioning on their lives.

Aristocracies of Skin: Douglass in Ireland, Historical Duty, and Donal O'Kelly's *"The Cambria"*

> To judge properly of the negro, you must see him educated, and treated with the respect due to a fellow-creature—uninsulted, by the filthy aristocracy of skin, and untarnished to the eye of the white by any associations connected with his state of slavery.
> —DANIEL O'CONNELL, speech given at a meeting of the Repeal Association, Dublin, October 11, 1843

> Whatever may be said of the aristocracies here, there is none based on the color of a man's skin. This species of aristocracy belongs preëminently to "the land of the free and the home of the brave."
> —FREDERICK DOUGLASS, *My Bondage and My Freedom* (1855)

On April 2, 2008, a documentary entitled *Frederick Douglass agus na Negroes Bána (Frederick Douglass and the White Negro)* screened on the Irish-language television channel TG4. While political pundits were furiously debating Fianna Fáil's—and, by extension, Ireland's—political future in an extended news program on RTÉ1 following Taoiseach Bertie Ahern's shocking resignation earlier that day, TG4 was also concerned with a story that, it claimed, was "for today and for the future." In the television listings, Douglass was described as "the 19th century Martin Luther King," a cleverly timed construction because the fortieth anniversary of King's assassination would be marked just two days later ("Schedule" 2008). The documentary, which was directed by John J. Doherty, featured contributions from several Irish and American academics, including Noel Ignatiev and Douglass scholar Patricia Ferreira. It traced Douglass's early life as a slave, his escape, the authorship of his 1845 *Narrative,* and his subsequent interactions and encounters with the Irish, both in Ireland and in the United States. In many ways, the documentary uses Douglass as a lens through which to recapitulate the Grand Narrative of Irish emigration to the United States, a narrative characterized by the "grievances" of the Great Famine and participation in the American Civil War (K. O'Neill 2001, 118). However, the film does not ignore the more ignominious moments in Irish emigration history, covering (as the presence of Ignatiev indicates) their sometimes violent assertion of whiteness culminating in the New York Draft Riots of 1863.

At the same time that it traced Irish interactions with African Americans in the nineteenth century, the program was also clearly providing a commentary on contemporary Ireland. The film begins with shots of contemporary Belfast and ends with shots of contemporary Dublin. In one striking scene, sociologist Bill Rolston paraphrases Douglass's claims regarding his treatment as an equal in Ireland: "I employ a cab—I am seated beside white people—I reach the hotel—I enter the same door—I am shown into the same parlor—I dine at the same table—and no one is offended. No delicate nose grows deformed in my presence" (Douglass 1994, 689).

Rolston's voice-over accompanies images of contemporary multicultural Dublin: when Rolston mentions Douglass's not having faced discrimination in any restaurant, the camera pans across Lemon, a crêperie on Dawson Street. This shot provides a neat geographical link to the following scene in which Marcus Valentine, the actor who plays Douglass, is set against the backdrop of the Mansion House, where, the narrator tells us, Douglass dined with the lord mayor. The Mansion House is almost directly opposite Lemon on Dawson Street. Viewers are also informed of Douglass's friendship with Daniel O'Connell, with whom he shared the platform at a repeal rally at Dublin's Conciliation Hall on September 29, 1845. "Ironically," the narrator observes, "the National Garda Immigration Bureau is located where the Conciliation Hall used to be." The implication is that what was a space of equality and mutual respect has been replaced by a space of hierarchy and exclusion. Toward the end of the film, a Valentine-as-Douglass voice-over is accompanied by images of multicultural crowds in contemporary Dublin: several nonwhite subjects appear in the frame and in the background; a sign in Chinese is visible over a storefront.

As the film suggests, Frederick Douglass has become an important figure in cultural negotiations of race and immigration in contemporary Ireland because he has actual historical links to Ireland and Irish America and wrote relatively extensively of his experiences with the Irish in both Ireland and America.[4] Because Douglass was sympathetic to the Famine-stricken Irish and subsequently surprised by and critical of their ruthless pursuit of white status in the New World, he wields a particular moral power in contemporary Ireland, challenging native-born white Irish to (re)consider the position of recent immigrants to Ireland, especially the ones who are not white. Doherty's

4. An earlier example is the *Irish Times* editorial of April 20, 1998, which compares the welcome Douglass received with the hostility with which one African American visitor to Ireland was confronted in 1998, "anecdotal impressions" that nonetheless "raise timely questions about Ireland's much-vaunted hospitality and friendliness to strangers" (Brady 1998, 15).

documentary thus exemplifies another one of the "mixed strategies of self-criticism and historical retrieval" that Michael Malouf has identified in recent attempts to build a tradition of Irish antiracism (2006, 321). This section examines a slightly earlier manifestation of this renewed, though always oblique, Irish interest in Douglass—Donal O'Kelly's *"The Cambria"*—attempting to determine where we might locate it in relation to the dilemma of acknowledging the oppression of Irish subjects without overstating Irish–African American solidarity in the past or, indeed, in the present.

"The Cambria" depicts Douglass's journey to Britain and Ireland aboard the eponymous ship in 1845. It dramatizes the events described by Douglass in "American Prejudice Against Color," an address delivered in Cork, and in *My Bondage and My Freedom* (1855), whereby Douglass faced a mob of angry white Southerners who threatened to throw him overboard after he delivered a powerful antislavery lecture aboard *The Cambria* (Douglass 1979, 59; Douglass 1994, 370–72). On O'Kelly's *Cambria*, Douglass's fellow passengers include the fictional white slaveholder Dodd, his daughter Matilda, and a white woman, Cecily Hutchinson, a member of the abolitionist Hutchinson Family Singers who did, in fact, travel aboard *The Cambria* with Douglass. Upon arrival in Cobh (*The Cambria* actually docked in Liverpool before traveling on to Cobh), Douglass is greeted rapturously by Daniel O'Connell, who introduces him to the assembled crowd as a man who has lived his life in pursuit of the principles of "freedom and self-determination" (O'Kelly 2005, 50). Directed by Raymond Keane and performed by O'Kelly and Sorcha Fox, O'Kelly frames *"The Cambria"* with the story of a Nigerian student recently deported from Ireland, thus explicitly contrasting the welcome that Douglass received in 1845 with the contemporary treatment of African immigrants to Ireland. In so doing, he effectively responds to Luke Gibbons's call for narratives that retrieve "emancipatory projects for alternative political futures" (2006a, 60).

The play opens in the present-day with Colette, a history teacher, sitting despondent in an airport lounge, recounting the deportation of one of her students to Vincent, a painter. The airport scene provides what O'Kelly calls the "springboard into the story of Frederick Douglass' voyage to Ireland aboard the Cambria in 1845" (2005, 2). The play concludes with Colette's naming of Douglass as a "one-time asylum-seeker and refugee" (52). In an uncanny real-life parallel, three days before the premiere of O'Kelly's play, nineteen-year-old student Olukunle Elukanlo was deported from Ireland on a charter flight to Nigeria with thirty-four other "failed" asylum seekers. After a public outcry, especially by school friends from Palmerstown Community College in West Dublin, the minister for justice, equality, and law reform allowed Elukanlo to return to Ireland on April 1 and granted him a six-month visa to enable him to sit for his leaving-certificate examinations that summer.

While Jason King's work has proven extremely helpful in contextualizing O'Kelly's play within contemporary Irish theater trends more generally, he does not discuss *"The Cambria"* specifically. On the other hand, Fionnghuala Sweeney's article on O'Kelly's play anticipates many of my concerns here, particularly regarding its original performance as part of the St. Patrick's Festival. However, because Sweeney's focus remains firmly on "unpicking the extent and meaning of [Ireland's] historical implication in the Atlantic [slave] trade," her article lacks an engagement with O'Kelly's impressive body of work predating *"The Cambria,"* which facilitates a deeper understanding of the play (2008, 279).[5] She also omits the way in which O'Kelly engages the often troubling racial politics of minstrelsy, an

---

5. "Having embraced the free market and emerged as a member of the global economic elite," Sweeney continues, "the Republic of Ireland has yet to attend to the ways in which that inheritance might begin to be reflected in the emerging political and cultural narrative of the present" (2008, 280). It is curious, then, that she does not mention English playwright Elizabeth Kuti's *The Sugar Wife*, which premiered in Dublin just a couple of weeks after O'Kelly's play, on April 8, 2005. Set in the nineteenth century, the play is concerned with the arrival of an African American slave orator, Sarah Worth, and her English abolitionist companion in the Dublin home of the Tewkley family, tea merchants likely based on the Bewleys. The play quite explicitly links the trade in human flesh with global capitalism.

issue that Lonergan raises in his review of *"The Cambria"*: "What does it mean for the white O'Kelly to play an African-American liberator? Is O'Kelly's conflation of the contemporary asylum seeker and Douglass fair to both?" (2005, 63). With the assistance of King and Sweeney, then, I hope to produce a more comprehensive analysis of *"The Cambria,"* situating it within a wider Irish theatrical context while also analyzing the specifics of the play.

At the conclusion of *Frederick Douglass agus na Negroes Bána*, images of Dublin's increasingly multicultural St. Patrick's Day parades accompany the rolling credits. The sequence, which pertains in no way to Douglass's involvement with Ireland and the Irish, confirms that the primary concern of Doherty and of Camel Productions is with contemporary multicultural Ireland rather than with Douglass. First staged as part of the St. Patrick's Festival on March 17, 2005, O'Kelly's play exists where the always controversial performative spaces of Irish theater and St. Patrick's Day parades collide. Nine years prior to the staging of O'Kelly's play "marked a significant turning point in the anniversary's history" because 1996 was the first year in which a concerted effort was made "to move the St. Patrick's Day celebrations in Dublin away from being 'just a parade'" (Cronin and Adair 2002, 241, 243). While the parade is still the focus of what has become the St. Patrick's Festival, other events—such as a Céilí Mór, a fireworks display (Skyfest), Irish-language workshops, art, music, comedy, and theater—also feature in the five-day program. Interestingly, 1996 was also the year in which Ireland became a country of net immigration (Garner 2004, 50). If, as Michael Cronin and Daryl Adair claim, the attempt "to reappropriate St Patrick's Day" from 1996 on was "a reaction to, and in some ways in defiance of, the diaspora-based St Patrick's celebrations that have claimed virtual 'ownership' of the festivities abroad," the changes to the Dublin format are also inextricable from the arrival of "other people's diasporas" in Ireland (2002, 241–42).

In fact, as Katherine O'Donnell argues, the reconceived festivities arose in part from a self-conscious attempt on the part of Irish authorities to promote the Irish St. Patrick's Day parades as inclusive and tolerant compared with the one in New York, the biggest global parade. Beginning in 1991, New York parade organizers, the Ancient Order of the Hibernians (AOH), repeatedly rejected applications by the Irish Lesbian and Gay Organization to march in the St. Patrick's Day parade. Reacting to events in New York, thirty-two lesbians marched in the 1992 Cork parade under a banner that read "Hello New York" (O'Donnell 2007, 138). In 1995 the Supreme Court ruled that the AOH, as a private organization, was entitled to exclude anyone they wished from the parade. But according to O'Donnell, "The unquestioned assumption that being homosexual is antithetical to being Irish provided the fundamental premise for which it was successfully argued in US courts that the Irish Lesbian and Gay Organization is a violent, obscene enemy bent on the destruction of Irish ethnicity and Irish communities" (2007, 128). (In response, a St. Pat's for All parade has been held in Queens, New York, every year since 2000 [Corrigan 2009, 5].) The then artistic director of the Abbey Theatre, Patrick Mason, weighed in, noting that it would be fitting to allow gays and lesbians to march on the centennial of Oscar Wilde's trial for homosexual offenses (Lonergan 2009, 148–49). Mason's intervention in the debate confirms how closely bound up Irish national theater is with St. Patrick's Day parades and issues of inclusivity.

When, in late 1995, the Irish government set up a steering committee to investigate alternative arrangements for subsequent Dublin parades, the brief of the resulting St. Patrick's Festival was to "'project, internationally, an accurate image of Ireland as a creative, professional, and sophisticated country with wide appeal, as we approach the new Millennium'" (O'Donnell 2007, 138). In 2007, the Dublin City Council launched its City Fusion initiative, a project that "brings together Irish and other nationalities to create an artistic spectacle for St. Patrick's Festival Parade" in which Polish, Lithuanian, Indonesian, Nigerian, and Sikh communities participated (McGreevy 2007, 6). As Sweeney warns, however, it would be easy to see the multiculturalist agenda of recent St. Patrick's Day festivities as "creating a political comfort-zone for a state eager to demonstrate its liberal credentials but less interested in structural reform" (2008, 282). After all, if the Irish Sikh Council marched for the first time in 2007, joining regular participants such as the Garda Band, it is also true that barely four months later, a row erupted over the wearing of the *dastaar* by Sikh members of the Garda Reserves (Thornburg 2007, n.p.; O'Brien 2007, 14).

In "Interculturalism and Irish Theatre: The Portrayal of Immigrants on the Irish Stage," King does not comment on the significance of the fact that two of the six plays he discusses were performed as part of the St. Patrick's Festival. In fact, *"The Cambria"* represents at least the third occasion in recent memory that Irish theater, St. Patrick's Day celebrations, and a concern with new immigrants to Ireland were yoked together, and King examines two of these. In 2003, Calypso's production of Maeve Ingoldsby's *Mixing It on the Mountain* ran at Trinity College's Samuel Beckett Theatre from March 18 to 22. The play explores the early life of Ireland's patron saint and featured a St. Patrick played by a Nigerian student named Solomon Ijigade. In that same year, a group of African actors led by Bisi Adigun performed a scene from Jimmy Murphy's *Kings of the Kilburn High Road* (2000) (King 2005, 26). Adigun's version of the play, which depicts the experiences of Irish laborers who emigrate to London in the 1970s, casts African actors in the roles of the Irish men. The play was subsequently staged in full as part of the Dublin Fringe Festival in 2006 and was taken to North America's Irish studies hub, the Keough-Naughton Institute at Notre Dame, to be performed as part of the events for a conference entitled "Race and Immigration in the New Ireland" in October 2007.

The opening of *"The Cambria"* at Liberty Hall Theatre in Dublin on March 17, 2005, must be viewed within the context of St. Patrick's Day as an occasion upon which the Irish in Ireland and abroad reflect on their own and "other people's" diasporas. The play's conjunction of Irish and other people's diasporas, in particular, is borne out by the other venues and contexts in which *"The Cambria"* has, to my knowledge, been performed. I saw the play on October 21, 2006, as part of the Liverpool Irish Festival and Black History Month at the Merseyside Maritime Museum on Albert Dock. Liverpool has strong ties to both Ireland and transatlantic slavery.[6] The play was also performed as part of the University of Southern California's conference on the Black and Green Atlantics in March 2007. Most recently, the play was staged at the Irish Arts Center in New York, again to coincide with St. Patrick's Day, from March 17 to 22, 2009.

In *"The Cambria,"* O'Kelly mobilizes the symbolism of St. Patrick's Day to establish St. Patrick as himself an oppressed subject and thus to create affinities between Ireland's patron saint, Frederick Douglass, and African asylum seekers in contemporary Ireland. As O'Kelly notes in an interview, "There's [sic] a lot of little ironic parallels between Patrick's story and the story of visitors arriving to [sic] Ireland now and finding themselves to be asylum seekers" (2009, 200). According to Nini Rodgers, Ireland "produced the most famous runaway slave in the history of the western world"—the man who would become St. Patrick (2007, 12). In the fifth century AD, Patrick, a sixteen-year-old Christian, was captured from his home in Roman Britain and sold into slavery in pagan Ireland. Devoting himself to prayer during his enslavement, Patrick eventually "heard a voice telling him that he would soon return to the fatherland, that a ship was ready for him" (ibid., 12). After traveling extensively across Ireland, Patrick boarded a ship and embarked on a troubled journey to freedom, his relationship with the captain and crew fraught by their paganism and his Christianity (ibid., 13).

For St. Patrick, then, the ship is an ambivalent space, one that both enslaves and subsequently liberates him. Similarly, in Frederick Douglass's multiple self-constructions, ships also emerge as ambivalent. They remind him of his condition as a slave, but they also symbolize, or even facilitate at times, his transition from slave to free working man. In *"The Cambria,"* O'Kelly paraphrases one particularly memorable

---

6. At least "two out of every three emigrants from Ireland during the 1830s and 1840s passed through Liverpool whether their ultimate destination was Manchester, London, New York, Quebec, or the Antipodes" (Scally 1995, 184).

passage from Douglass's 1845 *Narrative:* "Our house stood within a few rods of the Chesapeake Bay, whose broad bosom was ever white with sails from every quarter of the habitable globe. Those beautiful vessels, robed in purest white, so delightful to the eye of freemen, were to me so many shrouded ghosts, to terrify and torment me with thoughts of my wretched condition" (1994, 59). By contrast, when Douglass is hired out by his master as a ship's caulker while still a slave, Douglass "sought [his] own employment, made [his] own contracts, and collected the money which [he] earned," thus giving him a taste of freedom (983). He finds that "whenever my condition was improved, instead of its increasing my contentment, it only increased my desire to be free, and set me to thinking of plans to gain my freedom" (83). Indeed, Patricia Ferreira points to Douglass's encounter with two Irishmen while working at the Durgin and Bailey shipyard in Baltimore as one of several interactions with the Irish that "bolstered, and perhaps sparked, his resolve to become a free man" (2001, 54).

The ambivalence of the space of the ship for Douglass culminates in the *Cambria* incident, the subject of O'Kelly's play. As Alan Rice and Martin Crawford observe, "The recounting of his triumph aboard the *Cambria* was a refiguring of the Atlantic crossing from a historically enslaving experience into a literally liberating one" (1999, 3). In other words, while ships "focus attention on the middle passage," as Gilroy puts it (1993, 7), *The Cambria* provides Douglass with a means of exiling himself from his legal status as a slave. Rice and Crawford argue that "on the *Cambria* the racial world is turned upside down in a carnivalesque picture of enchained slaveholders and free-speaking African Americans that only becomes possible away from American mores in the liminal zone of the sea" (1999, 3). In a letter to Thurlow Weed in December 1845, Douglass himself recognizes the liminality of the sea in his musings on the *Cambria* incident: "But who has the right to say what subject shall or shall not be discussed on board of a British steamer? Certainly not the slaveholders of South Carolina, nor their slaveholding abettors in New-York or elsewhere. If any one has such a right, the ship's commander has" (Foner 1975, 124).

As in chapter 1, Michel Foucault's notion that the ship is the heterotopia—or "effectively enacted utopia in which the real sites, all the other real sites that can be found within the culture, are simultaneously represented, contested, and inverted"—par excellence is helpful here (1986, 24, 27). Like O'Connor's *Star of the Sea*, O'Kelly's *"The Cambria,"* as the title suggests, similarly foregrounds the ship as an ambivalent space in which competing ideologies and identities jostle. This point is neatly summed up by the Irish steward Dignam, who, in understated fashion, pronounces a ship at sea "a complicated place" (O'Kelly 2005, 34). Captain Judkins admits that his own father, who captained a slaver, "may have shipped [Douglass's] very ancestors to a life of slavery" (48), while Douglass—in a speech lifted from his *Narrative*—sees ships as "swift-winged angels, that fly around the world" and longs to be "under [their] protecting wing" (O'Kelly 2005, 36–37; Douglass 1994, 59).

If the links between St. Patrick and Douglass are emphasized through the representation of the ship as a space of both enslavement and liberation, O'Kelly suggests a further connection between Patrick, the fictional Nigerian deportee of 2005, and Douglass, the historical African American fugitive slave of 1845 via the mythohistorical figure of St. Patrick. O'Kelly even specifies that this student played St. Patrick in a school pageant (2005, 4). Significantly, the patron saint of Nigeria is none other than St. Patrick, a little-known fact that immediately gives the lie to the supposed incongruity of an African playing the saint in a school pageant or, indeed, in Ingoldsby's *Mixing It on the Mountain*. Although he was himself enslaved, the "real Patrick did not reject the institution of slavery," as Rodgers demonstrates. In his *Confessio*, "he speaks of an irreligious youth and hints that such behaviour merited his fall." His own family owned slaves, and the church that he established "did not directly attack the institution which was so important for securing prestige and advantage for the upper classes, from which its professionals came" (2007, 15–16).

O'Kelly's treatment of the St. Patrick analogy reflects the overall tone of the play. In other words, for the most part, O'Kelly maintains the delicate balance between "self-criticism and historical retrieval," taking care not to imply a simplistic correspondence, or even a sense of solidarity, between Irish and African American experiences in this period. In fact, with the Irish character Dignam, O'Kelly deflates Irish proclamations of empathy. When Douglass is moved from first class to steerage, Dignam tells him he is "outraged." Instead of pandering to audience expectations that his indignation arises from the unjust treatment of Douglass, however, Dignam adds that he feels strongly about Douglass's removal only because of the weight of his case that he, as steward, has to carry (O'Kelly 2005, 19). At the same time, O'Kelly gestures toward the possibility of cross-racial exchange through the character of Solomon. Though not explicitly stated in the stage directions and not immediately evident in the play's transcript, it is clear from the accent that Fox assumes while playing him that Solomon is cast as an African Caribbean character rather than an African American one. (Incidentally, St. Patrick is also the patron saint of the Caribbean island of Montserrat.) Solomon recognizes Douglass even though he is dressed like "a posh gobshite" (26), an expression he has picked up from Dignam. Both Dignam and Solomon are free working men, but both Douglass and Solomon are African diasporic subjects. Solomon, the black, colonized subject, thus functions as a mediating character between Dignam, the colonized Irishman, and Douglass, the African American former slave.

According to Sweeney, the distinctiveness of O'Kelly's play is that it posits identity as "derived from the reciprocal engagement of subjects, individually and collectively, with political morality, through participation in the space of a common narrative," a fact that is evident in "structures of characterisation" (2008, 285). Sweeney is not the only critic to recognize that O'Kelly's work serves to deconstruct traditional notions of identity. In Llewellyn-Jones's brief discussion of some of O'Kelly's plays, she observes that he often works "in a surreal intensely physical mode, which challenges notions of identity," though she fails to elaborate as to what precisely this process entails (2002, 152). In fact, O'Kelly's performance strategies in *"The Cambria"* represent the culmination of shifts that have taken place over the course of his playwriting career. In his critique of O'Kelly's earliest intervention into the politics of refuge, *Asylum! Asylum!* (1994), Victor Merriman argues that because the play is staged in a realistic mode, with realism being "the *lingua franca* of dominant cultural production," the "pull of the conventions of theatrical realism diluted its impact as a cautionary statement to a social order beginning to awake to the potential pleasures of flirtations with consumer capitalism" (2000, 284, 290). In his next refugee-themed play, *Farawayan* (1998), O'Kelly abandoned realism in favor of "the suggestive powers of dynamics of light/darkness, sound/silence, music/cacophony, stillness/movement . . . actual/virtual" (ibid., 289). By 1998, in other words, O'Kelly had come to the conclusion that naturalism in the theater—perhaps most particularly in the themes he revisits—"is a bit musty at this stage. It's had its century. Now is the time to shake it off" (O'Kelly 1998, 12).

In *"The Cambria,"* there are two actors—O'Kelly and Fox—who play painter Vincent and teacher Colette, respectively, who in turn subsequently enact the roles of the nineteenth-century characters. They each play some historical characters and some fictional characters; they each play a black character—Solomon in Colette's case, Douglass in Vincent's. Colette plays both male and female characters, while Vincent plays only male characters. Alternately and simultaneously, they both play Judkins, the captain of *The Cambria.* In her analysis of groups of boys in the work of Frank McGuinness, Brian Friel, and Tom Murphy, Aideen Howard identifies the prevalence of the trope of the duo compared with the "relative absence of single leading male characters from Irish drama." She argues that "the creation of two characters who, together, form a whole man has fostered, and is symptomatic of, the tendency to perceive Irish culture in terms of a duality; a schizophrenic inhabitation of two languages, two cultures and in some cases two incompatible political territories." For Howard, one of the limitations of the Irish stage duo is that "the scope of self is confined to the range of imaginative possibilities created by the other and the potential for unique individual experience is curtailed" (1997, n.p.).

At first glance, Colette and Vincent might appear to be just such a duo, a latter-day variation on Vladimir and Estragon, inhabiting a minimalist stage and preoccupied by the absent presence of Godot/Patrick. However, when they subsequently "morph" into their various nineteenth-century characters, Colette and Vincent function to disrupt both the single character *and* the duo in a similar way to the groups of boys discussed by Howard: Vincent plays *both* master *and* fugitive slave; Colette plays *both* British sea captain *and* Irish steward. The binary either-or is thus replaced by a shifting multiplicity. Colette and Vincent unite to create "a powerful destabilising theatrical device which complements the playwright['s] thematic concern with an Ireland of multiple parts." In O'Kelly's vision, an "Ireland of multiple parts" is, of course, an Ireland that is willing to concede that it is composed not only of its own diaspora beyond the borders of the nation-state, but also of other people's diasporas within the borders of the nation-state.

Although I absolutely concur, with Fintan O'Toole, that revisiting Douglass's journey to Ireland in *"The Cambria"* is not simply "an exercise in self-congratulation," I am nonetheless uneasy about some aspects of the play (2005, 2). The remainder of this section is devoted to unpacking these aspects in the hope of demonstrating that the historical-duty argument must be approached with caution. One of them is the way in which O'Kelly engages the often troubling racial politics of minstrelsy through actor-character layering. While O'Kelly, a white actor, performs as Douglass (without, it should be noted, blacking up), Douglass's character is assumed to be a (black) blackface minstrel by the other passengers aboard the ship. According to Sweeney, Douglass's two possible identities aboard *The Cambria* as far as the other passengers are concerned—slave or minstrel—"are peculiar forms of non-identity: one legal, the other a projection of social and racial desire" (2008, 287). If minstrelsy is a "non-identity," it is nonetheless a particularly powerful one that the Irish strategically deployed in the nineteenth century as a means of maneuvering themselves into a favorable position within the American racial hierarchy. As Eric Lott puts it, the history of minstrelsy "highlights the *necessarily* exploitative making of the Irish as 'white' even as that privileged category often oppressed the Irish themselves" (1995, 94). If O'Kelly's performance as Douglass in whiteface requires the audience "to discard the visual contradictions with which they are presented," it also unwittingly reinforces the power relations inherent in the history of American blackface minstrelsy by which the performance of blackness became a means of asserting Irish whiteness (Sweeney 2008, 285).

Although this outcome is clearly not O'Kelly's intention, its effect is underlined by the different understandings he has of blackface versus whiteface minstrelsy. At one important juncture in the play, according to Sweeney, Douglass "appears about to capitulate to the pathology of subjective absence suggested by the other passengers belief that he is a minstrel" by performing a minstrel song (ibid., 287). However, just at this moment, he is recognized by one of the ship's crew, Solomon, with whom he worked on the ships in New Bedford. Solomon calls Douglass by name, rather than by the alias under which he is traveling, and refuses to deny him. O'Kelly seems to suggest here that Douglass is awakened from the temptation to succumb to whites' perception of him by a fellow African diasporic subject who reminds him of their shared past and potentially positive future. Certainly, Sweeney shares this interpretation of the scene. However, I believe that the minstrelsy scene betrays O'Kelly's assumption that blackface is a degrading negation of self for black subjects but that his own endeavor—of performing Douglass in whiteface—represents a clever deconstruction of a unified white Irish self. On the contrary, Douglass himself recognized the "limitations, possibilities, and ultimate importance" of minstrelsy when he attended a show featuring black minstrels, Gavitt's *Original Ethiopian Serenaders,* in 1849:

> Partly from a love of music, and partly from curiosity to see persons of color exaggerating the peculiarities of their race, we were induced last evening to hear these Serenaders. The Company is said to be composed entirely of colored people, and it may be so.

We observed, however, that they too had recourse to the burnt cork and lamp black, the better to express their characters and to produce uniformity of complexion. Their lips, too, were evidently painted, and otherwise exaggerated. Their singing generally was but an imitation of white performers, and not even a tolerable representation of the character of colored people. (1849, n.p.)

As Lott argues, by emphasizing the artifice of the performance ("burnt cork and lamp black," "exaggerated," "imitation," "representation"), Douglass "inverts the racist logic of minstrelsy and locates its actual function of staging racial categories, boundaries and types, even when these possessed little that a black man could recognise as 'authentic'" (1995, 36). While O'Kelly seems to regard black blackface as representing "the insidious violence of colonial mimicry as the racist stereotype becomes internalized and commodified by those most harmed by it," African American minstrels in fact "appropriated from whites the very right to perform and symbolically possess 'the Negro'" (Chude-Sokei 2006, 4–5).

The delicate balance of "self-criticism and historical retrieval" is equally undermined by the program for *"The Cambria."* The first two pages constitute an overview of the supposed "Tangled Roots" of Irish and African Americans and Douglass's account of the *Cambria* incident excerpted from a letter he wrote to William Lloyd Garrison on September 1, 1845 (Foner and Taylor 1999, 14–15). Written by Jim Vincent of Robert Morris University in Pittsburgh who, according to the author's note, first alerted O'Kelly to Douglass's Irish connections, "Tangled Roots" traces the "unbroken chords [*sic*] of solidarity between Nineteenth-Century Irish Emancipation and American Civil Rights Movement."[7] Vincent concludes: "Forced from their land by slavery or hunger, crossing the same Atlantic Ocean, building a new life in America based on a remembered past,

---

7. "Tangled Roots" is also the title of a Yale University project "exploring the histories of Americans of Irish Heritage and Americans of African Heritage" (http://www.yale.edu/glc/tangledroots/).

relishing dance and story telling, finding strength in blues and ballads, excelling at oration, savoring community, Irish Americans and African-Americans have much to celebrate in their tangled roots." The fact that Douglass's words follow Vincent's have the effect of authenticating them. Because the spectator knows that the *Cambria* incident "really happened," she or he may also assume unquestioningly the veracity of Vincent's "Tangled Roots." In fact, many of the examples Vincent cites confirm Catherine Eagan's suspicion that contemporary appeals to black and Irish affinities often work in the interests of a hegemonic whiteness.

Ultimately, the cross-racial sympathy encouraged by Noone corresponds to a form that Elizabeth Spelman condemns, configured as follows, "I acknowledge your suffering only to the extent to which it promises to bring attention to my own" (quoted in Davis 2004, 407). Meanwhile, O'Kelly's play, though it strenuously avoids suggesting a simplistic analogy between white Irish and African diasporic subjects, still raises important and troubling questions about the nature and limitations of cross-racial sympathy. By having a white actor play Douglass, does the play truly demand that its (predominantly white) audiences identify with the struggles faced by a black character and historical figure? In her article on Oprah's Book Club, Davis notes that white readers of Lalita Tademy's multigenerational African American saga *Cane River* (2001) "moved beyond co-suffering to take pride in the black characters' insurgency against white domination" (2004, 411). But how "radically unsettling" can this kind of retrospective sympathy, demanded of readers only after the major battles have been won, really be? Similarly, O'Kelly's audiences know that Douglass and O'Connell are dead, African American slavery was long ago abolished, and Irish independence was (at least partially) achieved. Even in the service of building a tradition of Irish antiracism, then, the appeal to cross-racial sympathy is a strategy that poses all sorts of representational problems and must be handled sensitively if structures of white power and privilege are to be, if not dislodged, at least challenged.

4

Stand(ing) Up for the Immigrants

The Work of Comedian Des Bishop

> I came here in fuckin' 1990. You can be sure I was the only
> fuckin' immigrant that year. Times were different then. There
> was a sign at Shannon Airport that said "Wrong Way."
> —DES BISHOP, *Fitting In* (2006)

> I fuckin' hate when people give out about Ireland all the time
> these days. It's like "The country's gone to shit." Yeah? Well,
> how come no one's leaving anymore?
> —DES BISHOP, *Fitting In* (2006)

In the first episode of the third and final series of *Father Ted,* which
aired on Britain's Channel 4 on March 15, 1998, Ted and his hap-
less sidekick, Dougal, are obliged to tidy the living room because
their housekeeper, Mrs. Doyle, is incapacitated after falling off the
roof. Ted picks up a wide-brimmed lampshade, puts it on his head,
and embarks on an impression of a Chinese person. To his horror,
Ted realizes that the scene has been witnessed by three members
of the local Chinese community who, in typically surreal *Ted* fashion, are peering in the living room window. Informed by Dougal
that they are the Yin family from the Chinatown area of Craggy
Island, Ted replies incredulously: "There's a Chinatown on Craggy
Island?" ("Are You Right There, Father Ted?"). Branded a racist, he
attempts to placate his Chinese neighbors by hosting a celebration of
Craggy Island's ethnic diversity in the form of a slide show, followed
by "a limited supply of free drink" at the local pub. Ted's efforts
at appeasing the Craggy Island's Chinese community are ultimately

133

foiled when he invites them back to the parochial house that, in his absence, Mrs. Doyle has decorated with assorted World War II memorabilia that, unbeknownst to Ted, he has just inherited from a Nazi-loving fellow priest.

Father Ted screened on Channel 4 between 1995 and 1998. While several episodes satirized events from Ireland's recent past— revelations that Bishop Eamon Casey had fathered a child with a distant American cousin, the divorce referendum, successive *Eurovision Song Contest* victories, and so on—this particular episode is remarkably prescient. The notion that eight years subsequently, 10 percent of Ireland's residents would be foreign born would for many, in 1998, have seemed as remote as the possibility to Ted that there could be a Chinatown on the famously insular Craggy Island.[1] Although Arthur Mathews and Graham Linehan, the writers of the show, insist that they never intended for Craggy Island to be interpreted as a microcosm for Ireland, in this episode, it is difficult not to make the connection. The "Chinese" episode of *Father Ted* is a useful segue into this chapter because it foregrounds the key question that demands to be addressed in relation to the work of Irish American stand-up comedian Des Bishop: in an Ireland of rapidly changing demographics, how effective a weapon against racism can comedy possibly be?

Born in November 1975, Bishop is a white Irish American from Queens, New York. Expelled from his American school at the age of fourteen, his parents sent him to St. Peter's College in Wexford, a boarding school, and he has lived in Ireland since August 26, 1990. He first performed stand-up comedy while a student of English and history at University College Cork. Since then, he has become a very well-known personality in Irish popular culture, his contributions ranging from stage playwriting and performance to reality TV and

---

1. The 2006 census found that Ireland's population was 4,239,848, of whom 420,000 were born outside the state, an increase of 87 percent over the 224,000 non-Irish nationals recorded in the 2002 census ("Census 2006" 2008, 25, 37).

immersion journalism. He is, however, fundamentally a very popular stand-up comedian. As Davin O'Dwyer explicates, Bishop's comedy is founded upon observing "a peculiar Irish idiosyncrasy" and then crafting "a monologue of sustained humour, and we laugh at the insight and punchline" (2007, 20). The Irish idiosyncrasies that Bishop explores range from their obsession with immersion heating, his signature routine, to their difficulty with expressing emotions ("If there was an emotional Olympics, Ireland would be in the Special one, which is great because you're a winner just for taking part" [*Stop You're Killing Me 2*]) and from Ireland's drink culture ("Everyone's like: 'Ooh, all of a sudden, we have a problem with booze.' Oh, *now* it's a problem. The only thing that's changed is that it's a problem now. The booze hasn't fuckin' changed at all!" [*Des Bishop: Live at Vicar St.* 2005a] to the peculiarities of Irish accents ("Where's the fuckin' *T*? Where do you hide the *T*'s in Dublin? Shi', righ', gi's a ligh'. Where's the fuckin' *T*? I said to him, 'Where's the *T,* bro?' He said, 'Wha'?'" [ibid.]).

Here, though, I focus on the ways in which Bishop positions himself as a canny critic of Irish racism. The "Irish idiosyncrasy," in this case, is that having exported vast numbers of their own people for generations, the Irish have been far from welcoming of immigrants generally, and immigrants of African descent in particular, who have been arriving since the mid-1990s. In one discussion on RTÉ's Friday-night program *The Late Late Show*, which took place on September 16, 2005, prominent liberal columnist and critic Fintan O'Toole responded to scaremongering claims about immigration to Ireland by noting that "the biggest single category of immigrants into Ireland, even now, is Irish people. The largest national group of immigrants into Ireland—and it's been consistently the case over the last ten years—has been Irish people. And that tells us something, doesn't it: that the largest group of immigrants coming into the country are Irish emigrants. We have always migrated as a society. We have a society which has actually been formed and shaped by migration. It ill behoves us, of all people, to start this kind of stuff." O'Toole's last comment, that it "ill behoves us, of all people, to start this kind of stuff," is a version of Garner's "historical duty" argument. However, O'Toole's observations are a particular manifestation of this argument, one that evokes the returned emigrant as a reminder of Ireland's far-flung diaspora. To prick the consciences of those Irish who oppose immigration to Ireland, O'Toole not only points to the history of Irish emigration, but also the contemporary reality that many immigrants to Ireland are themselves Irish. The returned emigrant thus wields a double moral power in contemporary discussions of race and immigration because she or he embodies both historical emigration *and* contemporary immigration. Bishop, as the returned (descendant of) emigrant(s), is thus uniquely placed to engage with issues of race and immigration because he is a member of Ireland's own diaspora—he is an Irish American—living in Ireland at a time when "other people's diasporas," in Garner's terms, are settling on Irish soil: there is now, unquestionably, a Chinatown on Craggy Island. In this chapter, I consider the ethics and efficacy of the "historical duty" argument in relation to Bishop's stand-up comedy routines and the way in which Irish national identity is framed in his television documentaries. Does Bishop, like O'Connor, see in *transnational* identity the potential to transcend the narrow terms in which Irish national identity has historically been defined?

Irish Stand-Up Comedy: At Home and Abroad

The field of stand-up comedy has proven remarkably resistant to academic inquiry. This point is true, in part, because it poses difficulties in terms of disciplinary classification. Comedy, humor, and joking have been discussed from a variety of disciplinary and theoretical perspectives—anthropological (Mary Douglas, Victor Turner), psychoanalytical (Sigmund Freud, John Limon), philosophical (Simon Critchley), and performance studies (Philip Auslander). As Allison Fraiberg notes—specifically in relation to women's stand-up, but it could apply equally to all stand-up—it is "too performance- or drama-oriented for the social sciences; it's not dramatic enough for drama studies; it's too popular and non-fictional for literary studies."

The whole scenario, Fraiberg sums up, "can begin to look like a game of disciplinary cat and mouse" (1994, 318). The ideological leanings of stand-up, in particular, have been probed by feminist critics who have wondered if it is inevitably politically conservative or whether it might have the potential to be subversive. As Andrew Stott puts it, "The question of what we laugh at, and how it is censored or condoned by authority, is a highly politicized area, and comedy can be the site of manifest ideological struggle" (2005, 105).

The only existing study of Irish stand-up comedy is Stephen Dixon and Deirdre Falvey's *Gift of the Gag: The Explosion in Irish Comedy* (1999). The period during which *Father Ted* appeared on television constituted boom years for Irish comedy, even if, like *Ted*, much of this comedy was performed and produced in Britain. Before then, the "dearth of stand-up comedy in Ireland" had "long been an anomaly in a country with such a strong oral culture and . . . a reputation, accurate or not, for having a garrulous and literate population" (Boyd 1991, 15). Although *Ted* was a television comedy series, one of its stars, Ardal O'Hanlon, is a stand-up comic who, when he was given the part of Dougal Maguire, had recently won the Hackney Empire New Act of the Year, and several episodes guest-starred Irish stand-up talent: Tommy Tiernan, Kevin Gildea, Anne Gildea, Michael Redmond, Jason Byrne, Ed Byrne, and Patrick McDonnell. Since then, a thriving indigenous comedy scene has developed in Ireland, and Bishop has both contributed to and reaped the benefits of this phenomenon.

The diasporic resonances, the leave-takings and homecomings, of Des Bishop's experience relate not only to his life—as an Irish American who has returned to the Old Country—but also to the trajectory of his career. Bishop came of age as a comedian in a 70-seat venue upstairs in the International Bar on Dublin's Wicklow Street. The venue, previously called the Comedy Cellar, was founded by young comedians Barry Murphy, Ardal O'Hanlon, and Kevin Gildea in February 1988 and has been variously described as the "birthplace" and the "nursery" of Irish comedic talent (Dixon and Falvey 1999, 95). By the mid-1990s, however, those comedians who wanted real success left Dublin for London where, as O'Hanlon puts it, "the streets were paved with comedy gold" (quoted in ibid., 98).

Ten years older than Bishop, O'Hanlon and Sean Hughes made stand-up careers for themselves in Britain, while Dylan Moran and Tommy Tiernan, only six years older than Bishop, succeeded Hughes as Edinburgh Fringe Festival award winners, which catapulted them to success on the British comedy circuit. It was only in the late 1990s, as Dixon and Falvey observe, that "it became possible at last to forge a career in new comedy in Ireland" (ibid., 98). Bishop may be an Irish American exiled in the Old Country, but the Old Country can now support its comic offspring in a way that was impossible twenty years ago. The first purpose-built comedy club in Ireland, the Laughter Lounge, opened in Dublin in January 1998, and Ireland now hosts several high-profile comedy festivals, notably the Cat Laughs in Kilkenny in late May and early June, a four-day event in Dublin's Iveagh Gardens in July, and the Bulmer's Comedy Festival in Dublin in September. In the preamble to his *Live at Vicar St.* DVD, Bishop traces the evolution of his comedy career from the International Bar to Vicar Street over five years. Where his comic forebears traveled from the International to London via Edinburgh, Bishop has traveled from the tiny Dublin 2 bar, where, in 1998, he performed in front of ten or fifteen people, to the 950-seat Dublin 8 venue in 2003.

Brian Boyd, writing in 1991 about the popularity of Irish stand-ups in Britain, observes that there is "a practical motive behind the absence of political material in Irish comedy: coming from a small country, Irish comedians need to travel to find audiences, and can't afford to do parochial material" (1991, 15). Two decades later, it is precisely Bishop's brand of "parochial" humor that appeals to Irish audiences. For example, on his *Tongues* DVD (2008), Bishop recounts his experiences of living in the Connemara Gaeltacht learning how to speak Irish. Studying Ireland's second official language is a compulsory part of the Irish primary and secondary curricula, but an exemption applies to those students, such as Bishop, whose primary education up to eleven years of age was received in Northern Ireland or outside Ireland. His catalog of mishaps in learning

Irish—including a segment about its conditional mood (an modh coinníollach)—is funny only to those persons who have come through the Irish educational system and, more important, to the people who have at least a basic understanding of the language. It is difficult to imagine that *Tongues* would be a source of great amusement to non-Irish audiences.

Although Bishop won the 2002 Tap Water Award for comedy at the Edinburgh Fringe Festival,[2] compared with Irish contemporaries such as Dara Ó Briain, Ed Byrne, Jason Byrne, Andrew Maxwell, and the most recent Edinburgh award winner, David O'Doherty (2008), he rarely performs in Britain or appears on British television shows, and his audiences are almost exclusively located in Ireland.[3] Arguably, Bishop is all the more popular in Ireland *because* his comedy cannot travel. The exception to this point is Bishop's diasporic appeal. Bishop is virtually unknown in the United States because, he explains, "New Yorkers don't find it funny when an American can do an Irish accent" (*Live at Vicar St.* 2005a). When he is back in his home city, the only people who recognize him are those Irish women he sees in Macy's, who have come to New York on shopping trips. However, he has performed to Irish and Irish American audiences in New York and Boston. Only when this transatlantic context is considered do the limitations of the "historical duty" argument as deployed by Bishop and others become fully clear.

2. The Tap Water Awards were founded in 2001 by a group of comedians who objected to the sponsorship of the Edinburgh awards by Perrier on the basis that its parent company, Nestlé, encourages women in developing countries not to breast-feed, but to buy their powdered milk products instead. In June 2006, Perrier announced the withdrawal of its sponsorship from the Edinburgh awards and was replaced by the Scottish bank Intelligent Finance, hence the If.Comedy Awards. As a result, no Tap Water Awards have been held since 2006.

3. There are indications that this situation is beginning to change, however. More recently, Bishop has traveled to Australia, performing his *Desfunctional* at the 2009 Sydney and Melbourne Comedy Festivals, as well as *Tongues* dates in September 2008. In 2010 Bishop performed a show entitled *My Dad Was Nearly James Bond* at the Edinburgh Fringe.

To a great degree, the Irish idiosyncrasies on which Bishop insists are rather hackneyed stereotypes. In *Tongues,* for example, Bishop holds forth on the Irish reluctance to line up, their tardiness, and their inability to construct a work of engineering that is fit for its intended purpose. On his *Fitting In* DVD (2006), Bishop recounts the culture shock he experienced as a teenager when confronted with Irish attitudes toward game playing. In America, he claims, playing games for fun require three simple things: "rules, regulation, and organization." In Ireland, however, this restriction seems to mean that the games are no fun. In Ireland, there is only one rule for game play, and that is, "Sure, we're only having a laugh" (*Fitting In*, 2006). On his 2005 *Live at Vicar St.* DVD, Bishop proposes to write the first Irish self-help book, to be entitled *Ah, Sure, Fuck It.* Bishop thus trots out some of the most shopworn "Paddy"-style clichés about the Irish: that they are feckless and inefficient, lawless and unruly, laid back to the point of being negligent, and so on. The question is: why do Irish audiences laugh? One answer is, of course, that the Irish have always laughed at Irish jokes and stereotypes, though perhaps not when they are delivered by British comedians. Christopher Wilson distinguishes between "private ridicule," in which "the joker directs humourous abuse or criticism at a butt who is absent and unlikely to hear of the wit," and "shared ridicule," in which "the joker appears to deride himself and his audience simultaneously" (1979, 213, 217). In the latter scenario, Bishop becomes an honorary Irishman: his ridiculing of Irish foibles is also a ridiculing of himself or, at the very least, his Irish ancestors.

Another crucial issue is that Bishop has become known for his ability to assume convincingly a range of recognizable Irish accents, notably the accents of Cork, where he lived for several years, and Dublin, both "posh" and "working class." This detail becomes significant on two levels: first, the incongruity of an American speaking with an Irish accent is humorous in and of itself; second, when Bishop lampoons the Irish while speaking with an Irish accent that cannot be criticized for its accuracy or authenticity, Irish audiences are more inclined to accept what he is saying, no matter how stereotypical or hackneyed. Irish judgments on the *in*ability of British or American performers to assume an Irish accent is, I would argue, a vivid example of the empire "talking back" or, perhaps more accurately, laughing back. As Luke Gibbons observes, "Given the absence of any obvious visible marks of 'inferiority' (such as racial traits or skin colour), colonial stereotypes of the Irish were forced traditionally to rely on auditory rather than visual discrimination: the brogue, the 'Irish bull' and the blarney became the signs of cultural retardation" (Rockett, Gibbons, and Hill 1987, 215). Indeed, Pierce Brosnan has repeatedly spoken of the prejudice he suffered for his Irish accent after moving to London in 1964. He claims to have been "made to feel ashamed of being Irish, so I buried my Irishness and I buried my accent" (Lacey 1997, 26). The stigmatization of Irish accents acquires even greater significance in the context of comedy. According to Maureen Waters:

> There is considerable variation in the qualities eventually associated with the nineteenth century comic Irishman, but one feature remained constant: he spoke with a *brogue*, that is, the Irish English dialect attributed to the country people. The term is from the Irish word *bróg*, meaning shoe. Hence a person with a "brogue" sounded as if he had a shoe in his mouth; his speech was regarded as clumsy and unclear. The differences between Irish English and standard English were largely due to the influence of native idiom and syntax as well as to the fact that for many country people, English was a second language, imperfectly understood. (1984, 2)

Perhaps as a means of countering the historical mockery of Irish accents, the Irish now set very high standards when it comes to assessing the attempts of British and American performers to imitate Irish accents on stage and screen. In a review of the romantic comedy *P.S. I Love You* (2007), for example, Donald Clarke of the *Irish Times* ridicules Scottish actor Gerard Butler's "tortured vowels." Noting that Butler's accent "flits around like a fairy dancing to a fiddle waxed with the dew from a Killarney morn," Clarke claims that Butler sounds "sometimes rural, sometimes urban, sometimes

Swedish" (2007, 32). In the *Sunday Independent,* Donal Lynch writes that Butler's accent "surpasses that of Tom Cruise in *Far and Away* (1992) as the worst ever heard in a film (think: the Lucky Charms leprechaun with a speech impediment)" (2007, 13). By contrast, Bishop's ear for and ability to reproduce Irish accents lend credibility to his statements on Irishness more generally.

More significant, perhaps, is the fact that Bishop's brand of observational comedy capitalizes on a mood of introspection that became pervasive in Ireland during the Celtic Tiger years. When Bishop claims, for example, that the Irish are happiest when they are miserable, he is not simply reinforcing the age-old notion of the Irish as begrudgers, but also intervening in a discourse of self-analysis that acquired a great deal of currency in the latter years of the Celtic Tiger moment. This discourse, more often than not, took the form of the probing question: "We're richer now. But are we happy?" There are several examples of this discourse in operation in Irish culture during the boom. Since 2005, Joe Duffy, host of the RTÉ radio phone-in show *Liveline,* has presented a New Year's Day show entitled *How Was It for You?* in which he counts down the top-ten "highs" and "lows" of the previous year as voted by the public. In the summer of 2006, alongside Bank of Ireland's "Wealth of the Nation" report, which found that Ireland ranked as the second wealthiest in a survey of the top-eight nations of the Organization for Economic Cooperation and Development, the national broadcaster aired "a major retrospective on the last 20 years of Irish life," a week of programming under the theme "The Time of Our Lives? Ireland '86–'06." In June 2007, the Economic and Social Research Institute launched a book entitled *Best of Times: The Social Impact of the Celtic Tiger in Ireland,* which received a considerable degree of attention in the Irish media ("Heart of Nation" 2007, 28; Melia and Hogan 2007, 8). In August 2007, the *Irish Times* magazine ran an eighteen-page cover story entitled "Don't Worry, Be Happy." The subheading of the lead story, "What's the Craic?" claims that "the Celtic Tiger has been replaced by Celtic anxiety: falling property prices, a roller-coaster stock market, rising interest rates and a depreciation of the feel-good factor. Are we happy yet? Do we even know what happiness is?" (Gaffney 2007, 10). In the same week, a member of the Catholic hierarchy entered the debate, when Archbishop (now Cardinal) Seán Brady identified the "real captivities of the 'new' Ireland": the increase in alcohol and drug abuse, the pressure to work and consume, the pressure to look good and have the right image, and the increase in suicide and violence ("Brady" 2007). On his *Tongues* DVD, recorded in September 2008, Bishop confirms the Irish inability to be content with prosperity when he claims that he has "never met a nation of people more happy to be in a recession than Irish people," because those Irish who had been predicting for years that the bubble would burst would "rather be poor and right" (*Tongues* 2008).

If many of Bishop's stand-up routines trade on the peculiarities of Irish identity during the Celtic Tiger (and now post–Celtic Tiger) moment, my interest lies specifically in his treatment of one consequence of Ireland's unprecedented prosperity from the mid-1990s on: immigration. His engagement with this issue relies on strategies that are both characteristic of stand-up comedy generally and of Bishop's own persona in particular. Crucial to O'Dwyer's explication of "the Bishop formula" is the fact that Bishop is "an outsider." He is, moreover, "an amped-up David Attenborough, and we are both the wildlife and the viewer. A beautiful relationship is born" (2007, 20). O'Dwyer's summation of Bishop is insightful. Bishop has indeed established himself as an outsider and as such continues a long tradition in stand-up comedy. As Lawrence Mintz observes, "Traditionally, the comedian is defective in some way, but his natural weaknesses generate pity, and more important, exemption from the expectation of normal behavior. He is thus presented to the audience as marginal" (1985, 74). When Bishop performs his signature routine—regarding the confusion he felt when he arrived in a country that relies on the immersion switch in order to generate hot water for a shower—audiences laugh benevolently because Bishop, an outsider to the culture, fails to understand and observe the rules of immersion heating in a place that, at least in 1990 when Bishop arrived in Ireland, did not have the reputation for being as wasteful as the country of his birth: that it needs to be switched on well in advance of the shower, that it must be switched off immediately after having a shower, and so on. Bishop's marginal status thus derives from the fact that he is an immigrant, a white Irish American immigrant, but an immigrant nonetheless.

O'Dwyer's claim that Bishop's Irish audiences are both wildlife *and* viewer is also fundamental because the analogy recalls Stephanie Koziski's elucidation of the relationship between the anthropologist, as "sympathetic outsider," and stand-up comedian, as "cynical outsider" (1984, 63). Further, it captures the effect of defamiliarizing the normative, in a Brechtian sense, that characterizes so much stand-up comedy, including Bishop's. As Koziski puts it, "Many standup comedians jar their audience's sensibilities by making individuals experience a shock of recognition. This occurs as deeply-held popular beliefs about themselves—even the hidden underpinnings of their culture—are brought to an audience's level of conscious awareness" (57). Consider, for example, the following monologue from Bishop's *Live at Vicar St.* DVD:

> Irish people are happiest when they're miserable. It was better when everyone had fuck all because there was no jealousy. The only person you were jealous of was the fella in front of you at the dole queue: "Look at that fucker, getting his money before me." Those were the days, man. Everyone had a 1976 Ford Fiesta, great fuckin' car. Better days, man. Then the Celtic Tiger kicked in: "Look at that cunt with the Lexus next door. Who does he think he is?" The jealousy kicked in, and you hated it. Everyone was going: "Ah sure, it's never gonna last. The bubble's gonna burst. You bought a house? You fuckin' eejit!" You're happiest when you're miserable. . . . I think Irish people were happiest during the Famine. You walk up to your friend: "Howya, Shamie?" "Ah, sure you know yourself: fuckin' starvin'!" "Me too, let's go and eat some nettles. Come on, buddy. Those pussies going off to America! Fuckin' stick it out!"

Audiences laugh because they are experiencing the very "shock of recognition" that Koziski describes.

Theorizing the "Returned Yank"

If much of the humor in Bishop's performances derives from his supposed marginality to the culture in which he is living, the particularities of his outsider status rely on his construction of a "returned
Yank" comic persona. He thereby toys with a figure that is prominent, in its many manifestations, in the Irish and Irish American
imagination. Historically, the returned Yank has served a variety
of purposes. According to Liam Harte, many returned Yanks "are
shown to be responding to the siren call of emigrant nostalgia. Having failed to realize the American dream, they seek sanctuary in a
romanticised Ireland" (2006, 11). Sean Thornton, from John Ford's
The Quiet Man (1952), falls into this category: having accidentally
killed a man in a prizefight, Sean finds refuge in his mother's idyllic
homestead at Inisfree in the West of Ireland. Although Sean marries
Mary Kate Danaher and settles in Ireland, the arrival of such figures
in Ireland often reminds returned Yanks "of the real reasons why
they first left, and must do so again" (ibid., 11). Another version of
this figure appears in *The Field* (1990), which dramatizes the obsession of Bull McCabe (Richard Harris) with purchasing, finally, the
rented field he has lovingly cultivated for several years, only to have
the arrival of a wealthy returned Yank (Tom Berenger) threaten to
thwart his dreams.

Indeed, Bishop refers specifically to this film, which appeared in
the same year that he moved to Ireland, on several occasions in his
stand-up routines. On his *Des Bishop Live* DVD (2005b), Bishop
recalls an adolescent sexual fantasy inspired by a scene from the
film that takes place at the local dance hall, in which a Traveller
woman asks the men present if any of them is "man enough" to
dance with "the tinker's daughter" (*Des Bishop Live* 2005b; *The
Field* 1990). Recalling the scene, Bishop imagines himself taking the
place of the Yank in the film who is more than happy to dance with
the woman. In a discussion in *Fitting In* of a particularly congested
Dublin roundabout, Bishop draws a comparison between frustrated
commuters "trying to move traffic with their soul" and Bull McCabe

"trying to fight back the Atlantic Ocean at the end of *The Field*."
Furthermore, his reference to "those pussies going off to America!"
during the Great Famine is likely an allusion to one of the most dramatic scenes in *The Field*, in which Bull tells his son that the Yank's
"family lived around here, but when the going got tough, they ran
away to America. They ran away from the Famine. But we stayed.
Do you understand? We stayed! We stayed! We stayed!"

Since Ireland began to enjoy the fruits of a sustained economic
boom, however, there are indications that the figure of the returned
Yank and reactions to him or her also began to undergo a transformation. For Martina Devlin, Michael Flatley is the most vivid
contemporary embodiment of the big-spending, brash Irish American. What is notable about Flatley, though, is that the Irish admire
rather than resent him. Devlin even suggests that, insofar as the
Irish are "trying as hard as [they] can to become like [Michael Flat-
ley]. And to spend . . . like him," they're "turning into a nation of
Irish-Americans" (2007, n.p.). For Devlin, then, the returned Yank
is a somewhat anachronistic figure or, at the very least, has become
indistinguishable from the acquisitive, materialistic native Irish. In
Celtic Tiger Ireland, it became more likely that the returned Yank
him- or herself will feel rather than be the object of resentment.
In Maeve Binchy's *Tara Road* (1998), for example, returned Yank
Sheila Maine is "astounded at how well Ireland was doing, how
prosperous the people were, and how successful were the small busi-
nesses she saw everywhere" (1998, 106). As Binchy's protagonist,
Ria, correctly intuits, Sheila is "not entirely pleased to see the upturn
in the economy." Similarly, Bishop notes in *Tongues* that "there is no
one more bitter than the Irish person who emigrated in 1988–1989
because they think: if I'd only hung on for another couple of years,
I'd own two houses in Lucan and three apartments in Budapest that
I've never even seen!"

The stereotypical returned Yank, according to Philip O'Leary,
is characterized by "flashy clothes, conspicuous wealth, ignorance,
bombast, and a distressing accent" (2000, 259). Brought up middle class in New York, Bishop's being sent to a boarding school in

Ireland after being expelled from his American school was a measure of his parents' economic success. Bishop recalls being labeled "the Yank" at school and being the locus of his peers' resentments: "I came here, you were all broke as fuck: [assumes Irish accent] 'Fuckin' Americans with your fuckin' money.' You were all jealous of me because I had 'things'" (*Live at Vicar St.* 2005a). He reports that Irish people "didn't like me coming over here with my arrogant New York ways" (ibid.). Irish people have, moreover, repeatedly accused him, as an American, of being "t[h]ick," with a dropped *H*. (ibid.). Perhaps, though, the most striking parallel between Bishop's persona and the "returned Yank" figure is the one described in Heidi Hansson's discussion of returned exiles in nineteenth-century Irish novels. Hansson argues that she or he—and it is usually he—"combines an outsider's view with an insider's authority and is therefore often used to express critical ideas" (2005, 90). Because the returning exile has had "experiences of other countries and other kinds of social organization," she or he is "often described as an instigator of reform" (ibid., 89). From Queens, New York, "the most culturally diverse place on the planet," Bishop presents himself as possessing the expertise to comment on Ireland's newfound multiculturalism (*Des Bishop Live* 2005b).

For example, he recalls that, as a teenage "Yank" in Ireland, his school friends would excoriate him for perceived American racism: "What's going on? What's going on in America? You're all fuckin' racist over there. What you did to the blacks was fuckin' terrible. What you did to the American Indians is not fuckin' right," only for those same people to eat their words many years later: "Jesus, Des, we're fuckin' sorry. We never knew that Irish people were racist because there were no black people here" (*Live at Vicar St.* 2005a). Having been exposed to Irish racism in New York, however, Bishop claims that the fact of Irish racism came as no surprise to him: "I could have told you. I remember working with Irish guys on the building sites in New York, you know, during the summer. And the Irish guys would be there, working away on the site, ninety-degree heat, no shirt on the back, sun beating down, skin bubbling away.

'You'd want to put some sunblock on that, bro.' 'Do you think I'm fuckin' gay, do you? Sunblock is for women!' He turns to his friend, another Irishman, and he says: 'Do you know what the problem is in this country, Paddy? Fuckin' immigrants'" (*Live at Vicar St.* 2005a). In this anecdote, Bishop refers indirectly Garner's "historical duty" argument, indicting the Irish for their anti-immigrant rhetoric even while they themselves continue to reap the economic benefits of emigrating to another country.

In some examples, Bishop's views on historical emigration and contemporary immigration are communicated less overtly. On his *Live at Vicar St.* DVD, for instance, he opens the show by claiming that he is "having a bit of an identity crisis." He has lived in Ireland since he was fourteen years old, yet Irish people still tell him he is not Irish. Bishop asserts his connection to Ireland on the basis of having lived there for fifteen years, but for some Irish people, it is still not enough to render him "Irish." This show was performed in Ireland throughout 2004. In June of that year, a referendum on Irish citizenship was held, and, considered in this context—though Bishop makes no mention of it—his remarks become significant. Until 2004, Ireland, like the United States, had observed *jus soli*, in which citizenship is automatically granted to anyone born on national soil. (In 1998, under the terms of the Good Friday/Belfast Agreement, this right was extended to anyone born in the six counties, if they so wished.) In June, 79 percent of the Irish electorate voted to accept the government's proposed *jus sanguinis* model so that anyone born on the island of Ireland to non-Irish parents is entitled to citizenship only if at least one parent has been living in Ireland for three of the previous five years. The referendum was instigated at the behest of then minister for justice, equality, and law reform Michael McDowell to counterbalance the burden on the state of what he termed *citizenship tourists:* women from "eastern Europe and elsewhere in the world who have come here on holiday visas, given birth, collected the birth certificate and the passport for the child and returned home" (quoted in Brennock 2004, 1).

As Suzanna Chan argues, "Because the change to the Constitution re-conceives Irish citizenship to have a basis in bloodline, it precludes the belonging of recent immigrants to Ireland yet concurrently supports that of the 'Irish diaspora'" (2006, 4). In other words, there is a double standard implicit in the referendum, in which many immigrants with a *territorial* tie to Ireland that is of less than three years' duration may not claim citizenship for their Irish children, while the right to citizenship of Irish diasporic subjects, who have no *territorial* tie to Ireland and a *blood* tie that may, in some cases, be a single grandparent, is upheld. When Bishop professes hurt at not being considered Irish enough by Irish people, he, consciously or not, inserts himself into these debates. Like recent immigrants to Ireland, his territorial tie is not enough for him to be considered Irish. It is, however, essential to recognize the privileged position in which Bishop finds himself relative to recent immigrants to Ireland. In his personal experience, he is not considered Irish according to *popular cultural conceptions,* but recent immigrants to Ireland and their children are not considered Irish *according to the Constitution.* As a member of the Irish diaspora, he benefits from his blood tie to Ireland, however remote. In other words, he is more "unlike" than "like" recent immigrants to Ireland.

Rachel Lee argues that "stand-up comics make political knowledge evident in everyday life amusing to ponder, and also render political aggression—expressions of desire for power—both palpable and palatable" (2003, n.p.). Indeed, Bishop's comedy both highlights the predicament of immigrants to Ireland and diffuses the tensions that this situation has occasioned. While working in a fast food restaurant in Waterford as part of *The Des Bishop Work Experience* documentary, Bishop complained that Irish customers, unlike their American counterparts, never clear their trays. Bishop reports that some Irish people reacted angrily to this claim, telling him: "If you don't like the fuckin' trays, fuck off back to your own country" (*Des Bishop Live* 2005b). Bishop thus invokes one of the most hackneyed racist rejoinders in existence, yet audiences laugh because it is directed at Bishop—a white Irish American—rather than Bishop's Chinese coworkers. When a drunken customer *does* call one of his Chinese coworkers a "Chink," Bishop takes issue with him, telling him, "Bro, don't call 'em 'Chinks,' trying to be the hero." The drunk turns on Bishop and says: "You Yankee bastard! I wish Iraq won!" (*The Des Bishop Work Experience* 2004, episode 1).

Yankee bastard is obviously not nearly as charged a racial slur as *Chink,* but clearly, Bishop's strategy is as follows: by implying that he himself—a white member of the Irish diaspora—has suffered bigotry in Ireland, he encourages white Irish audiences to question their attitudes toward "other people's diasporas" in Ireland. Bishop is simultaneously one of "us" (white Irish) *and* "them" (foreign-born immigrant). Two key questions arise from Bishop's strategy: first, how ethical is it to draw comparisons between his experiences of living in Ireland as a white Irish American and the experiences of nonwhite immigrants to Ireland? By too closely identifying his experiences with the circumstances of nonwhite immigrants to Ireland, Bishop runs the risk of encouraging his audiences in both Ireland and the United States to partake of an analogy that does not do justice to the particular status of immigrants of color in contemporary Ireland. The second question that presents itself relates to the efficacy of this strategy. In other words, does Bishop's approach ultimately leave his audiences firmly ensconced in their comfort zone?

"Undocumented" or "Illegal"?

The dangers of the "historical duty" argument, which are bound up with issues of whiteness, become particularly visible when transatlantic Irishness is brought to bear on the question. Such problems are exemplified in the aftermath of the events of September 11, 2001, debates in which Bishop has himself explicitly intervened. As Diane Negra argues, although the tendency "to use Irishness as a way of speaking a whiteness that would otherwise be taboo was well underway before the events of September 11," the experience of national trauma after 9/11 "clearly necessitated and triggered new ways of speaking regionalism and whiteness through Irishness" (2006a, 355, 358). In particular, Negra draws attention to the reaction to New York firefighter Mike Moran's invitation to Osama Bin Laden to "kiss [his] royal Irish ass" (365). According to Negra, after 9/11, Irishness became associated with white, male, working-class heroism, a means of laying claim to a white identity that was also "innocent." To take Negra's argument even further, it seems that these discourses of victimhood and innocence are mutually reinforcing. The Irish were victims in the past, which ensures they are now innocent, which leaves them vulnerable to further victimization in the future. I am referring, specifically, to the deployment of Irish heroism rhetoric in debates on immigration reform that ensued in the post-9/11 era. In a September 2006 article in the *Irish Independent*, Caitriona Palmer reports on Steve MacSweeney, one of the "Irish 9/11 heroes" who "risked his life and identity to search for survivors" (2006, 8). Now, because MacSweeney is living in the United States illegally, he may be forced to leave the country. In the accompanying images, MacSweeney is photographed at Ground Zero wearing a "Legalize the Irish.org" T-shirt.

The slogan is that of the Irish Lobby for Immigration Reform, which was established in December 2005 and on whose behalf Bishop performed benefit gigs in New York in September 2006 and January 2008. Like the *Irish Independent* article, the ILIR participates in and consolidates a discourse of Irish victimhood established well in advance of 9/11. On the ILIR website's home page, above photographs of former US presidents Ronald Reagan and John F. Kennedy reads the question "No Irish Need Apply?" Invoking the oft-referenced NINA signs, which were immortalized in song by John F. Poole in 1862, the ILIR claims that "under the current immigration system, neither Ronald Reagan or John F. Kennedy's Irish ancestors or relatives could come to America legally today." The implication is, of course, that the Irish have a unique history of providing America with ideal citizens—the president is the ultimate citizen—and should, thus, enjoy special privileges in current debates on immigration reform. Although there are a few examples of newspaper advertisements containing the "No Irish Need Apply" caveat,

Richard Jensen disputes the very existence of these signs at commercial establishments across America (2002, 405). In appealing to these mythical signs, the ILIR bears out what Catherine Eagan identifies as "the Irish and Irish American tendency to link 'Irishness' to a heritage of oppression that is in many ways very distant from their present-day lives" (2006, 21).

My point here is not to sanction the scapegoating of undocumented immigrants in a post–Homeland Security America. Rather, it is to point out that contemporary Irish American claims to victimhood ring rather false given the opportunities available in Ireland over a boom period that lasted some fifteen years compared with the experiences of other immigrants in the United States and, indeed, previous generations of emigrating Irish. For example, in a *Sunday Tribune* article in February 2006, Sarah McInerney reports that thirty-eight-year-old Mary Brennan "has recently been diagnosed with asthma, but because she can't get health insurance without a social security number, she can't afford the $5,000 test that could help her condition. As she explains this, her phone credit runs out. You also can't a billed phone in the United States without a social security number." Even sympathetic McInerney is moved to ask: "So why does she stay?" (2006, 9).

In his stand-up routines, then, Bishop repeatedly appeals to his own status as an Irish diasporic subject in order to expose the hypocrisy of contemporary Irish attitudes toward immigration. However, given the nature of the ILIR's campaign and the status of Irishness as "a category of racial fantasy," as Negra puts it, in the United States more generally, the "historical duty" argument can assume more problematic undertones (2006b, 1). In an interview with Ryan Tubridy, Bishop claims that the "New Irish" are "an obsession" of his, because he himself is "an immigrant" (*Tubridy Tonight* 2006). In an *Irish Voice* article about Bishop's ILIR benefit gig in January 2008, April Drew observes, "An immigrant himself . . . he knows first hand what the immigrant experience is like" (2008, n.p.). With equal claims, or so he and others frame it, to an interest in ILIR's campaign (as the descendant of Irish immigrants to the United

States) *and* "other people's diasporas" in Ireland (because he, too, is an immigrant to Ireland), Bishop risks eliding the experiences of so-called undocumented Irish in the United States and illegal immigrants to Ireland. For Luke Gibbons, emphasizing connections between the Irish and other oppressed peoples "is not to indulge in the self-absorption of victim culture but the opposite: to engage in an act of ethical imagination in which one's own uneven development becomes not just a way in, but a way out, a means of empathising with other peoples and societies in similar situations today" (2002, 104). As with O'Connor's Irish American novels, Bishop's comedy suggests that such acts of "ethical imagination" must be approached with caution in order to acknowledge the privileges that Irish and Irish diasporic subjects now enjoy.

The second question, regarding the efficacy of the "historical duty" argument as a rhetorical strategy, relates to the potential of stand-up comedy, as a cultural form, for social critique. In his analysis of the stand-up comic's monologue, David Marc argues that "a monologue, like a sermon, asks the anonymous members of the assembly to spontaneously merge into a single emotional organism capable of reacting uniformly to the metaphor, wisdom, and worldview of one appointed personality" (2002, 11). Echoing Marc, Mintz observes that "the comedian is almost always establishing agreement, consensus within his or her specific audience" and that his or her most important role is "to orchestrate a sense of homogeneity, community, and shared values and perspectives" (2005, 577–78). Equally, Mary Douglas argues that "the disruptive comments which [the joker] makes upon [the structure] are in a sense the comments of the social group upon itself. He merely expresses consensus" (1999, 158).

In his 2007–8 show *Tongues*, Bishop claims that he willingly learned Irish so that "the next time some fat Dublin prick tells [him he's] not Irish, [he] can respond in a language that this man doesn't understand." Bishop thus explodes one of the most powerful properties of national identity, language. In order to do so, however, he creates a community of listeners who identify uniformly with "the peculiar Irish idiosyncrasy" he is unpacking. In mocking certain aspects of Irishness, does Bishop thus ultimately endorse a particular version of national identity that is, by its very nature, exclusive and exclusionary? In other words, in order to lampoon "Irish" characteristics, Bishop necessarily takes for granted the preexistence of a coherent, unified "Irish" identity. As Werner Sollors argues, "In all cases the community of laughter itself is an ethnicizing phenomenon, as we develop a sense of we-ness in laughing with others" (1986, 132). Bishop's stand-up comedy, performed to predominantly white, Irish-born audiences, risks reinforcing Irishness as white, even if this whiteness (in Bishop's case, at least) is tolerant and embracing of a multicultural Ireland.

On the *Des Bishop Live* DVD, Bishop envisions a multiethnic County Clare hurling team by embarking on an impression of legendary Gaelic games commentator Micheál Ó Muircheartaigh. When Bishop as Ó Muircheartaigh stumbles over the Nigerian surname of one of the imaginary hurlers, it is the very *incongruity* of this scenario that appeals to audiences. Audiences laugh because it is almost inconceivable to them that a man of Nigerian descent could participate in a sport so distinctly and parochially "Irish." In contrast to Bishop's tongue-in-cheek utopianism, the reality is that Nigerian youngsters on underage Gaelic Athletic Association teams have been subjected to racist abuse from players on opposing teams (J. Corcoran 2007, n.p.). Ultimately, though, if Bishop's well-intentioned comedy may at times appear ethically suspect and hopelessly utopian, his own awareness of its limitations mitigates somewhat the criticism to which he can justly be subjected. On *The Des Bishop Work Experience* DVD, Bishop mocks his own aspirations to victim chic:

I was born white and middle class from [*sic*] Queens, New York. There was no persecution associated with my life. Nobody hates you. You're just like one of those people that sail through life. I wanted to be a black comedian who's going, like: "We were so poor, we had peanut butter and jelly, or jelly and peanut butter. Those were our options." That's the life I wanted, but no, no, no, middle class. . . . I got no struggle, no struggle in my life at all.

So what do I do? I end up working minimum-wage jobs for four months just to feel like I'm a victim. And then I end up in Superquinn, and it ain't even minimum wage! (*The Des Bishop Work Experience* 2004, episode 4).

In order for Bishop's comedy to be really effective, his predominantly white audiences on both sides of the Atlantic need to join him in recognizing their own racial and class privilege.

From Immersion Heating to Immersion Journalism

Bishop's treatment of race and immigration in contemporary Ireland in his stand-up comedy represents only one aspect of his social consciousness.[4] Indeed, he cites Michael Moore, Mark Thomas, and Bill Hicks as important influences, although he ultimately proclaims himself to be "more of a comedian than an activist" (quoted in O'Dwyer 2007, 21). His social conscience is best elucidated by drawing attention to his three documentary series for RTÉ: *The Des Bishop Work Experience* (four episodes, 2004), *Des Bishop: Joy in the Hood* (six episodes, 2006), and *Des Bishop: In the Name of the Fada* (six episodes, 2008). All three follow the same format, in which Bishop undertakes his own version of immersion journalism to highlight the struggles faced by various marginal communities in contemporary Ireland: in *Work Experience*, he takes four different minimum-wage jobs over a four-month period, alongside Irish-born and migrant workers; in *Joy in the Hood*, he runs comedy workshops with locals in disadvantaged urban areas, both in the Republic and in Northern Ireland; and in *In the Name of the Fada*, he spends a year living in the Connemara Gaeltacht learning how to speak Irish and challenging himself to perform the first-ever stand-up comedy gig in Irish.

---

4. With this section's subheading, I am riffing on Davin O'Dwyer's claim that with Bishop's Irish-learning project, he has "swapped immersion heating for immersion learning" (2007, 20).

The format of the shows represents a hybrid of several strands found within contemporary broadcast media. Most obviously, they borrow elements of the "group-challenge" reality-TV format, though since Bishop is very much a solitary celebrity contestant, the challenges he sets himself are individual rather than group oriented. The shows also deploy the "video diary" segments that are a feature of many survival and competitive reality shows (Biressi and Nunn 2005, 72). As Anita Biressi and Heather Nunn observe, "The seeming contrasting intimacy of the to-camera disclosure of the ordinary individual signifies a switch of power relations, as the 'real' individual speaks to the audience without the interference of camera crew, television hosts or coaches, and so on" (ibid.). The video-diary segments of the documentaries function to reveal Bishop's "true" feelings as to how he is progressing with the challenge at hand. Interspersed with footage of Bishop interacting with the people among whom he is working and living and the video-diary segments are excerpts from live stand-up shows. Accompanying each of the documentaries, then, is a stand-up show in which Bishop explains his motivations for and experiences in doing the documentaries: *Fitting In* is the show that accompanied *Joy in the Hood*; *Tongues* is the stand-up counterpart to *In the Name of the Fada*. The excerpts from actual stand-up shows complement the documentary format, it could be argued, because both have been promoted as forms of popular anthropology.

What interests me, however, is the shift that takes place from the focus on class as the most powerful tool of marginalization in contemporary Ireland in *Work Experience* to a preoccupation with the *connections* between class and ethnocultural identity in *Joy in the Hood* (while episodes 1, 2, and 3 deal with regional working-class communities in Dublin, Cork, and Limerick, episodes 4, 5, and 6 are devoted to Travellers in Tuam, County Galway, and the loyalist and nationalist working-class communities, respectively, of Belfast's Mount Vernon and Derry's Bogside). By the time *In the Name of the Fada* is broadcast on RTÉ in March 2008, Bishop appears to have abandoned class altogether in favor of his interest in "language and culture," a phrase that recurs persistently throughout the series. This section explores episode 5 of *In the Name of the Fada*, in which Bishop returns to New York and is seen interviewing students of Irish at New York University's Glucksman Ireland House, meeting emigrants who are native speakers of Irish in Boston, performing a benefit gig for the ILIR at Rory Dolan's pub in Yonkers, and speaking to a Korean American who has learned Irish from a CD (*In the Name of the Fada* 2008, episode 5). The episode reflects the tensions of the show's attitude toward the Irish language and the ambivalence of Bishop's statements on Irish identity more generally. Though not alluded to explicitly, *In the Name of the Fada* implicitly raises questions about Irish identity and the future of the Irish language in an increasingly diverse Ireland. The show's significance within this context is borne out by the fact that Bishop won the Foras Na Gaeilge—a body responsible for the promotion of the Irish language on the island of Ireland—award for *In the Name of the Fada* at the Media and Multicultural Awards in November 2008.

On the one hand, Bishop's intervention into debates on the Irish language might be interpreted in terms of the embrace of Gaelic culture that became "hip" during the Celtic Tiger years. In *The Pope's Children: Ireland's New Elite* (2005), economist David McWilliams coined the term *Hibernian Cosmopolitans* or *HiCos* to describe a group of people who epitomize the hybridization of Hibernians, "those Irish people who regard themselves as Irish first, expressed by the Catholic religion, Irish culture, history and language," and the Cosmopolitans, "who are those people born on the island who regard themselves first as citizens of the world and secondly as Irish" (2006, 216). For McWilliams, this group—or "class"—of people emerged in the 1990s, taking "the best elements of each, blending them into one identity" (222). HiCos are generally white-collar professionals and urban dwellers, but they also give their children Irish names, enroll them in Gaelscoileanna, and are devotees of the Gaelic Athletic Association. As part of this "elevation of all things Hibernian," the Irish language has enjoyed something of a renaissance (224). According to McWilliams, "Irish-speaking Raidió na Life is the trendiest radio station in Dublin, . . . enrolments for courses in

Irish language diplomas are full, Gael Linn is bursting at the seams yet Chinese is the lingua franca of Moore Street" (223). As Edna Longley puts it, writing about the same phenomenon, "The spiritual capital of the Celtic Twilight is now being invested by the Celtic Tiger" (Longley and Kiberd 2001, 19).

Interestingly, McWilliams argues that the rise of the HiCo has been greatly bolstered by two factors: return emigration and immigration. If so, it is unsurprising that Bishop, who promotes himself as *both* returned emigrant (or descendant of emigrants) *and* immigrant, should take on the issue of the Irish language. Returned emigrants who found their cosmopolitan sensibilities nurtured in London, New York, and other world cities also cultivated "an acute sense of Irishness" in their adopted homes. As such, "they arrived back with a stronger sense of Irishness than they had originally taken away" (2006, 230). Second, immigration has, according to McWilliams, prompted Irish people to ask themselves: "Who are we? Are we just a province of the USA? Are we simply Boston with bad weather?" (ibid.). If McWilliams attributes the increased enrollment in Irish classes to immigration, at least in part, it is unsurprising that immigrants have also been cited as a cause of the perceived decline of the language. *In the Name of the Fada* aired on RTÉ between March 13 and April 17, 2008, a period during which a number of articles appeared in the Irish press regarding this apparent decline.

On April 3, Minister for Community, Rural, and Gaeltacht Affairs Éamon Ó Cuív told an audience at City University of New York that Ireland needs a quarter of a million Irish speakers by 2028 to save the future of the language (Hogan 2008, n.p.). In an opinion piece in the *Sunday Independent* on April 13, Marc Coleman criticizes the Department of Education's policies on the language and explicitly scapegoats immigrants as a new "threat" to Irish:

> The first [problem facing native speakers of Irish] is what can only be described as a second plantation of the Gaeltacht whereby native Irish speakers are becoming strangers in our own environment. Ironically, the Cabinet recently decided to issue a stamp to

commemorate the 400th anniversary of the Plantation of Ulster
. . . ,a generous gesture towards the million Irish Protestants whose
history and origins deserve respect and recognition. Were a second wave of incomers not threatening the Gaeltacht's existence, it
might be easier to celebrate this commemoration. (2008, n.p.)

Coleman's views are worryingly reminiscent of the Immigration
Control Platform's injunction to "stop the invasion and colonization
of Ireland," positioning recent immigrants to Ireland as the rapa-
cious successors to the forces of British colonialism (Luibhéid 2004,
339). In the documentary, then, Bishop is faced with a difficult task:
embracing the Irish language while simultaneously avoiding the historical baggage—of nationalism and separatism some would say borders on xenophobia—it brings with it.

RTÉ's other scheduling decisions during the period in which *In
the Name of the Fada* aired also bear mentioning. Most notably,
it promoted a week of "special programming" devoted to interculturalism on both its television and its radio platforms from April 7
to April 14, 2008. One of them was a series of one-minute documentary vignettes, under the rubric *The Richness of Change*, which
aired between television programs throughout the week. Produced
in association with the Forum on Migration and Communications,
the vignettes highlight "the diversity of origin and of profession,
amongst Ireland's immigrant population" (http://www.fomacs.org).
Between *Prime Time,* a current-affairs program, and the fifth episode of *In the Name of the Fada,* RTÉ screened the sixth of ten
vignettes, about Anna Kowalska, a Polish woman who works as a
team leader for the Bank of Ireland's Polish Helpdesk. As Kowalska
explains, many from the Polish community in Ireland (estimated at
around 230,000 in 2008) work more than one job and thus do not
have an opportunity to visit their local branch in person. Having a
Polish Helpdesk means that Polish customers can not only avail of
Banking 365 (Bank of Ireland's telephone and Internet banking service), but also conduct their business in their mother tongue. How
significant is it that RTÉ preceded one (episode of a) documentary

preoccupied with linguistic diversity in Ireland with a shorter documentary *also* preoccupied with linguistic diversity in Ireland? How are we to reconcile Kowalska's assertion that the five members of the Polish team at Banking 365 are "well integrated" with her claim that she will "always be Polish" and will "never say [she is] Irish"? Can the vignette shed light on some of the ambivalences of the episode of Bishop's documentary that followed?

In the fifth episode, which aired on April 10, 2008, Bishop and Antoine Phat Willie—the man with whom he has been boarding in Connemara—travel to New York to uncover the phenomenon of Americans learning Irish in the United States. At New York University's Glucksman Ireland House, Bishop asks students of Irish why they have decided to learn the language. Two out of three respond that they are of Irish descent, so if anyone will "carry on the language" in the United States, it makes sense that it would be those individuals who have Irish ancestors. Bishop concurs that learning Irish has been a powerful experience for him, because the language has "a genetic connection to who I [am] as a human being." Bishop then travels to Boston to meet emigrants from Connemara who still communicate in Irish, despite living in the United States for many years. Upon his return, Bishop visits the offices of the *Irish Voice* and speaks to the newspaper's founder, Niall O'Dowd. (It should be noted, if only because the episode does not, that O'Dowd is also one of the founders of the Irish Lobby for Immigration Reform.) In an interview carried out through Irish, Bishop reflects on his experience of learning the language: "When you speak Irish, it's . . . I don't know the word for it but it's deep. It's deep in my stomach and inside my head." For most of the episode, then, Bishop seems to espouse the importance of learning and speaking Irish on the basis of a biological ("genetic") or visceral connection to Ireland and Irish cultural identity, a point reinforced by Bishop's visit to his childhood home in Queens and the introduction of Antoine to his family.

However, two of Bishop's encounters in episode 5 seem to suggest that "language" and "cultural identity" *can* be divorced from one another and, by extension, that one need not be "genetically" Irish in order to feel a connection to the language. On a New York street, Bishop raps in Irish, and a Hispanic man raps in Spanish. Here, a *cultural* form that is perceived as African American—hip-hop— is hospitable to translation into *languages* other than the African American English dialect in which it is usually performed. Second, toward the end of the episode, Bishop meets a Korean American man who learned Irish from a CD and who sings a *sean-nós* song to Bishop in Irish of the Donegal dialect. This man has no "genetic" connection to Ireland, but he felt a desire to learn the language none- theless. If, as Werner Sollors argues, "the conflict between contrac- tual and hereditary, self-made and ancestral" definitions of identity is the central drama in American culture, this ethnic American man's relationship to the Irish language is governed by *consent* rather than *descent* (1986, 5–6). In both cases, Irish proves to be malleable and porous, not insular and closed. As Negra argues in a different con- text, "Destabilizations of 'cultural authenticity' provide new oppor- tunities for it to be made transferable" (2006b, 16).

Like in the stand-up shows, in episode 5 of *In the Name of the Fada,* Bishop gestures toward alternative ways of "being Irish" or of participating in "Irish culture" other than being normatively white and "genetically" Irish. However, he is ultimately unwilling or unable to perform the radical relinquishment of a sense of stable Irishness that would facilitate such alternative possibilities. Bishop's encounter with the Korean American man is reminiscent of the short film *Yu Ming Is Ainm Dom* (Daniel O'Hara, 2003), which drama- tizes in comic fashion the experiences of a young Chinese man who learns Irish only to find, after arriving in Ireland, that only a minor- ity of Irish people actually speak the language, especially in Dublin. The success of O'Hara's film, which won the Temple Bar Diversions Festival Short Film Award, and Steph Green's adaptation of Doyle's story "New Boy" (2007) lends credence to the suggestion that the most complex examinations of nonwhite immigrant experiences in Ireland occur in short films. In the final chapter, I turn to representa- tions of race in contemporary Irish cinema.

5

To Hell's Kitchen and Back

Migration Between Ireland and America
in Contemporary Cinema

> O'Leary, O'Reilly, O'Hare and O'Hara
> There's no one as Irish as Barack Obama.
> —CORRIGAN BROTHERS (2008)

In February 2008, a little-known Irish folk band called Hardy Drew and the Nancy Boys, inspired by reports that US presidential candidate Barack Obama had ancestry that could be traced back to Moneygall, County Offaly, wrote a song called "There's no one as Irish as Barack Obama." The song received much airplay in Ireland, and, in January 2009, the group—now renamed the Corrigan Brothers—was invited to perform it on the Irish American float of the Inauguration Day parade and at the Irish American Democrats' Dinner that evening. Although most viewed the song as a humorous and whimsical take on the new president's multiethnic ancestry, Fintan O'Toole took issue with the "endless game of claiming everyone as Irish," expressing concern that doing so "ceases to be a way of opening up history and showing the complexity of Irish identity and becomes a way of hijacking history and muscling in on other people's identity" (2009, n.p.). Here, O'Toole effectively paraphrases many of the concerns articulated in this book. However, in a letter to the *Irish Times* the following week, Canon Stephen Neill protested O'Toole's "toxic commentary," claiming that the song does not seek to displace Obama's African American identity. As Neill points out, the lyrics of the song explicitly state that "He's Hawaiian, he's Kenyan American too" (Neill 2009, n.p.).

It is helpful to consider Obama's multiple identity positions—as a man of mixed-race ancestry, as the son of an emigrant to the United States—as I begin this chapter, in which I examine two films that foreground intersections between Irishness and blackness, emigration and immigration. Indeed, one of the late controversies in the first presidential campaign was the revelation just four days before the election that Obama's aunt Zeituni Onyango, from Kenya, had had her application for asylum rejected in 2004 and had been living in the United States "illegally" every since. Consistent with the rest of this book, in which "returned Yank" narratives and narratives of emigration to the United States *from* Ireland are viewed as significant in the context of contemporary immigration *to* Ireland, this chapter interrogates the ways in which race and immigration figure in two films by, respectively, actor-producer Pierce Brosnan and writer-director Jim Sheridan, both Irish-born but having spent periods of their professional lives—in Brosnan's case, most of his career—in the United States. *The Nephew* (1998) is, like the Corrigan Brothers' song, about mixed-race identity; *In America* (2003) is about the process of emigrating to the United States ("illegally") and becoming American.

Although neither *The Nephew* nor *In America* is "about" African immigrants to Ireland, the fact that the first features the arrival of a mixed-race Irish American in Ireland and the second juxtaposes Irish and African immigrants to the United States enables the films to be interpreted as "parables," as Kathleen Vejvoda puts it, of race and immigration in contemporary Ireland (2007, 373). In fact, Vejvoda—the only scholar who has, to my knowledge, compared these two films—maintains that *The Nephew* and *In America* "reflect the filmmakers' fledgling attempts to come to terms with the role of race in Ireland's—rather than in America's—future" (ibid.). While Vejvoda's article is astute in many ways, my reading will emphasize the *inextricability* of the Irish from the American contexts of the films. In other words, although the films certainly raise important questions about the ways in which race figures in Ireland's present and future, it is the contention of this book that Irish attitudes toward race have been so profoundly influenced by American racial ideologies (and

Irish emigrant experiences within those ideologies) that it is virtually impossible to separate the two.

Whereas Vejvoda organizes her comparison of the films around such thematic commonalities as the need to let go of Ireland's past, racial heterogeneity as the catalyst for spiritual conversion, and a strong identification between racial "otherness" and Irish womanhood, I am more interested in the trope of the Irish American who either does (*The Nephew*) or does not (*In America*) return to Ireland, for both have found themselves the objects of powerful analogies in contemporary Ireland (ibid., 369, 368, 366). During the period spanning the appearance of these films, the makeup of Ireland's immigrants changed dramatically: in 1998, 53 percent of all immigrants to Ireland were returning Irish; by 2004, this figure was 34 percent; by 2008, it had dipped as low as 16 percent (M. Corcoran 2003, 304; "Population and Migration Estimates" 2008, 1). As I argue in relation to Des Bishop's stand-up persona, the emigrant—or descendant of emigrants—who returned during the boom years wields a double moral power in discussions of race and immigration because he or she embodies both historical emigration *and* contemporary immigration. It is in this context that I read *The Nephew*.

However, those Irish who emigrated to the United States during the 1980s, in many cases illegally, who *did not* return to Ireland during the Celtic Tiger era and who are now lobbying to regularize their status in the United States, are often compared with those migrants who have come *to* Ireland in relatively large numbers since the mid-1990s. For example, in his April 2008 address to a joint meeting of the United States Congress, former *taoiseach* Bertie Ahern observed:

> The New Ireland—once a place so many left—is now a place to which so many come. These newcomers to our society have enriched the texture of our land and of our lives. We are working, as are you, to welcome those who contribute to our society as they lift up their own lives, while we also address the inevitable implications for our society, our culture, our community and our way of life. So we are profoundly aware of those challenges as we ask you

to consider the case of our undocumented Irish immigrant community in the United States today. We hope you will be able to find
a solution to their plight that would enable them to regularise their
status and open to them a path to permanent residency. ("Ireland
and America" 2008, n.p.)

A heated exchange of letters to the editor of the *Irish Times* in
March and April 2007 provides another case in point. W. Dudgeon
quips on March 22, "Pardon my ignorance, but what exactly is the
difference between the 'undocumented' Irish in the United States and
the 'illegal' immigrants in this country?" (2007, 19). Denis Murphy
writes on March 24 in defense of himself and others who emigrated
to the United States in the 1980s and early 1990s because "this
state had nothing for us" (2007, 17). As I argue in chapter 3, Ronan
Noone also exploits the comparison in *The Blowin of Baile Gall*. It is
in this context of an implied relationship between "New Irish" (those
Irish who emigrated to the United States in the 1980s) and the "New
Irish" (those immigrants who have been arriving in Ireland since the
1990s) that I read *In America*.

Before turning to the films, it is useful to consider the critical
context in which these films appeared. A fairly significant body of
scholarship focuses on Irish films that emerged during the boom
years, much of it characterized by a discomfort about the effects
of globalization. Many critics are unequivocal that globalization
equals Americanization. As Debbie Ging argues, for example,
Celtic Tiger cinema falls into two categories: "a pastiche of hip yet
politically vacuous images of 'Ireland as Anyplace'" and "a series
of nostalgic Tourist Board images aimed primarily at an American
marketplace" (2002, 185; 2008, 184). The first category comprises
films such as *About Adam* (Gerard Stembridge, 1999), *Flick* (Fintan Connolly, 1999), *When Brendan Met Trudy* (Kieron J. Walsh,
2000), *Goldfish Memory* (Elizabeth Gill, 2003), and *Intermission*
(John Crowley, 2003), which, for Martin McLoone, exemplify "a
new hip hedonism" in Irish cinema (2008, 46). Unlike the rural-cen-
tered productions that have dominated cinematic representations of

Ireland in the past, these films are all set in contemporary Dublin and feature twentysomething protagonists who are stylish and cosmopolitan, urbane and sophisticated. Ging finds that such productions favor "a marketable vision of Irishness, whereby Irish identity has become more a global commodity than a means of critical self-questioning" (2002, 177). Similarly, Michael Gillespie concludes that films such as Kieran Hickey's *Exposure* (1978) and *Criminal Conversation* (1980) simply could not be made in the "the homogenized atmosphere of the present environment" (2008b, 43). Gillespie attributes such homogenization and the "erosion of an Irish film identity" to the choice of film projects made by Irish directors such as Neil Jordan and Jim Sheridan, whose "exposure to Hollywood has blunted their abilities to bring Irish identity to their work" (2008a, 235–36).

The second category of films, which Ging finds equally lacking, includes one of the films to be discussed here, *The Nephew* (Eugene Brady, 1998) as well as *Into the West* (Mike Newell, 1992), *Circle of Friends* (Pat O'Connor, 1995), *Waking Ned Devine* (Kirk Jones, 1998), and *The Closer You Get* (Aileen Ritchie, 1999). Ruth Barton terms this cinematic trend "the new 'heritage' cinema" characterized by a preoccupation with an "'imaginary' past, a kind of glorious Celtic never-never land" (1997, 42–43). For Barton, these films "satisfy a deeper set of desires shared by their largely metropolitan targeted audience (Irish, British or otherwise). That is, the recreation of a pre-industrial, uni-racial society, similar to the peasant community of Peter Mayle's Provence" (51). Although *The Nephew* features a nonwhite protagonist, his "difference" from the Inis Dara locals reinforces Barton's point. Chad is, as Kathleen Vejvoda points out, a "fish-out-of-water" (2007, 375n11).

In contrast to Ging, some critics argue that there are productions that challenge images of Ireland as personified either by "breezy, prosperous urbanites" or by "simple, fun-loving yokels," by exposing the underbelly of the Celtic Tiger (2002, 186). The work of the writer-director team Mark O'Halloran and Lenny Abrahamson, for example, deals with heroin addiction (*Adam and Paul* [2004]), rural isolation (*Garage* [2007]), and, in the four-part RTÉ television series *Prosperity* (2007), single motherhood, adolescent bullying, alcoholism, and the challenges faced by an African immigrant to Ireland (Gillespie 2008b; Schreiber 2008). Meanwhile, Seán Crosson (2008a) contends that the recent cycle of Irish-set horror films (*Dead Meat* [Conor McMahon, 2004], *Boy Eats Girl* [Stephen Bradley, 2005], *Isolation* [Billy O'Brien, 2005], and *Shrooms* [Paddy Breathnach, 2006])—a very new venture in Irish cinema—confronts the failures and complacencies of the Celtic Tiger by providing a countertourist vision of rural Ireland.

Although this project is primarily concerned with imaginative parallels, oblique or overt, between emigration *from* Ireland and immigration *to* Ireland, it is worth mentioning some of the few Irish feature films that confront the issue of immigration. Roddy Doyle has taken his interest in recent immigrants to Ireland into the realm of film, as well as fiction and drama. His screenplay for *When Brendan Met Trudy* (2000) features a Nigerian immigrant who is eventually deported to Germany. The film sends up Irish assumptions that nonwhite people at home must be "medical students" or, abroad, "black babies."[1] When Brendan asks Edgar awkwardly if he is "one of those medical students," Edgar responds pointedly, but cheerfully, "I am one of 'those' refugees." Ciarán O'Connor's *Capital Letters* (2004) depicts the trafficking of African women to Ireland for prostitution, and David Gleeson's heist thriller, *The Front Line* (2006), is the story of Congolese refugee Joe Yumba's attempt to rescue his family from gangsters who seek his assistance in robbing the Dublin bank where he works as a security guard.

---

1. As Ronit Lentin argues, the 1960s "'Black Babies' phenomenon—when images of black babies were used on church collection boxes to aid Irish missionaries—conditioned Irish Catholics to regard black people in a particular way, as passive victims who could only be saved by the good offices of the Catholic Church" (2003, 312).

Transnational Tragic Mulatto:
Eugene Brady's *The Nephew* (1998)

Produced by Irish Dreamtime, the company formed by Pierce Brosnan and Beau St. Clair in 1996, and directed by Eugene Brady from his own original story, *The Nephew* tells the story of nineteen-year-old Chad Egan-Washington's (Hill Harper) arrival in Ireland from America to scatter his dead mother's ashes in her birthplace of Inis Dara. His mother, Karen, emigrated to New York in the 1970s, married Chad's father, and ran a grocery store in Hell's Kitchen. Taking up residence on his uncle Tony's farm, Chad's appearance is the catalyst for the uncovering of long-buried secrets concerning and connecting Karen; her brother (Donal McCann); local publican Joe Brady (Pierce Brosnan); his mother's former best friend, Brenda (Sinéad Cusack); and her son Peter (Luke Griffin). The film premiered in Ireland at the Galway Film Fleadh in July 1998, where it was inevitably (and unfavorably) compared with the Quinn brothers' "returned Yank" film, *This Is My Father* (Paul Quinn, 1998). According to Hugh Linehan, *This Is My Father* "was rapturously received by an audience which expressed its approval by voting it Best First Film of the Fleadh. By comparison, the Pierce Brosnan–produced and, on the surface, similarly-themed *The Nephew*, in which another American returns to Ireland—to scatter the ashes of his mother on the island where she was born—was a sorry affair" (1998, 13). It is likely that the critics preferred *This Is My Father* because it deconstructs in a forceful manner, partly by revising *The Quiet Man* (1952), the notion of Ireland as a pastoral idyll. On the other hand, *The Nephew* appears to reinforce, rather than challenge, some of *The Quiet Man*'s most troubling conceits. In the United States, the film failed to get a release in cinemas and went directly to video.

In *Race in Modern Irish Literature and Culture*, John Brannigan argues that "the political narratives and cultural productions" of 1960s and 1970s Ireland "evince the existence of prescribed narratives of so-called 'multi-racial' experience in pre-'Celtic Tiger' Ireland, and that these narratives leave a problematic legacy for the attempt to recognise and celebrate a 'cosmopolitics' of heterogeneity in contemporary Ireland" (2009, 183). Indeed, one continuity between the 1970s and the Celtic Tiger years is the importance of Irish rock star and Thin Lizzy front man Phil Lynott in discussions of race and Irishness. As I suggest in chapter 1, Lynott has become overdetermined in the contemporary Irish imagination as the mixed-race embodiment of the possibilities for contemporary multicultural Ireland. Nowhere is this more apparent than in *The Nephew*.

What is striking about extant discussions of the film is the degree to which they insist on Chad's *blackness*. Martin McLoone summarizes *The Nephew* as a story about "the impact back in Ireland of the returning Irish-American, this time with the added frisson that the returning nephew is also African-American" (2000, 186); Stephanie Rains writes that the film "concerns the arrival on an island off the west coast of Ireland of Chad, a black Irish American teenager" (2006, 146); Maria Pramaggiore describes *The Nephew* as a film in which "a young African American man visits Ireland to meet the family of his dead Irish mother" (2007, 25–26); Debbie Ging's synopsis of the film is that "a black stranger is introduced and accepted but only on white terms" (2002, 186); Luke Gibbons writes that Chad is "an African-American teenager" (2005b, 566); Vejvoda observes that the film "defies the traditional narrative of return by making its Irish-American character African-American as well" (2007, 366). Only Ruth Barton is perceptive enough to recognize the importance of Chad's *mixed raceness* to the plot of the film (2006, 198). Not only is Chad's *national* identity hyphenated (Irish American), but so too is his *racial* identity (black-white, or mixed race). That Chad's mixed raceness is crucial to the film is reflected in the character's "double-barreled" name: he is Chad Egan-Washington, inscribing *both* his parents' identities equally.

There are few in-depth commentaries on *The Nephew*, and the most sustained and substantial of them is Vejvoda's. Her contention that Chad is not only racialized but gendered female (through his artistic and musical talents) provides a convincing foundation for her argument that Chad is represented as a "magical Negro" whose "ultimate purpose is to heal and transform the lives of the white Irish male characters" (2007, 368). Although Vejvoda demonstrates convincingly the limitations of the "magical Negro" archetype, in this chapter, I wish to pursue Chad's affinities with a different cinematic and literary archetype: the "tragic mulatto." Although Vejvoda is correct in identifying the resonances of the film in contemporary Ireland, it would be misleading to entirely discount its status as a Hollywood film. *The Nephew* was, after all, financed almost entirely outside Ireland (Ging 2002, 186). Moreover, one of Pierce Brosnan's stated aims for his production company, Irish Dreamtime, is to find "young writers and actors and directors and put back into the cinema community, *whether in L.A. or in Ireland,* a little of what we got out" (Brosnan quoted in Lacey 1997, 20; emphasis added). Therefore, *The Nephew* can be usefully interpreted only if *both* Irish *and* American contexts are considered, and the mixed-race protagonist provides the key to recognizing this need.

Although the mixed-race subject and the tragic mulatto are by no means synonymous, the tragic mulatto is overwhelmingly pervasive in American cultural imaginings of biracial and multiracial identities. Indeed, black-white interraciality is wholly overdetermined in discussions of American mixed raceness more generally. A prominent trope in white- and later black-authored nineteenth-century sentimental fiction in the United States, the tragic mulatto was commonly portrayed as a white-looking woman of mixed racial ancestry who has been raised as a genteel southern lady. After her father dies, her "black blood" is discovered, and her father's failure to regulate his affairs in his lifetime results in her being sold off as a slave with the rest of his property. For white abolitionist women writers, the tragic mulatta—as she most often was—served a political function: if such a refined, virtually white, woman could be condemned to a life of slavery—where, of course, she was vulnerable to the unwelcome sexual advances of lascivious white men—surely it was time to abolish this inhumane institution. In the postbellum period, the trope of the tragic mulatta persisted, but in a different form. According to Hazel Carby, writing about African American women of the late nineteenth and early twentieth centuries who deployed the tragic mulatta in their work, she was "a narrative device of mediation, allowing a fictional exploration of the relation between the races while offering an imaginary expression of the relation between them" (1987, 89). The mulatta's death, when it happens, occurs "through grief, murder, childbirth, abortion, [or] suicide," but even her life is characterized by "remorse, despair, bitterness, alienation and insanity" (Berzon 1978, 102). Hollywood cinema adopted the trope with zeal, the tragic mulatta appearing onscreen as early as 1912 (Bogle 2001, 9).[2]

Just as he or she exists at the intersection of blackness and whiteness, so the mulatto or mulatta tests the limits of "nation." The tragic mulatto is often conceived as a peculiarly American archetype. This perception owes much to the uniqueness, compared with other slave societies, of the 1662 law enacted by the Virginia assembly, which dictated that children of interracial couples would follow the condition of their mother (Williamson 1980, 8). Because the vast majority of children born of such unions were to black (slave) women and (free) white men, mulatto offspring became slaves like their mothers. This fact, combined with the "one-drop rule" in operation in many states, according to which any trace of African ancestry made an individual "black" under law, makes for the dramatic and sudden "reversal of fortune" in such narratives that will topple the beautiful mulatta from the pedestal of white mistresshood to the degradation of black female slavery (Zanger 1966, 67). As Eve Allegra Raimon argues, "'Tragic mulatto' narratives lend themselves to imaginative representations of the nation's future racial composition," a situation that played out vividly in the late 1990s in the United States (2004, 8; Beltrán and Fojas 2008, 12). In 1998, when *The Nephew* appeared,

---

2. However, the most famous mulatto in the history of early Hollywood cinema is not "tragic" but menacing. Silas Lynch in D. W. Griffith's *Birth of a Nation* (1915), a film adapted from Thomas Dixon's novels *The Leopard's Spots* (1902) and *The Clansman* (1905), reflects the contemporaneous discourse of hybrid degeneracy, or the notion that in mixed-race individuals, the worst attributes of both "races" would be united (Beltrán and Fojas 2008, 9–10).

the mixed-race figure was at the center of deeply politicized and divisive debates, where a campaign was being staged to have the category of "multiracial" included in the 2000 census. The effort was ultimately unsuccessful, but in 2000, for the first time, respondents were permitted to check more than one category when describing their racial identity on the census form. The visibility of the "multiracial" person in such debates was the culmination of a trend in which there was a resurgence of interest in mixed-race subjects. In the fall of 1993, for example, *Time* produced a famous special issue, ostensibly celebrating the possibility of America's interracial future. A computer-generated image of a white-looking female—dubbed "Eve"—graced the cover, apparently embodying and announcing the "new face of America." As several critics observe, there was nothing "new" about Eve; she was merely an "odd computerized updating of the typological categories of the nineteenth and early twentieth centuries" (Haraway 1997, 239). Ultimately, as Suzanne Bost notes of the renewed preoccupation with the mixed-race figure in 1990s America, "fear and celebration work in tandem: the fascination with mixture corresponds to (and potentially masks) racist efforts to contain fluidity and to reinstitute categories" (2005, 185).

While the mixed-race (especially black-white) subject has historically featured prominently in political debates within the specific national context of the United States, narratives of American black-white interracialism also lend themselves quite easily to a transnational dimension. It usually takes the form of characters extolling the virtues of other national contexts that they perceive to be more accepting of mixed-race subjects or interracial marriage (or both). Most often, this context is France or South America (usually Brazil). In *Kings Go Forth* (Delmer Daves, 1958), for instance, Monique Blair (Natalie Wood) is the daughter of an interracial American couple whom they choose to bring up in France. American racist ideologies still impinge on her life, however, when she falls for a WASP American GI played by Tony Curtis. At the end of *Guess Who's Coming to Dinner* (Stanley Kramer, 1967), interracial couple Johanna Drayton and John Wade Prentice leave for Zurich. In Danzy

Senna's novel *Caucasia,* Deck Lee conceives of Brazil as a "Xanadu," a "grand Mulatto Nation," and takes his (darker-skinned) mixed-race daughter there to live (1998, 355). Deck's choice recalls Brian Redfield's desire to move his family to Brazil in Nella Larsen's *Passing* (1929), in order to escape the rigid racial order with which they have to contend in New York. In Larsen's other novel, *Quicksand* (1928), mixed-race protagonist Helga Crane spends time in Copenhagen with her maternal relatives but leaves when she realizes that there, she is merely looked upon as a fetishized exotic.

As should be clear, the "whole subtradition" of the tragic mulatto "centers on the figuration of a specific racial type in decidedly *feminine* terms" (Harper 1996, 103). The ambivalence of Chad's gender identity in *The Nephew*—his empathy for women characters and his artistic talents juxtaposed with his obvious heterosexuality and masculine physique—owes itself to the grafting of the mulatto's story, traditionally a feminized one, onto the narrative of diasporic return, usually a masculinized one (Pabst 2003, 191). *The Nephew* is, as Luke Gibbons notes, a "returned Yank" narrative "in the time-honoured tradition of *The Quiet Man*" (2005b, 566). Like *The Quiet Man,* which represented a homecoming of sorts for Irish American director John Ford, the notion of the "returned Yank" resonates with the public persona of actor-producer Pierce Brosnan as well as with the film's narrative. As Ruth Barton observes, "Irish Dreamtime's policy seems to be to alternate between producing commercial Hollywood fare that exploits Brosnan's reputation as Bond and low-budget, Irish-themed works that reflect on his own somewhat traumatic relationship with the country of his birth" (2006, 194). Navan-born Brosnan, whose father left his mother when he was a young child, was passed between relatives until he joined his mother in London at the age of eleven (ibid., 181). For Barton, the paternity- or orphan-themed *The Nephew* and *Evelyn* (2002) reflect "the influence of the actor/producer's own ambiguous attitude to the country of his birth" (ibid., 197–98). By contrast, Brosnan has, in interviews, constructed America as a haven from his traumatic past in Ireland and Britain: "I felt at home once I got off that plane in America. I felt connected—with the country, the openness of the people. Ambition wasn't a dirty word here; wanting to be successful was not something to be ashamed of. And there was an acceptance of me as a man, as an actor. . . . I just felt very at home" (O'Connor 1996, 129). It is not surprising, therefore, that Brady's story of a very together young Irish American returning to the Old Country to help his uncle and cousin to heal their psychic scars appealed to Brosnan.

Like Des Bishop, Chad's "returned Yank" persona corresponds most faithfully to the version described in Heidi Hansson's discussion of returned exiles in nineteenth-century Irish novels. Hansson argues that she or he—and it is usually he—"combines an outsider's view with an insider's authority and is therefore often used to express critical ideas" (2005, 90). Because the returning exile has had "experiences of other countries and other kinds of social organization," she or he is "often described as an instigator of reform" (89). Unlike *The Quiet Man* and the "therapeutic narratives" it has spawned, in which "the romantic appeal of the Irish countryside and the search for home is offset against the disenchantment of life in the metropolis [and] traumas from the past for which modernity has no answer," the young mixed-race man from New York City provides therapy for the Irish rural dwellers beset by their own traumatic pasts (Gibbons 2006b, 97). This point is reflected in a key scene in the film in which Chad symbolically wrests authority from the priest, a figure who would, historically, have provided advice and counsel for parishioners in emotional distress. Chad enters the confessional box not to unburden himself of his sins, but to elicit from the priest information on the rancor that exists between his uncle and Joe Brady. He takes advantage of the Catholic confessional as a space of disclosure, but reverses the usual power dynamic by subjecting the priest to an interrogation rather than vice versa.

As Vejvoda observes, despite having lost both his parents, "Chad arrives on Inis Dara as a centred, self-realised whole person" who has "no emotional problems of his own" (2007, 369). At first glance, then, Chad would seem to have little in common with the archetypal tragic mulatto as elucidated by several key scholars. Indeed, as a kind of *emotionally* heroic character, he might sit more comfortably among the multiracial action heroes, played by Vin Diesel, Dwayne Johnson (the Rock), Keanu Reeves, and Jessica Alba, who Mary Beltrán and Camilla Fojas argue have "become a trend in their own right" in contemporary Hollywood cinema (2008, 11). However, through the parallels the film constructs between Chad and Irish rocker Phil Lynott, the film finds it impossible to envision a positive future for its mixed-race protagonist, despite appearances to the contrary. Phil Lynott, who died at age thirty-five in 1986 from complications arising from drug abuse, himself persists in the Irish imagination as a version of the tragic-mulatto archetype. In her article, Vejvoda emphasizes the importance of Chad's association with music, "both with rap . . . and with traditional Irish song" (2007, 367). Though she mentions Patsy's attempt at a rap version of "Whiskey in the Jar," she fails to recognize that it is one of three occasions in which Thin Lizzy is explicitly referenced on either the film's soundtrack or in the visual frame. Meanwhile, although Ruth Barton observes that "a further layer of meaning enter[s] the frame via the use of a number of Phil Lynott's songs on the soundtrack," she does not explicate what this "further layer of meaning" might be (2006, 199).

The first allusion occurs just after Tony reads of Karen's death. That night, he wakes abruptly from a nightmare, imagining he hears snatches of Thin Lizzy's "Dancing in the Moonlight," and shouts: "For God's sake, Karen." Given what the viewer subsequently learns about Karen, it is likely that her admiration for Thin Lizzy and 1970s rock music is bound up with her general rebelliousness and refusal to abide by the strictures of the society in which she was raised. Karen's appreciation for Thin Lizzy is confirmed when Chad opens her wardrobe door, untouched since her departure from Ireland, and the camera pans over, among other 1970s paraphernalia, a Thin Lizzy poster. Most significantly, just before Patsy embarks on his execrable rap version of "Whiskey in the Jar," the famous opening riff from Thin Lizzy's 1973 version of the song is heard over the soundtrack. Patsy is thus doing a rap cover *of the Thin Lizzy cover* of a traditional Irish song. As Gerry Smyth argues, "Whiskey in the Jar" became "Thin Lizzy's signature tune for a number of years, and has been widely interpreted ever since as an attempt—self-conscious or not—to marry the values and practices of two very different traditions: one (the ballad) old and established, the other (rock) new and evolving" (2005, 38). Patsy's rap cover of the Thin Lizzy cover of "Whiskey in the Jar" represents the film's attempt to emphasize the possibility of being both African American and Irish (American). Moreover, the film's references to Thin Lizzy provide a temporal link between the 1970s, when Karen left Ireland, and the present day, the late 1990s, and, through the tropes of mixed raceness and singing, between Lynott and Chad.

It is unsurprising that the ghost of Lynott is evoked in *The Nephew*, given the way in which he has been represented in Irish culture since his death in the mid-1980s. I have already mentioned, for example, Joseph O'Connor's configuration of Lynott as a convenient avatar for multiple crossings and identities—transatlantic, racial, musical—in *The Secret World of the Irish Male* (1994b). The notion of Lynott as the incarnation of multiple hybridities probably owes much to Fintan O'Toole's 1986 obituary first published in *Magill* magazine. O'Toole opens by observing that Lynott grew up in a newly built Dublin Corporation estate in "new territory" that was "not known before," thus immediately positioning Lynott at a geographical frontier. Lynott's heroes were people "of the Wild West or of Celtic Mythology"; he "learned the peculiar mixture of an arty romanticism and macho hardman strutting"; he married the local and the global musically.[3] Similarly, John Kelly writes that Lynott "managed to come across as a mixture of a cowboy, a comic-book hero, a gigolo, an American, a rake, a romantic, a hard man and an old softie" (1998, 14). Echoing

---

3. O'Toole's obituary first appeared as "Don't Believe a Word: The Life and Death of Phil Lynott," *Magill* (January 1986): 40–43. I quote from the reprinted version in *A Mass for Jesse James: A Journey Through 1980's Ireland* (Dublin: Raven Arts, 1990), 176–83.

O'Toole and Kelly, Smyth constructs Lynott as "a contradiction, an insider who was also an outsider, someone in whom the most basic of human experiences (such as belonging and exclusion) and emotions (such as identification and alienation) were in conflict" (2005, 39). In *The Nephew,* Chad comes to embody the same crossings and identities—transatlantic, racial, musical—as Lynott.

In *Racism in the Irish Experience,* Steve Garner emphasizes the importance of constructing (or inventing) an Irish antiracist tradition to which those individuals engaged in antiracist work in contemporary Ireland can look for inspiration (2004, 214). He argues that there is "alongside the hostility outlined elsewhere, a stream of positive work . . . and, moreover, of mainstream normalization of difference, particularly in the field of popular culture, the two key areas being music and sport" (236–37). Garner points to Phil Lynott and Irish Zambian Samantha Mumba as examples of this trend in music and Irish Fijian Seán Óg Ó hAilpín, Irish Asian Jason Sherlock, black Briton Chris Hughton, and "the key figure," Irish Nigerian Paul McGrath, in Irish sport (237–38). Garner is only one of several commentators and, indeed, artists to hone in on, in particular, Phil Lynott and Paul McGrath as evidence of the existence of a tradition of antiracism in Ireland.

According to Declan Kiberd, for example, "Many people have been shocked by racist attacks on foreigners (not all of them confined to black visitors) and some have wondered whether this is a new phenomenon. Back in the 1970s, when the late Phil Lynott sang 'Whiskey in the Jar,' there was little evidence of such intolerance: or even in the 1980s when soccer fans sang the praises of Paul McGrath (although the famous 'ooh-aah' chant had something slightly iffy about it)" (Longley and Kiberd 2001, 47). In Roddy Doyle's "Guess Who's Coming for the Dinner" (2001), Larry Linnane questions whether he might be racist when his daughter, Stephanie, brings her Nigerian boyfriend home to meet the family: "He wasn't a racist. He was sure about that now, positive—he thought. When he watched a footballer, for example, he didn't see skin; he saw skill. Paul McGrath, black and brilliant. Gary Breen, white and shite. And it was the same with music. Phil Lynott, absolutely brilliant. Neil Diamond, absolutely shite. And politics. Mandela, a hero. Ahern, a chancer" (2007, 8). Even in *Once* (John Carney, 2006), when the Guy (Glen Hansard) and Girl (Markéta Irglová) decide to record an album, their backing group are a Thin Lizzy–loving trio who congregate at the Phil Lynott bronze statue just off Dublin's Grafton Street. The three are disappointed when Guy informs them that, unfortunately, they will *not* be recording covers of Lizzy songs. Who better to facilitate this intercultural musical collaboration (and unconsummated romance) than Lynott? In a very fundamental way, then, Phil Lynott has become liberal shorthand for the possibilities offered by a multicultural Ireland.

There are essentially two interrelated problems with the Lynott-Chad connection and, indeed, with the appeal to Lynott in contemporary Irish culture more generally. The first is that Lynott, along with Paul McGrath, has been persistently constructed as an Irish version of the tragic mulatto in popular culture.[4] In his obituary for Lynott, Fintan O'Toole juxtaposes the "happy homes and happy families" of other children living in Lynott's neighborhood with Lynott's comparatively more difficult childhood by quoting from his song "Black Boys on the Corner":

> I'm a little black boy
> And I don't know my place
> I'm just a little boy
> I just threw my ace
> I'm a little black boy
> Recognise my face.
>   (1990, 176)

---

4. McGrath, who never quite fulfilled his promise in a soccer career marred by alcoholism and depression, wrote in his 2006 autobiography, *Back from the Brink,* of "a largely loveless childhood with the attendant problems of bed-wetting, chronic insecurity and a deep unhappiness that culminated in two bouts of catatonic resignation in his teens" (Duggan 2006, 11).

The little black boy who doesn't know his place recalls Sterling Brown's configuration of the tragic mulatto as "miserable" because of his "divided inheritance" (1933, 195–96) and with Judith Berzon's assertion that she or he is "an outcast, a wanderer, one alone . . . a fictional symbol of marginality" (1978, 100). O'Toole goes on to assert that music "never completely filled the gap left by his [absent] father," which is consistent with a general obsession with paternity and paternal abandonment in the wider context of tragic-mulatto narratives. The tragic mulatto is, as Raimon puts it, commonly depicted as "somehow abandoned" because he or she either is literally an orphan or has been separated from his or her parents (2004, 8). According to O'Toole, "Thinking of himself as an orphan, he had himself been adopted by the heroic loners of his dream world. . . . Phil Lynott, the fatherless child, never grew old and withered. But he never stopped thinking of himself as an orphan" (1990, 177). Like Lynott and the archetypal tragic mulatto, Chad is also an orphan, his father murdered when he was ten years old, his mother only recently deceased. Casting Lynott—and by extension Chad—as a tragic mulatto is problematic because it represents a dilution of "otherness"—and any attendant perceived threat—into a more acceptable form: blackness becomes mixed raceness (or pseudowhiteness); power becomes passivity; beauty and youth become (in Lynott's case) death. The white Irish viewer of *The Nephew* is not unsettled by his or her confrontation with racial otherness in the film not because it has been deconstructed, but because it has been domesticated.

The second problem with the Lynott-Chad connection is suggested by Garner in his discussion of Lynott and McGrath: "The experiences of not-so-famous black Irish people have been of life-long rejection and marginalisation" (2004, 238). In other words, at the root of the acceptance of Phil Lynott in Ireland was his exceptional talent and success: he was, in many respects, the first Irish superstar. According to O'Toole, Lynott's "black skin and lithe style had an exotic air" that were important in the construction of Thin Lizzy as a rock spectacle (1990, 180). Equally, John Kelly writes that "Phil Lynott undoubtedly possessed that elusive quality called style, and he was perfect subject matter for photographers and artists. He threw all kinds of shapes and he had a great face—one that was easy to capture as a striking image" (1998, 14). Similarly, in *The Nephew*, Brenda's twin sons are fascinated by Chad's hair and clothing, perceiving him as the embodiment of "cool." The exceptionality of Chad, and his concomitant exoticism, is intimately connected to his relatively unproblematic welcome by the Inis Dara community.

Given the historical contexts of the film on both sides of the Atlantic—the "multiracial" debate in America, the influx of non-white immigrants to Ireland—it is reasonable to suggest that in *The Nephew*, Brady transplants the American mixed-race subject to the fictional Irish setting of Inis Dara in order to envision *Ireland's* multicultural future just as he or she was being deployed in similar and contemporaneous debates in the United States. Yet as several scholars argue, and as Bost recapitulates above, there is every reason to be skeptical of appeals to the mixed-race subject—in the Irish case, Phil Lynott—in contemporary culture, even if they are well intentioned. As David Theo Goldberg puts it, although "'mixed race' may seem adequately to capture prevailing demographic heterogeneity, . . . it does so only by silently fixing in place the racializing project. It naturalizes racial assumption, marking mixed-ness as an aberrant condition, as transgressive, and at the extreme as purity polluting" (1997, 63). Importing the American mixed-race subject to contemporary multicultural Ireland may thus provoke more questions than it resolves. As negotiations of race and immigration in contemporary Irish culture become more prevalent and urgent, liberals need to be attentive to such dangers in order to avoid reproducing the very hierarchies and stereotypes they wish to overturn.

In Ireland? Jim Sheridan's *In America* (2003)

In the only (to date) full-length study of Sheridan's oeuvre as director or writer, which predates the release of *In America*, Ruth Barton claims that the subtitle to her book *Jim Sheridan: Framing the Nation* (2002) draws attention to the ways in which Sheridan's films "capture and articulate the national mood" (2002, 5). In particular, Barton emphasizes the extent to which "the family becomes metonymic for the nation" in Sheridan's work (77). In *In the Name of the Father* (1993), for example, debates over Irish Republican violence versus peaceful resistance to British colonial occupation in Northern Ireland are dramatized as a father-son conflict between Gerry and Giuseppe Conlon. In *Into the West* (1992), directed by Mike Newell from Sheridan's script, Ossie and Tito are "the lost children of the nation/family" (128, 124). Barton's observations on the importance of family as a microcosm for nation, and especially the "idealisation of the maternal figure," in Sheridan's oeuvre are equally true of the film that was in production when she completed her study: with the working title *East of Harlem*, the film became *In America* (25). In fact, *Into the West* and *In America* are, thematically, very similar. Two siblings—brothers in *Into the West*, sisters in *In America*—feel neglected by their emotionally distant fathers, a situation that, in both cases, is attributable to grief: Papa Riley (Gabriel Byrne) has descended into alcoholism after the death of his wife; Johnny Sullivan (Paddy Considine) is mourning the death of his son. Both families attempt to overcome their sorrow by escaping to mythical Wests: the West of Ireland in *Into the West* and even farther west, the United States, in *In America*.

The film is concerned with the Sullivan family from Ireland—Johnny, Sarah (Samantha Morton), and their two daughters, Christy and Ariel (Sarah and Emma Bolger)—who move to New York as illegal immigrants after the death of their son and brother, Frankie. The family rents an apartment in a Hell's Kitchen building occupied by junkies, transvestites, and a black, AIDS-afflicted artist called Mateo (Djimon Hounsou). Initially intimidated by Mateo's angstridden screams emanating from the apartment below theirs, the two girls and their mother eventually befriend him. At first, Johnny, a struggling actor, resents the intimacy that develops between Mateo and his family. However, he, too, is won over in due course. When Sarah becomes pregnant for the fourth time, the doctor warns her that if she carries the baby to full term, she will be endangering both her own life and the life of the child. However, both mother and baby live, and the family comes to terms with their grief over Frankie. Lacking health insurance, the Sullivans' medical bills are miraculously taken care of by Mateo, and Baby Sarah's struggle for survival is explicitly crosscut with images of Mateo dying.

Even at first glance, Sheridan's film seems to satisfy the criteria for what Donald Bogle calls "the movies' huckfinn fixation," whereby "the white hero [Johnny] grows in stature from his association with the dusty black. Blacks seem to possess the soul the white man searches for" (2001, 140). Certainly, existing scholarship on the film relies very much on this kind of interpretation. For Catherine Eagan, "Mateo serves as a conduit to bring the family together again, even as he is dying of AIDS" (2006, 34). Vejvoda finds that in both *The Nephew* and *In America,* the racial Others are "paragons of integrity and self-knowledge who minister to the needs of the Irish characters" (2007, 366). Meanwhile, Beth Newhall argues that Sheridan's portrayal of Mateo "embraces a representational strategy that draws upon tropes of imperialist and racist discourse" (2005, 145). For Newhall, the use in the soundtrack of "primitive" music to accompany or suggest Mateo's presence and the depiction of Mateo as possessing "magical" and "spiritual" qualities translate into "two stereotypes encoded in opposing images: the uncontrollable, beastlike savage, and the innocent, servile saint" (150). Although I agree wholeheartedly with these analyses—and draw upon them in this discussion—they are not extensive enough to do justice to the complexity of the discourses in which the film is embedded.

If Sheridan's families tend be "metonymic for the nation," it must be understood that "family" in *In America* means "white Irish family." In other words, the film's focus on maternity and reproduction implicates it deeply in historical and contemporary discourses surrounding race, immigration, and citizenship on both sides of the Atlantic. According to Richard Dyer, as "the literal bearers of children and because they are held primarily responsible for their initial raising, women are the indispensable means by which the group—the race—is in every sense reproduced" (1999, 29). Thus, Laura Doyle has argued that because the mother figure embodies borders of nation, sex, and race, she becomes mobilized precisely at those moments in which these borders are being reconsidered or problematized. So for Doyle, after the passage of the Johnson-Reed Immigration Act in the United States in 1924, "the contemporary development on the one hand, of eugenics, and on the other, of the Harlem Renaissance and modernism—with their common focus on racialized mother figures—emerges as no mere coincidence" (1994, 9).

The racialized mother figure was equally evident in the run-up to Ireland's referendum on citizenship, which took place some eight months after *In America* was released in Ireland on October 31, 2003. As Eithne Luibhéid demonstrates, such rhetoric was developed, circulated, and legitimated in the two or three years prior to the referendum through discourses on sex and childbearing (2004, 338–39). Such discourses regarding, in particular, asylum-seeker women's pregnancy "commonly conveyed beliefs and concerns about crime, welfare abuse, cynical exploitation, cultural 'dilution,' economic difficulties, and a crisis of national sovereignty" (340). It is not surprising, therefore, that the culmination of this rhetoric, the 2004 referendum, "took as its iconographic and anecdotal bogey woman the spectre of a pregnant black woman, who threatened to swallow up, devour and incorporate the economy if she was allowed to claim Irish citizenship by way of her child" (Sullivan 2007, 194).

Like my reading of *The Nephew,* my interpretation of *In America* relies on the dual Irish and American contexts of the film. While set exclusively in New York, the city of Dublin doubles for New York in several interior scenes: the family's Hell's Kitchen apartment was an apartment on Dublin's Parnell Street (C. Dwyer 2003, n.p.), and Sheridan and his crew shot for only two weeks in New York compared with twelve weeks in Dublin (M. Dwyer 2004, n.p.). However, Sheridan's film has the added complication of two (implied) historical settings. The "deliberate lack of historical specificity" in *My Left Foot* (1989) and *The Field* indicates the degree to which both films, but especially *The Field*, "aspire to the mythic and, therefore, the timeless" (Barton 2002, 41). The same is true of *In America.*

Although it supposedly refers to Sheridan's own experiences as an illegal immigrant to the United States with his family in the early 1980s, and despite the fact that the film's autobiographical premise was heavily emphasized in the publicity for the film and in the accompanying "pictorial moviebook," the director is adamant that he "wasn't interested in doing a period film" (Sheridan 2003).[5] The present-day setting is confirmed early on when the deejay on the Sullivans' car radio announces hits from the sixties, seventies, eighties, and nineties. Furthermore, the family's trip to the cinema to see Steven Spielberg's 1982 film *E.T.* is plausible in a contemporary setting because *E.T.* was rereleased for its twentieth anniversary in 2002. My reading of Sheridan's film therefore emphasizes the interconnectedness of the two historical moments (the 1980s and 2002–3) and the two geographical locations (Ireland and America) in which it positions itself.

I am particularly interested in the ways in which the film was promoted by both reviewers and Sheridan himself as a post-9/11 film. As Seán Crosson reveals, reviews of *In America* in the United States presented the film as providing "the means through which Americans, and in particular the citizens of New York, could come to terms with their own recent trauma, the tragedy that has become known as 9/11" (2008b, 68). These reviews were consistent with the ways in which narratives of Irishness were circulating more generally in American culture at that particular historical juncture. Both Diane Negra and Luke Gibbons have drawn attention to the construction of Ireland and Irishness as therapeutic, a trend that was "well underway before the events of September 11" (Negra 2006a, 355). Nonetheless, the

5. In the accompanying book, cowriters Jim, Naomi, and Kirsten Sheridan provide forewords in which they recount their own individual memories from their time in the United States in the early 1980s. Strikingly, stills from the film are juxtaposed with real-life photographs of Naomi and Kirsten as children: in their school uniforms (Sheridan, Sheridan, and Sheridan 2003, 64–65) and playing in the snow (102–3).

notion of Irishness as therapeutic was deployed in significant ways in the traumatic aftermath of 9/11. Enya's New Age ballad "Only Time" became, according to Negra, "the soundtrack for national grief" (364). Equally, Georgina Brennan, writing for the magazine *Irish America,* described Chieftain Paddy Moloney's appearance at Ground Zero after playing at the funeral of one of the 9/11 victims:

> Paddy played his tin whistle. Surrounded by a small group of Irish cops, friends and his daughter Edín, Paddy played the haunting "Táimse i mo Chodladh" (I Am Asleep), an Irish wake song. And as the weight of devastation sat heavy on the crowd's hearts Paddy played "Dóchas" (Hope), lifting the spirits of all. The old Irish tradition that inspired Paddy to come to Ground Zero made a difference to the rescue workers as they stopped, in the midst of smoke rising from the pits, to gaze at the sight of a small man playing music larger than the city itself. (Brennan 2002, 20)

Again, Irishness functions as a means of enabling Americans to express and come to terms with their emotions. Citing reviews that claimed *In America* was "the perfect answer to 9/11" and the "best movie to address the way we live today" depicting "how humans respond to tragedy yet search for freedom," Crosson demonstrates effectively the extent to which the reception of *In America* is embedded in such therapeutic discourses.

Equally, Sheridan himself was not reluctant to draw attention to the film's post-9/11 resonances. In the accompanying screenplay, readers are informed that "*In America* was one of the first productions to shoot in New York following the events of September 11, lending the crew a strong sense of wanting to reveal the underlying soul of New York in the photography" (Sheridan, Sheridan, and Sheridan 2003, 25). In the director's commentary, Sheridan points out that he shot the opening image of the American flag on camcorder soon after September 11, 2001: "I quite like it," he says, "even though there was quite a lot of flag-waving at that time, which you could understand" (ibid.). The shot of the American flag cuts to the

Sullivan family's encounter at the Canadian border in their bid to be admitted to the United States. To post-9/11 audiences in the United States, moreover, the Hell's Kitchen setting of the film would resonate deeply because of the losses suffered by the area's firefighters during the September 11 attacks. The hardest-hit station in Manhattan was Engine 54/Ladder 4/Battalion 9, "The Pride of Midtown" in Hell's Kitchen, which lost fifteen men.

The problem with such assertions of *In America*'s post-9/11 resonances is that, when read in this context, the film becomes more problematic than the simple story of a family's recovery from grief as they assimilate in the New World. It becomes a tale of innocent (read: white) immigrants who survive in America at the expense of their more menacing (read: nonwhite) immigrant counterparts. The juxtaposition of a post-9/11 American flag with illegal immigrants entering US territory inevitably conjoins border crossing and immigration with the destruction wrought by the terrorist attacks on the United States in September 2001. However, any potential threat posed by this *white Irish* family, in particular, is quickly defused. The *deceit* that they practice upon the immigration officials—they tell them they are on vacation, although they are planning to stay and work—is counterbalanced by the awful *truth* that they have just lost a child. They are fleeing death, as Sheridan would have it. They themselves pose no such risk. Visually, the notion of the *officials'* malevolence—as those individuals with the power to hinder the family's entry to the United States—is reinforced by the way in which they encroach on the frame, flanking Johnny and Sarah on both sides of the vehicle. The car, so often a symbol of American freedom and expansiveness in the road-movie tradition, is, in this scene, static, and the roof bears down oppressively on its occupants. Once they have been welcomed to America, moreover, Sheridan underscores their admission to the United States by presenting the family crossing a series of domestic thresholds. When they enter their apartment building in Manhattan, they pass through two doors, walk up several flights of stairs, and confront Mateo's closed door with a sign reading "Keep Away" before eventually reaching their own apartment, which, after a close-up shot of an intricate lock system, Sarah observes is "like Fort Knox."

In the aftermath of 9/11, of course, a suspected new form of terrorist attack received wide coverage and credence: biological warfare. Over the course of several weeks beginning on September 18, only a week after the 9/11 attacks, letters containing anthrax were mailed to five news organizations and two senators. A week later, the World Health Organization confirmed and intensified US fears when it issued a warning urging Western governments to ensure their readiness to deal with a terrorist attack using biological weapons (Boseley 2001, n.p.). For the Soviets in the 1980s, AIDS represented "an American biological weapon gone amok and destroying its creator" (Gilman 1994, 264). In fact:

> The fear of AIDS can—and clearly has been—exploited in relation to notions of racial, as well as sexual, purity. The perceptible need is for a border, between the polluted (here diseased, contagious) and the pure (disease-free, taken in this case to be HIV negative). . . . The border can usefully be aligned, however, with national boundaries. AIDS was, in the understanding of many countries, an invasion from outside, which encouraged calls for clampdowns on immigration, as well as for legally enforced "testing" of the aliens within the midst of the country. Aliens could be literally understood, or identified, as those elements which the prevailing ideology deemed to be "other." (MacKinnon 1992, 191)

Given this context, it is important to understand the film's AIDS motif in terms of both its 1980s and its contemporary resonances. Mateo, who is suffering from an AIDS-related illness, comes to symbolize the immigrant who, quite literally, poses a threat to national health. Indeed, Barbara Browning notes that the metaphor of disease and contagion "is invoked—often in the guise of a literal threat—at moments of anxiety over diasporic flows [between Africa and the West], whether migrational or cultural" (1998, 6).

By locating AIDS on a black male body, Sheridan is—consciously or unconsciously—operating according to codes that are easily understandable to American audiences. For example, Mateo's country of origin is never specified. Even in the director's commentary, Sheridan only says he is "African." Neither the DVD's subtitles nor the screenplay provide further insight, with no attempt made to translate Mateo's occasional mutterings in a "foreign language" (Sheridan, Sheridan, and Sheridan 2003, 79). However, this does not prevent some reviewers from making a telling assumption about Mateo's nationality. Jessica Winter of the *Village Voice* describes Mateo as "a glowering Haitian artist" (2003, n.p.). In the early days of AIDS in the 1980s, Haitian immigrants were scapegoated as carriers of AIDS, and Winter appears to reinforce this myth in her review of the film. Sander Gilman suggests that shifting the perceived source of pollution to black Africans and Haitians assuaged "American 'liberal' sensibilities while still locating the origin of the disease within the paradigm of American racist ideology" (1994, 263).

As Sander Gilman further points out, during the 1980s in the United States, the typical person with AIDS was persistently constructed as a black male homosexual. Of course, prior to the adoption of the acronym AIDS in 1982 by the Centers for Disease Control, the epidemic was known as GRID (Gay-Related Immuno-Deficiency). As is the case with Mateo's nationality, Sheridan never specifies whether Mateo is gay. However, it is certainly implied, if only momentarily. In a key scene in the movie, Johnny confronts Mateo after Sarah, through Mateo's influence, decides to go through with a pregnancy that will endanger her own life:

JOHNNY: Are you in love with her? *(He leans in to Mateo.)* Are you in love with her?

MATEO: No. *(He leans toward Johnny.)* I'm in love with you. *(Johnny stares at Mateo.)* And I'm in love with your beautiful woman. And I'm in love with your kids. And I'm even in love with your unborn child. *(shouts)* I'm even in love with your anger! I'm in love with anything that lives!

(Johnny looks at Mateo.)
JOHNNY: You're dying. (Sheridan, Sheridan, and Sheridan 2003, 91)

The evocation of homosexuality in relation to Mateo—if only fleetingly—serves to defuse any potential threat of the sexually voracious black man to white, female sexual purity while simultaneously reinforcing the association between black male homosexuality and AIDS. In a further slippage, Sheridan notes in his director's commentary that the figure of Mateo—the black artist—is based on Jean-Michel Basquiat. Basquiat died, at age twenty-seven, of a heroin overdose, but he did not have AIDS. Curiously, in a building occupied predominantly by heroin addicts, it is the black man—whom we never see engaging in any "risk behaviors"—who has contracted AIDS. The suggestion that Mateo is homosexual also serves to reassure Johnny that the physically imposing black man (he is described as "a formidable black man" in the screenplay) poses no challenge to his own masculinity (ibid., 23). His roles as husband and father are slightly undermined by his inability to find acting work in order to provide for them. Once Johnny discovers that Mateo is dying, the black man acts as a vehicle that facilitates the restoration of Johnny's masculinity and, indeed, his emotional well-being. The pair are doubled throughout in their association with ghosts and haunting. When the girls, upon arrival in their new Hell's Kitchen apartment building, hear Mateo's cries, Christy observes: "Maybe he sees ghosts," to which Ariel responds, "Is this a haunted house?" (ibid., 26). Subsequently, Ariel tells Mateo that in his painting, their building "looks like a haunted house" (78). As Mateo responds, the house is, indeed, haunted but not, as Johnny initially believes, by Mateo, who gives him the "heebie-jeebies" (81). In his subsequent confrontation with Mateo, Johnny realizes that it is he, numbed with the pain of his son's death, who is "a fucking ghost. I don't exist. I can't think. I can't laugh. I can't cry. I can't . . . feel!" (91). Accordingly, when Christy performs the Eagles song "Desperado" at a school concert, she appeals to her father to "let somebody love you / Before it's too late" (93). The inclusion of this song also serves to establish the

Sullivans as desperadoes—illegal immigrants, and hence outlaws, if benign ones—in a very American tradition.

The diseased black African man thus comes to stand in contrast to the healthy, white Irish family. Mateo is inextricably aligned with death, whereas the Sullivan females are life givers. In the case of Sarah, this fact is portrayed quite overtly through her determination to go through with a troubled, but ultimately successful, pregnancy. Mateo's closeness to death ensures that he becomes cast in the role of prophet. He confides to Sarah, "The baby will bring its own luck." During Johnny's confrontation with Mateo, Johnny claims that "the baby could infect her, and two girls'll be left without their ma" (90). The metaphor of infection is key, because it is Mateo, the contaminated, raced outsider, and not the new baby, who poses a threat to the family in terms of contagion. The baby is born, an American citizen, and she does not "infect" her mother. However, she does need a blood transfusion. An agitated, postnatal Sarah refuses to sign a permission form to allow the transfusion to take place, saying, "All the blood is bad. Mateo said all the blood is bad. You're not giving my baby bad blood," one of the few occasions, perhaps, in which the film appears to reference the 1980s rather than the present day (112). The only alternative is for ten-year-old Christy to donate the much-needed blood. Christy has previously performed mouth-to-mouth resuscitation on Mateo and expresses a fear that she may have contracted his disease and will pass it on to her newborn sister. Sheridan quite explicitly suggests, therefore, that the danger is not that the new baby will infect her mother, but that Mateo—via Christy—could infect the new baby.

Mateo's knowledge that "all the blood is bad"—knowledge derived perhaps from his own experience as a person with AIDS—confirms his dual role in the film as both a threat to the pure, white, healthy (read: national) body *and* a kind of omniscient prophet, which goes some way toward tempering this threat. The film establishes a series of correspondences between "heaven" and "home," illegal aliens and aliens from outer space through its allusions to

Spielberg's 1982 film *E.T.*[6] Indeed, when the family first arrives in Manhattan, Christy's voice-over observes that it was "like we were on another planet" (20). After Ariel sees *E.T.* for the first time, she tells Marina—appropriately, at an ice cream parlor called Heaven— that "heaven" and "home" are not the same thing. However, in the case of Mateo, "heaven" and "home" become interchangeable. Mateo is both a Christ-like martyr—or "spiritual father," as Jim Sheridan describes him—and an undesirable immigrant who must be "sent home." As Mateo's health deteriorates, Ariel asks him why he has sores:

MATEO *(to Ariel, softly)*: If I tell you a secret . . . *(Ariel leans against a chair.)* . . . will you tell nobody else? *(Ariel shakes her head "no.")*
ARIEL: No, I won't.
MATEO *(softly)*: I'm an alien. *(She turns to look at him.)* Like ET. From different planet. My skin is too sensitive for this Earth. The air is too hard for me. *(Ariel thinks about this for a beat. Deep down she can sense what Mateo is saying to her even if she has to put it into her own way of thinking.)*
ARIEL *(softly)*: Are you going home like ET?
(This is the first time Mateo has really confronted this. He is very upset.)
MATEO *(softly)*: I suppose I'm going home. (101)

6. As Ruth Barton demonstrates, the films from which Sheridan visually quotes in his films are always deeply significant: in *In the Name of the Father*, the prisoners watch *The Godfather* (Francis Ford Coppola, 1974), "a film that links criminality with male bonding" (2002, 76); in *Into the West*, the boys watch *Butch Cassidy and the Sundance Kid* (George Roy Hill, 1969), a classic western, and *Back to the Future III* (Robert Zemeckis, 1989), a film that toys with the western form—as does *Into the West* (130, 133). The other film-within-the-film in *In America* is *The Grapes of Wrath* (John Ford, 1940), which, as Seán Crosson argues, is significant because the clip shown reflects one of the most dramatic changes Ford made to Steinbeck's novel: instead of Steinbeck's searing critique of American social policy in the 1930s, the Joad migrants emerge in Ford's film as optimistic and hopeful (2008b, 66).

Roger Ebert's assumption, in his review of *In America*, that Mateo is a Nigerian immigrant is interesting in an Irish context, because of 2,866 deportation orders signed by the minister of justice in 2004, 946 (one third) were issued to Nigerians ("Irish Asylum Statistics" 2005). Furthermore, the implications of "aliens" and "going home" also resonate within a 1980s *and* contemporary Irish American context, especially when we consider the demographic group to which Sheridan and his family—as illegal immigrants to the United States in 1982—belonged. As I argue in relation to the stand-up performances of Des Bishop and Ronan Noone's *The Blowin of Baile Gall,* the yoking together of "illegal immigrants" to Ireland and so-called undocumented Irish in the United States tends to benefit the latter group rather than the former by enabling an appeal to a rhetoric of victimhood that elides the historical and contemporary advantages that attach to the possession of white skin.

When read according to its 1980s (AIDS as a biological weapon) and contemporary (anthrax as a post-9/11 biological weapon), Irish (Citizenship Referendum), and American (post-9/11 immigration paranoia) contexts, *In America* becomes as much a dramatization of "Fortress Ireland" as a tale of Irish immigrants to America and their search for belonging, a suggestion that is immediately borne out by its present-day setting and its Dublin locations. This understanding confirms a shift in the status of the Irish as an ambiguously raced immigrant group in Britain, the United States, and elsewhere to a white, European ethnic group unwilling to share the spoils of sudden and unprecedented economic prosperity. The film's establishment of a dichotomy between "desirable" and "undesirable" immigrants recalls the immigration history of the United States, at the same time as it adds another layer of meaning to the label bestowed on Ireland by the *Economist* in January 2005, as the world's most "desirable" place to live (Kekic 2004, n.p.).

Epilogue

The Departees?

> Why was it, Síle wondered, that *emigration* sounded noble and
> tragic, *immigration* grubby and grasping?
> —EMMA DONOGHUE, *Landing* (2007)

This book is about reversals. In the course of writing it, yet another reversal took place, one that is most usefully illustrated by drawing yet again upon the emigration-immigration dialectic that has provided the impetus for this entire work. On June 23, 2007—some seven weeks after Donoghue's novel was published—the *Irish Times*'s Saturday magazine ran a feature on returning immigrants. "Making a Comeback" described the reverse migration of Irishmen and -women from Sydney, Los Angeles, Malaysia and Japan, Croatia and Brussels. Barely a year later, on June 28, 2008, the cover story in the "Weekend Review" section of the newspaper was a piece by Harry McGee entitled "Back to the Future?" With a prominently displayed photograph of Irishmen and -women lining up for visas at the US Embassy in Dublin in 1987, McGee asks, "Could it really get that bad again?" Since then, a flurry of newspaper features have appeared, addressing the possibility of renewed mass emigration in the wake of a global recession that has severely curtailed employment opportunities and worsened pay conditions in Ireland (Corrigan 2008, 2; Mulcahy 2008, 22–23).[1] The Central Statistics Office found that net

---

1. Mulcahy's article appeared in a magazine devoted to "the 1980s revisited," itself reflecting and perpetuating the public perception that the current recession

193

immigration plummeted from 67,300 to 38,500 in the year ending April 2008 ("Population and Migration Estimates" 2008, 2). By April 2009, Ireland was, once again, a country of net emigration.[2]

The impact of Ireland's economic crisis on its immigrant population quickly became palpable. In September 2008, Fine Gael T. D. Leo Varadkar called on the government to consider paying immigrant workers a lump-sum payment of up to six months' worth of unemployment benefits if they agreed to return home, a proposal that was roundly condemned by Minister for Integration Conor Lenihan (Edwards 2008, n.p.). The 2009 budget, published on October 14, 2008, announced an unprecedented 43 percent cut in funding for the Equality Authority, an independent body set up to uphold Ireland's antidiscrimination laws. The decision led to the resignation of its chief executive, Niall Crowley. Similarly, the office of the minister for integration had its budget cut by a quarter. In February 2009, on Joe Duffy's RTÉ Radio 1 program, a controversy arose over white Irish taxi drivers' displaying the tricolor on their vehicles, a move perceived as an invitation to white Irish customers to pass over taxis driven by Africans (Fottrell 2009, n.p.). On June 1, 2009, changes to the existing work-permit system came into effect. Although these changes primarily impact those individuals applying for permits to work in Ireland after that date, they also make it virtually impossible for existing non-EEA permit holders to remain in Ireland should they be made redundant (C. Taylor 2009, n.p.).

Vertiginous though the rapidly evolving economic and social conditions in Ireland may be, I wish to conclude by urging academics and scholars to continue to keep apace with cultural production that is (re)imagining and responding to the connections between historical

---

represents a "return" to the 1980s. In an *Irish Independent* article published some four months later, Karen Buckley concludes her piece on dole lines with "Deja [*sic*] vu—welcome to the Eighties. Sorry, the new Noughties" (2009, 4). See also P. Kenny 2009, 10–13.

2. Net outward migration rose from 7,800 in April 2009 to 34,500 in April 2010 ("Population and Migration Estimates" 2010, 1).

and contemporary flows of people to and from Ireland. By referring briefly to three texts—Roddy Doyle's "Guess Who's Coming for the Dinner" (2000), Sinéad Moriarty's *Whose Life Is It Anyway?* (2008), and Emma Donoghue's *Landing* (2007)—I wish to suggest some of the directions that this research might take. The changes to Ireland's work-permit system, for example, raise important questions about how appropriate the Irish adoption of a European guest-worker policy was in the first place. As Kieran Allen notes, the Irish work-permit system was modeled on the guest-worker system, which was devised by the major industrial powers after World War II. The system "assumed that immigration is temporary and that the individual worker should be treated as a guest who would eventually leave. Guests, of course, need particular hosts to invite them, and for workers this meant an employer on whom they were dependent. Hosts, of course, can only look after guests in times of plenty and in leaner periods they may have to ask guests to leave" (2007, 86). How significant, in this context, are Doyle's story and Moriarty's novel? These narratives borrow the premise of Stanley Kramer's US civil rights–era film *Guess Who's Coming to Dinner* (1967), and thus readily evoke European guest-worker policies as described by Allen. Doyle's and Moriarty's texts conclude with the departure of their African diasporic "guests": the first, from dinner; the second, from Ireland altogether.

Originally serialized in *Metro Éireann* and reprinted in a slightly altered form as "The Dinner" in the *New Yorker* in February 2001, Roddy Doyle's short story was subsequently adapted into a play, *Guess Who's Coming for the Dinner,* which premiered at the Dublin Theatre Festival in September of that year. In the story, white Irishman Larry Linnane, a father of four daughters and one son, is "surprised, and angry, and hurt, and confused" when his eldest daughter, Stephanie, informs the family that she has been seeing a Nigerian man named Ben (Doyle 2007, 5). Invited to dinner at the Linnane home, Ben is, as Doyle playfully notes, "more like . . . Sidney Poitier" than Eddie Murphy (11). Notwithstanding some tense moments and misunderstandings, Larry overcomes his suspicion of Ben, especially after the young man recounts how his sister Jumi "disappeared" in Nigeria. As it turns out, Ben and Stephanie are not romantically involved, but are "just friends" (25). The story ends happily with Ben's departure and a smile exchanged between him and Larry.

Strictly speaking, Ben is not a guest worker but an asylum seeker. However, this nuance merely serves to highlight the hierarchies that exist within Ireland's labor market, with Irish and other EEA nationals at the top, work-permit holders in the middle, and asylum seekers, who are not permitted to work, at the bottom. Indeed, when his wife and daughters first discuss Ben, Larry's attention is engaged only when he hears Stephanie's response to Vanessa's question:

> "What's he do for his money?"
> "He's an accountant," said Stephanie.
> Larry sat up: no daughter of his was going to get stuck with a bloody accountant.
> "At least, he would be," said Stephanie, "if they let him work."
> "What's that mean?" said Larry.
> They looked at him. The aggression and fear in his voice had shocked even him.
> "They won't let him work," said Stephanie. . . . "Because they haven't granted him asylum yet." (4–5)

At the fraught dinner that follows, Ben—unlike John Wade Prentice in *Guess Who's Coming to Dinner*—is the only guest. After one heated exchange, Larry tells Ben to "get out of [his] house," only for the situation to be defused by his wife, Mona (16). Eventually, and significantly, Ben leaves of his own accord. Like the updated *Guess Who's Coming to Dinner* scenario, as I argue below, the outcome of Doyle's story—if read as a parable of Ireland's work-permit system— is ultimately reassuring for white Irish readers. There may be a period of strained relations between native Irish and work-permit holders, but it can be easily overcome, they will get along nicely together, and the guest(worker)s will know the appropriate time to leave.

In the film, *Guess Who's Coming to Dinner,* a young white woman called Joey Drayton returns from a trip to Hawaii having met, fallen in love with, and become engaged to John Wade Prentice, an African American doctor who specializes in tropical diseases. On arrival in San Francisco, she and her fiancé travel to the opulent home of her parents, liberal journalist Matt and art curator Christine, to inform them of their plans to marry and to move to Geneva, where John will take up a position with the World Health Organization. After sustained opposition to the union by Matt and, subsequently, John's father, the couple finally receive the blessing of both sets of parents, and the Draytons and their guests withdraw to the dining room to enjoy a dinner prepared by the Draytons' African American maid, Tillie. The appearance of the film coincides with the *Loving v. Virginia* decision of 1967, in which the United States Supreme Court found individual states' antimiscegenation laws unconstitutional, thereby paving the way for the removal of restrictions on interracial marriage. Although Martin Luther King would not be assassinated until the following year, the shift from King's advocacy of nonviolent protest and civil disobedience to the Black Power ideologies of Stokely Carmichael and others was, by 1967, already palpable.

Although Doyle updates and transplants the *Guess* scenario to contemporary Dublin, he reproduces some of the film's most heavy-handed conceits. For example, in one important scene in the film, Matt and Christine go to a drive-in restaurant and order ice cream. Matt cannot recall the flavor of the ice cream he ordered at the same establishment on a previous visit, but when the waitress suggests "fresh Oregon boysenberry sherbet," he feels sure that it is the right one. When the ice cream arrives, he is initially dismayed to discover that he was mistaken, that it is not the flavor he wanted, but he soon realizes that he likes this new flavor very much nonetheless. With this analogy, according to Thomas Wartenberg, "the film proposes that a person's response to the race (i.e., skin color) of another is also a matter of taste . . . and so as ephemeral as a preference for one or another ice cream flavour. This undergirds the film's optimism that racism can be eliminated. Matt will eventually get used to the color of his daughter's husband, just as he got used to an unfamiliar flavor of ice cream" (1999, 125). In Doyle's story, Larry has a number of preconceptions regarding his daughter's Nigerian boyfriend, neatly summed up by Doyle as "AIDS, War, the Works." Initially disarmed by the well-dressed, well-spoken man who presents himself at the Linnane home, Larry is appalled when he notices that Ben is wearing aftershave. One of Larry's "rules" is that he "never put on anything that smelt—aftershave, bay rum, even talc if it was scented." For Larry, a "man with a smell was hiding something" (Doyle 2007, 12). Just as in the film, ice cream flavors substitute for racial attitudes, so in Doyle's story, Larry's anti-aftershave prejudice symbolizes his own racial preconceptions. At the end of the story, Larry inquires about Ben's cologne with a view to purchasing some for himself. For Doyle, as in the film, Larry's racism can be overcome as easily as his aversion to male perfume.

By presenting racial prejudice and tolerance as matters of individual taste, the story confirms Maureen T. Reddy's contention in the only extant critique of Doyle's *Metro Éireann* stories to date that racism "equates with prejudice and is entirely personal, not systemic or social, not intimately intertwined with all the basic conditions of daily life" (2007, 19), an interpretation that echoes Wartenberg's point that the film "understands racism as an effect of the prejudices of individual social actors" and fails to acknowledge "racism's systematic, structural aspects" (1999, 120). When it emerges that Stephanie and Ben are "just friends" (Doyle 2007, 25), the message seems to be, according to Reddy, that "African immigrants do not want to marry your daughters; they just want to work and live in peace in Ireland." This outcome compromises even further the story's already simplistic treatment of Larry's change of heart, for his "turnaround is not really tested" (Reddy 2007, 19). Ultimately, he does not need to confront the reality of his daughter entering into an interracial marriage. The literal nonrelationship in Doyle's story mirrors the virtual nonrelationship in the film, which, in its attempt "to prevent John from being seen as sexually voracious," offers "no visual evidence of his passion for Johanna" (Wartenberg 1999, 127). Famously, the spectator's only glimpse of the couple's physical intimacy is a kiss refracted through a taxi's rearview mirror.

Whose Life Is It Anyway? is the fifth novel by Sinéad Moriarty, who rose to prominence after her first book, *The Baby Trail*, was published in 2004. In the book, set in 1998–99, Niamh O'Flaherty is a twenty-eight-year-old Londoner born of white Irish parents who, having moved to Dublin years before to attend college and subsequently work as a newspaper columnist, falls in love with a forty-two-year-old black French phonetics professor named Pierre. The *Guess* scenario occurs roughly 300 pages into a 360-page novel, so the rest of the narrative is sustained by frequent flashbacks to the 1980s, when Niamh was a teenager growing up in London struggling to assert herself against her parents'—and especially her father's—insistence that their children be "Irish." Like in the film, there is a fourteen-year age gap between Pierre and Niamh; the couple propose to marry swiftly and move to Vancouver (it is Geneva in the film); the O'Flahertys have a priest friend who urges Niamh's father, Mick, to welcome Pierre into the family (Father Hogan in *Whose Life?* and Monsignor Ryan in *Guess*); Mick gathers the concerned parties in a room to communicate his eventual acceptance of the union and recalls "the way I felt about [my wife] Annie when we first met," just as in the film, Mrs. Prentice reminds Matt Drayton of what it is like to be young and in love (Moriarty 2008, 355). Finally, and most strikingly, Mick reports overhearing Pierre say to his father that Mick sees "him as a black man while [he sees himself] simply as a man" (354), which is exactly what John tells *his* father in *Guess Who's Coming to Dinner.*

Whose Life Is It Anyway?—like Moriarty's other novels—sits squarely in the "chick lit" tradition, a genre that has thrived both in Ireland and globally since the mid-1990s. Interestingly, the rise of Irish chick lit coincides with Ireland's economic boom and, for Ruadhán Mac Cormaic, is "the one genre that has tried to engage with the fast-track shifts of the Celtic Tiger years" (2007b, 15). This point may be attributed, perhaps, to the fact that chick-lit novels espouse a kind of neoliberal selfhood that accords rather neatly with the very economic policies that fueled Celtic Tiger–ism in the second half of the 1990s (Garner 2007b, 113). Or, put another way, one of the defining characteristics of chick lit also became one of the defining characteristics of Celtic Tiger Ireland: consumption, especially of the conspicuous variety. However, even in chick lit, according to Mac Cormaic, "migrants are invisible" (2007b, 15). In this respect, Moriarty's novel is interesting. She does engage with the issue of black immigration to Ireland. However, her fictional representative of black immigration is a middle-class, European-born and -raised man of African Caribbean descent rather than a refugee or asylum seeker from continental Africa. Nonetheless, a novel that dramatizes the marriage of a white woman of Irish descent to a non-Irish black immigrant to Ireland inevitably draws attention to the possibility of relationships between white Irish and nonwhite "New Irish," even as it scrupulously avoids the subject by displacing the familial conflict to London. If, as I argue in previous chapters, one of the most powerful analogies circulating in Celtic Tiger Ireland was the one between returned Irish emigrant and nonwhite immigrant, Moriarty's novel marries the two to one another.

The differences between Niamh and Pierre are not just "racial" but encompass the categories of class (though university educated, Niamh comes from a decidedly blue-collar background; Pierre's father and mother are, respectively, a university professor and an interior designer), age (a fourteen-year age gap), and religion (Niamh was raised Catholic; Pierre is agnostic). For the reader to accept the probability of an attraction between the two, therefore, Moriarty must subordinate these differences to Niamh's and Pierre's similarities, the two most important of which are: first, their status as, simultaneously, European *and* postcolonial subjects and, second, their views on gender. When Pierre and Niamh first meet, their difference from each other—and from the people who surround them in their Dublin setting—is registered in terms of their accents rather than their complexions. Pierre "doesn't sound French" because he moved to Oxford when he was ten years old (Moriarty 2008, 4); Niamh speaks English "with an English-Irish accent peppered with Irish sayings" because she grew up in London, the daughter of Irish parents (8). (It is only after this exchange that Pierre refers to his "tan" [8]—their racial difference from one another.) What Pierre and Niamh have in common, then, is their "mongrel" status as, simultaneously, European *and* postcolonial subjects: Niamh is the daughter of white Irish parents who, lacking opportunities in Ireland, emigrated to London in the 1960s; Pierre's parents are from Martinique, who, lacking opportunities there, emigrated to France (8).

Second, although there is no place in the novel for racial essentialism, Niamh makes a career out of perpetuating gender essentialism. Examples of Niamh's newspaper columns, on topics such as "what men want to say to women but are afraid to," men's and women's contrasting "bathroom habits," "shoe shopping," and "packing" rituals are interspersed throughout the novel. Indeed, it is Pierre's enjoyment of one of Niamh's columns that leads to their being introduced. The *racial* difference between Niamh and Pierre is overcome or neutralized by their common belief in the innate "difference between men and women," the title of the column that Pierre finds so amusing and leads to their being introduced (3). Just as Susan Courtney is concerned that *Guess Who's Coming to Dinner* can tolerate "the opening up of former restricted racial institutions only by refortifying sexual ones," so the same critique could be applied to Moriarty's novel. After all, Niamh willingly gives up her job at the *Irish Daily News* in order to facilitate the advancement of her fiancé's career in Canada.

At times, Moriarty appears to write with tongue firmly in cheek. She, through Niamh, seems to recognize that the diametric opposition Mick clings to between Irish ("authentic") and global ("inauthentic") is a thorough fallacy. "I was only allowed watch *Top of the Pops*," Niamh declares, "when Foster and Allen were on it in their leprechaun suits with my father howling along to 'A Bunch of Thyme'" (Moriarty 2008, 41). Moriarty could not have chosen a *less* authentic example of Irish music, which suggests that she does so very self-consciously. The duo caused quite a furor when they appeared on *Top of the Pops* in March 1982 dressed in green velvet, white ruffles, and black shoe buckles, a move that was perceived as pandering to degrading British and American stereotypes of Irishness (Courtney 2000, 12). Indeed, the trappings of Irishness that Mick so values—"We had a tricolour hanging from a flagpole in our garden, the hedge was cut in the shape of a shamrock, we had leprechaun gnomes with fishing-rods sitting around the pond and the doorbell was set to the tune of 'Danny Boy'" (37)—are almost all American fabrications.

Despite troubling these notions of authentic-inauthentic, Moriarty does not ridicule them or their most vocal mouthpiece, Mick. To do so would be to lampoon the driving conflict of the novel: whether Mick will accept his son-in-law even though he is not "authentically" Irish (white, Catholic). It is more likely that Moriarty emphasizes Mick's inauthentic authenticity in order to suggest the extent to which the Irish diaspora is invested in romanticized fantasies of the homeland. As one reviewer puts it, the O'Flaherty clan is "more 'Oirish' than the Irish" themselves (Looby 2008, 10). This point is certainly salient. As I note in the introduction, David Lloyd has argued that the very term *diaspora* is connotative of Irish Americans' "sentimental and fetishizing desire to establish their genealogy in the old country" and, as such, thoroughly depoliticizes the social and historical reality of emigration (1999, 102).

However, this strategy in Moriarty's novel produces two troubling effects. First, it projects Irish racism onto the diaspora, effectively absolving the Irish in Ireland of any culpability. In this respect, the novel echoes the problematic logic of Declan Kiberd's claim that "while Phil Lynott was being acclaimed in Dublin as the inventor of Celtic Rock, over in Boston the lace-curtain Irish who voted for the Kennedys were also quite capable of refusing to share buses and schools with black neighbours" (Longley and Kiberd 2001, 48). It is significant that the eventual meetings between Pierre and Niamh's aunt, sister, and parents take place in London, although Niamh's mother visits Dublin after the pair have already moved in together. The only member of the O'Flaherty clan to meet Pierre in Dublin is her brother, Finn. At no stage in the novel are readers informed of the couple being the object of racial abuse in Dublin, where they live. In a country whose population is only 1 percent black, it is reasonable to suggest that in the late 1990s, a black-white interracial couple would still raise some eyebrows, even in "cosmopolitan" and "multicultural" Dublin (Moriarty 2008, 294, 314). The second problem with this strategy is that it makes Irish diasporic racism a function of Irish diasporic subjects' postcolonial displacement, effectively absolving the diaspora of its participation in structures of white power abroad. In other words, what this novel tells readers is that the Irish in Ireland are not racist; the Irish abroad *are* racist, but this fact can be attributed more to an insularity forged as a consequence of having to settle in a foreign country than a seemingly unquestioning acceptance of the racial hierarchies embedded in the social and legal institutions of their host countries.

It may be significant that Pierre and Niamh move to Vancouver at the end of the novel, for Canada has had, since 1982, an official policy of multiculturalism and boasts one of the world's most diverse populations. In Toronto, the Indian Irish protagonist of Emma Donoghue's *Landing* feels, for the first time in years, "visually unremarkable" so full is the city of "Indian and Sri Lankan and Bangladeshi faces" (2007, 250). It is interesting to consider the possibilities that Canada represents as a model for Irish multiculturalism, for several critics find the US multicultural model extremely deficient. Kiberd, for example, cites Arthur Schlesinger's *Disuniting of America* (1991) to bolster his claim that in the United States, "multiculturalism has posed a problem" (Longley and Kiberd 2001, 56). In *Landing,* Síle O'Shaughnessy is a thirty-nine-year-old flight attendant who meets twenty-five-year-old Jude Turner, an Anglo-Canadian from Ireland, Ontario, aboard one of her transatlantic flights. An epistolary romance—punctuated by infrequent transatlantic visits—develops between the two, and, after a year, Síle decides to take voluntary redundancy from her job, sell her house in Dublin, and move to Canada to be with Jude. *Landing* provides an interesting twist on the "historical duty" argument that animates much of the cultural production discussed in this book. Here, it is not only the memory of *Irish* emigration that is evoked by Donoghue in relation to contemporary immigration, but also the imperfect memory of the experiences of Síle's, and her older sister Orla's, mother as an *Indian* immigrant to Ireland in the 1970s.

On the one hand, Donoghue suggests that such memory has the potential to generate a radical, politically active form of empathy for more recent arrivals to Ireland. Certainly, it is the case for Orla, who runs a drop-in center for new immigrants called Ireland of the Welcomes and rails against the 2004 referendum on Irish citizenship (Donoghue 2007, 188). On the other hand, the influx of immigrants to Ireland has virtually no impact on Síle, except insofar as she is "not the only brown face anymore," and "compared to the women in chadors [she] hardly look[s] foreign at all" (35). Immigration to Ireland affects her only to the extent that she is less racially "other" than she had previously been. Indeed, Síle's narcissism confirms the concerns I have expressed throughout this book regarding the potential of mixed-race subjects to challenge Irish whiteness. Even though Síle is a nonwhite, mixed-race Irish subject, she does not destabilize white Irish norms. She is even slightly scornful of her sister's efforts, finding the name of the drop-in center "unfortunately soupy" (79).

In contrast to her sister's preoccupation with the psychic, economic, and political effects of immigration, Síle sees herself as a transnational subject, a "nomad" (123) unencumbered by roots: "Flying's in my blood," she tells Jude in an e-mail, "because I was born at 30,000 feet" (67). All of Síle's Celtic Tiger friends are migrant cosmopolites: Marcus is a well-traveled Englishman who has lived in Ireland for several years; his lover, Pedro Valdez, is from Barcelona; Jael traveled extensively before returning to Ireland, marrying and "blagging" her way into public relations (42). What distinguishes Síle and her friends from the people who frequent her sister's drop-in center is their class positioning. Whereas most of these migrants are obliged to become mobile because of economic *necessity*, Síle and her friends are mobile because of economic *privilege*. When Síle books Jude on a flight to Ireland so they can attend a friend's wedding together, Jude objects to Síle's having spent eight hundred euros on a seat she had claimed was "an amazing Web bargain": "It cost me no more than a couple of good pairs of shoes," Síle tells Jude, "and god knows, I don't need any more shoes" (226).

Síle's global mobility as an Irish citizen, as reinforced by her career as a flight attendant, and her difference from the migrants with whom her sister works, serves as a reminder that Dublin Airport has become a highly charged symbol of Fortress Ireland, as we have already seen in relation to Donal O'Kelly's *"The Cambria"* (2005). Indeed, competing discourses of Irish entitlement (to travel and settle wherever they want, to deny others admission to Ireland) and Irish victimhood (when other countries exercise *their* right not to admit Irish people) become solidified during airport encounters. In 2006, Irish actor Rúaidhrí Conroy made headlines when he was refused entry to the United States because he overstayed a visa granted in 1998. One of the stars of the short film *Six Shooter* (Martin McDonagh, 2004), Conroy was en route to the Academy Awards ceremony, where the film was nominated for, and won, the Oscar for Best Live Action Short Film. In his acceptance speech, McDonagh commiserated with the absent Conroy, expressing his hope that he could be there "next time, if they let you into the country." In June 2009, two Irishmen— a "former Cork county senior hurler and his cousin"—were "placed in chains and forced to spend the night in a maximum security US [*sic*] prison in Boston," after having been stopped by Department of Homeland Security, Customs, and Border Protection officials (Downes 2009, 5). In a bizarre article by John Downes in the *Sunday Tribune,* Jonathon O'Callaghan's status as a hurler is repeatedly stated and highlighted by an accompanying photograph of him posing with a hurley stick. The article also notes that O'Callaghan had "previously been refused permission to enter the country" and that he works "in construction," encodings that point to the likelihood of O'Callaghan's having overstayed a vacation visa in order to work (illegally) in the United States on a previous occasion.

In these cases, the subjects' violation of the conditions of previously granted visas (admitted in the first, implied in the second) is the actual or likely reason for their having been denied entry to the United States. By way of contrast with what the O'Callaghans endured in Boston, Downes points to the case of three Texan backpackers refused entry to and deported from Ireland on July 3, who were subsequently offered "an all-expenses-paid trip from the D4hotels group" to encourage them to return (Healy 2009, n.p.). However, Downes fails to mention that the hotel group's response occurred in the context of concerns expressed by Tourism Ireland over the treatment of prospective tourists by the Garda National Immigration Bureau at Dublin Airport. It is difficult to imagine that the hotel group would have responded in this manner if the tourists had originated from destinations other than a country upon which Ireland's tourist industry relies heavily. Indeed, no comparable offer was made in September 2008 when a Nigerian Catholic priest in possession of a valid tourist visa was arrested, strip-searched, and brought to Cloverhill Prison upon arrival at Dublin Airport. He was released only after the Nigerian ambassador to Ireland offered guarantees on his behalf.

Síle's conception of immigration is based on her understanding of her mother's experience. As far as Síle is concerned, Sunita Pillay, also a flight attendant, met her father on a flight, they fell in love and married, and Sunita converted to Catholicism and moved in Ireland. When Orla and Síle were five and three, respectively, Sunita, a diabetes sufferer, died of hypoglycemia. For Síle, therefore, emigration, romance, and tragedy are intimately linked. If Síle's (mis)construction of her mother's immigrant experience is based on appearances and surfaces, it reflects her more general outlook on emigration. When Síle, walking along Grafton Street, is handed a flyer for Ireland of the Welcomes, she is "darkly amused" that her dark skin makes her a target. But apart from this response, her only reaction is to make "a note to tell Orla that whoever wrote her leaflets couldn't spell *adjustment*" (Donoghue 2007, 247). When Síle and Jude meet in New York City and take a trip to Ellis Island, Síle asks Jude to pose alongside some "unclaimed baggage" and "look sad" for a photo opportunity (259). It is not until Síle decides to emigrate herself that her sympathy for others is awakened. She recalls her father telling her of "Indian women, coming to join their fiancés in Britain, having to submit to virginity tests at Heathrow" and one of Orla's Nigerian clients who had "just had a backstreet abortion because she was terrified to go to England for a legal one while her application for asylum in Ireland was pending" (299).

However, unlike Orla, whose understanding of their mother's unhappiness encourages her to look outward and identify with the plight of others in similar circumstances or worse (as Luke Gibbons has suggested is possible), Síle's empathy is directed inward. It translates into the kind that Elizabeth Spelman condemns and one that, as I note in chapter 3, Ronan Noone's play also encourages: "I acknowledge your suffering only to the extent to which it promises to bring attention to my own" (quoted in Davis 2004, 407). Síle's "suffering"—the bureaucratic form filling that is required in order to apply for permanent residency in Canada—does not compare with the indignities, violations, and dangers of the cases cited above. Nonetheless, when she reports the challenges of form filling to Jude, her girlfriend tells her, "This reminds me of the Irish ships arriving at Quebec in the 1840s . . . the terror of the dirty, disease-spreading immigrants" (Donoghue 2007, 284), thereby closing the circle between the narratives of "historical duty" and Irish victimhood on which I insist throughout this book. Only Orla appears to recognize that *privilege* separates Síle from both contemporary immigrants *to* Ireland and nineteenth-century emigrants *from* Ireland. "Why don't you just buy a Porsche?" Orla asks Síle after a conversation about her sister's decision to emigrate. "You've got every other symptom of a classic midlife crisis" (292).

Jude's evocation of Grosse Ile is actually the culmination of a discourse of victimhood that pervades the novel, for Síle, her friend Marcus, and, to a lesser extent, Jude all imagine themselves to be victims because of the demands of being in a long-distance relationship. At one point, Síle presses "her face to Jude's small breasts, and roar[s], 'I demand asylum from a harsh world! I claim this as my true homeland!'" (192). Of his failed relationship with Pedro, Marcus says, "If love's a country, there's no such thing as a permanent visa. Deportation without notice" (307). Bizarrely, Donoghue herself—who, for the most part, positions her third-person narrator at a clear distance from Síle's affectations (232, 292)—appears to participate in this problematic elision of romantic self-indulgence and the denial of political rights to asylum seekers by including article 13 (2) from the Universal Declaration of Human Rights as an epigraph to the chapter entitled "Home Base," which describes Síle's first visit to Ireland, Ontario, to see Jude. Each of the twenty-five chapters has an epigraph, but this one is the only example that is so explicitly political. "Everyone has the right to leave any country, including his own, and to return to his country," the epigraph reads (111). Even Jude, who has a more nuanced conception of emigration because of her job as an archivist at a local museum, is given to the odd poor-me outburst. Jude claims, "I almost think it was better in the old days— simpler, anyway—when you just waved good-bye to the ship or train, pulled your shawl over your head and got on with surviving" (261).

The final straw for Síle is a revelation Orla makes just before Síle's planned definitive departure for Canada: her suspicion that their mother's death was a deliberate act of diabetic noncompliance. Síle is finally confronted with the possibility that her mother was simply one of many "depressed immigrants" who committed suicide (309). She wants "to wail aloud for Sunita Pillay, glamorous Air India stew, who'd swapped everything she'd known for a rain-green Dublin suburb: followed her man, gone into exile, surrendered her country and family and friends in the best tradition of womanhood. Who'd done it all for love, and discovered that love wasn't enough after all" (311). In an important book published in the mid-1990s, Benjamin DeMott critiques what he terms the "friendship orthodoxy" in American culture, whereby amity and "affirmative civility" between blacks and whites is put forth as the solution to racial inequality. The problem with this position, according to DeMott, is that "the evolution of the ideal color-blind society is imagined to occur more within feelings than in response to policy change" (1995, 35). Because Síle's understanding of her mother's experience as an immigrant is based entirely on "feelings" (love and romance), she is blind to the social and economic realities of emigration.

"When we were at college," Orla asks of Síle, "didn't it seem like everyone we knew was moving to New York or Brussels? But then the minute the Boom happened, most of them came rushing home. You've picked an odd moment to leave, I must say; you're pushing against the tide" (Donoghue 2007, 292). If *Landing* had been published only slightly later, Síle's move might not have seemed so "odd," though her motives (economics over romance?) might very well have been different. Indeed, the program of redundancies introduced by her airline, and the union mandate to strike as a result, foreshadows an Irish unemployment rate that rose to 13 percent in 2009 and the widespread labor unrest that accompanied it (246). If there is a return to the "bad old days" of high unemployment and emigration, how will it be captured in the cultural imagination? How will the relationship between the two types of "New Irish" be complicated by such developments? Will Roddy Doyle write a short story, entitled "The Departees," about a demographic comprising *both* white Irish-born and non-Irish subjects who leave Ireland to seek employment elsewhere? What new meanings will the term *other people's diasporas* take on? Will writers, dramatists, comics, and filmmakers continue to find in the Grand Narrative of Irish transatlantic emigration rich terrain on which to map their contemporary concerns? If so, what will the racial, political, and ethical implications of such engagements be?

Works Cited ✌ *Index*

Works Cited

"About Arambe." 2009. Arambe Productions. July 21. http://www.arambe
    productions.com/.

"About Calypso." 2009. Calypso Productions. Aug. 6. http://homepage
    .eircom.net/~calypso/about.html.

"About Us." 2008. *Metro Éireann*. Apr. 19. http://www.metroeireann.com
    /index.php?option=com_content&task=view&id=25&Itemid=45&limit
    =1&limitstart=1.

Allen, Kieran. 2007. "Neo-liberalism and Immigration." In *Immigration
    and Social Change in the Republic of Ireland,* edited by Bryan Fan-
    ning, 84–98. Manchester: Manchester Univ. Press.

Almeida, Linda Dowling. 2001. *Irish Immigrants in New York City,
    1945–1995.* Bloomington: Indiana Univ. Press.

Alvarez, Lizette. 2005. "Suddenly Rich, Poor Old Ireland Seems Bewil-
    dered." *New York Times,* Feb. 2, late edition, A4.

Anderson, Benedict. 1991. *Imagined Communities: Reflections on the
    Origin and Spread of Nationalism.* London: Verso.

"Are You Right There, Father Ted?" In *Father Ted: The Complete Third
    Series,* written by Graham Linehan and Arthur Mathews and directed
    by Andy de Emmony. DVD. Video Collection International.

Armitage, David. 2001. "The Red Atlantic." *Reviews in American History*
    29: 479–86.

Auslander, Philip. 1997. *From Acting to Performance: Essays in Modern-
    ism and Postmodernism.* Abingdon: Routledge.

Babb, Valerie. 1998. *Whiteness Visible: The Meaning of Whiteness in
    American Literature and Culture.* New York: New York Univ. Press.

Barton, Ruth. 1997. "From History to Heritage: Some Recent Develop-
    ments in Irish Cinema." *Irish Review* 21: 41–56.

———. 2002. *Jim Sheridan: Framing the Nation.* Dublin: Liffey Press.

———. 2006. *Acting Irish in Hollywood: From Fitzgerald to Farrell.* Dublin: Irish Academic Press.

Baucom, Ian. 2000. "Found Drowned: The Irish Atlantic." In *Victorian Afterlife: Postmodern Culture Rewrites the Nineteenth Century,* edited by John Kucich and Dianne Sadoff, 125–56. Minneapolis: Univ. of Minnesota Press.

Beltrán, Mary, and Camilla Fojas. 2008. Introduction to *Mixed Race Hollywood,* edited by Mary Beltrán and Camilla Fojas, 1–20. New York: New York Univ. Press.

Berzon, Judith. 1978. *Neither White nor Black: The Mulatto Character in American Fiction.* New York: New York Univ. Press.

Binchy, Maeve. 1998. *Tara Road.* London: Orion.

Biressi, Anita, and Heather Nunn. 2005. *Reality TV: Realism and Revelation.* London: Wallflower Press.

Blight, David W. 2002. *Beyond the Battlefield: Race, Memory, and the American Civil War.* Amherst: Amherst Univ. Press.

Bogle, Donald. 2001. *Toms, Coons, Mulattoes, Mammies, and Bucks: An Interpretative History of Blacks in American Films.* New York: Continuum.

Bolger, Dermot. 1993. Foreword to *Ireland in Exile: Irish Writers Abroad,* edited by Dermot Bolger and introduced by Joseph O'Connor, 7–10. Dublin: New Island Books.

Bolster, W. Jeffrey. 1997. *Black Jacks: African American Seamen in the Age of Sail.* Cambridge, MA: Harvard Univ. Press.

Booker, M. Keith. 1997. "Late Capitalism Comes to Dublin: 'American' Popular Culture in the Novels of Roddy Doyle." *Ariel: A Review of International English Literature* 28, no. 3: 27–45.

Boseley, Sarah. 2001. "Warning of Killer Diseases: Virus Attack WHO Tells West to Prepare for Terrorists Using Deadly Agents." *Guardian,* Sept. 26. http://www.guardian.co.uk/uk_news/story/0,,558245,00.html.

Bost, Suzanne. 2005. *Mulattas and Mestizas: Representing Mixed Identities in the Americas, 1850–2000.* Athens: Univ. of Georgia Press.

Boyd, Brian. 1991. "Off the Bar-Stool." *Independent,* Mar. 18, 15.

Brady, Conor. 1998. "A Welcome Here?" *Irish Times,* Apr. 20, 15.

"Brady: We've Become Land of 'Stocks and Shares.'" 2007. *Irish Examiner,* Aug. 23. http://archives.tcm.ie/irishexaminer/2007/08/23/story40666.asp.

Brannigan, John. 2009. *Race in Modern Irish Literature and Culture.* Edinburgh: Edinburgh Univ. Press.

Brennan, Georgina. 2002. "The Chieftains Hold New York's Hand." *Irish America* (Dec.–Jan.): 20.

Brennock, Mark. 2004. "'Citizenship Tourists' a Tiny Group, Statistics Indicate." *Irish Times,* Apr. 22, 1.

Brown, Sterling A. 1933. "Negro Character as Seen by White Authors." *Journal of Negro Education* 2, no. 2: 179–203.

Browning, Barbara. 1998. *Infectious Rhythm: Metaphors of Contagion and the Spread of African Culture.* New York: Routledge.

Buckley, Karen. 2009. "Back in the Dole Queue—after 20 Years." *Irish Independent,* Feb. 7, "Weekend Review," 4.

Burke, Mary. 2009. "Writing of a Different Country." *Irish Literary Supplement: A Review of Irish Books* 28, no. 2: 14.

Carby, Hazel V. 1987. *Reconstructing Womanhood: The Emergence of the Afro-American Woman Novelist.* New York: Oxford Univ. Press.

———. 2001. "What Is This 'Black' in Irish Popular Culture?" *European Journal of Cultural Studies* 4, no. 3: 325–49.

Casey, Natasha. 2002. "*Riverdance:* The Importance of Being Irish American." *New Hibernia Review* 6, no. 4: 9–25.

Castle, Terry. 1986. *Masquerade and Civilization: Carnivalesque in Eighteenth-Century English Culture and Fiction.* Stanford, CA: Stanford Univ. Press.

"Census 2006: Non-Irish Nationals Living in Ireland." 2008. http://www.cso.ie/releasespublications/documents/population/non-irish/pages1-22.pdf. Cork: Central Statistics Office.

"Census 2006: Principal Demographic Results." 2007. http://www.cso.ie/census/Census2006_Principal_Demographic_Results.htm. Dublin: Central Statistics Office.

Chan, Suzanna. 2006. "'Kiss My Royal Irish Ass': Contesting Identity: Visual Culture, Gender, Whiteness, and Diaspora." *Journal of Gender Studies* 15, no. 1: 1–17.

Chude-Sokei, Louis. 2006. *The Last "Darky": Bert Williams, Black-on-Black Minstrelsy, and the African Diaspora.* Durham, NC: Duke Univ. Press.

Clarke, Donald. 2007. "Gerard Butler: Irish or Swedish, Asks Donald Clarke." *Irish Times,* Dec. 21, "Ticket," 32.

Cleary, Joe. 2003. "'Misplaced Ideas'? Colonialism, Location, and Dislocation in Irish Studies." In *Ireland and Postcolonial Theory,* edited by Clare Carroll and Patricia King, 16–45. Cork: Cork Univ. Press.

Cohen, Robin. 1997. *Global Diasporas: An Introduction.* Florence, KY: Routledge.

Coleman, Marc. 2008. "Total Immersion Is Critical If Irish Is to Be Rescued." *Sunday Independent,* Apr. 13. http://www.independent.ie/opinion /analysis/total-immersion-is-critical-if-irish-is-to-be-rescued-1346149 .html.

Connolly, Claire. 2003. "The Turn to the Map: Cartographic Fictions in Irish Culture." In *Éire/Land,* edited by Vera Kreilkamp, 27–35. Boston: McMullen Museum of Art.

Corcoran, Jody. 2007. "Why Racism and Violence Cannot Be Tolerated on Any GAA Pitch." *Sunday Independent,* July 1. http://www.independent .ie/opinion/analysis/why-racism-and-violence-cannot-be-tolerated-on -any-gaa-pitch-892479.html.

Corcoran, Mary P. 2003. "The Process of Migration and the Reinvention of Self: The Experiences of Returning Irish Emigrants." In *New Directions in Irish-American History,* edited by Kevin Kenny, 302–18. Madison: Univ. of Wisconsin Press.

Corrigan, Conn. 2008. "Young Irish Drifting Back to US." *Irish Times,* Oct. 18, "Weekend Review," 2.

———. 2009. "Taking to the Streets of New York with Pride." *Irish Times,* Feb. 28, "Weekend Review," 5.

Coulter, Colin. 2003. "The End of Irish History? An Introduction." In *End of Irish History? Critical Approaches to the Celtic Tiger,* edited by Colin Coulter, 1–33. Manchester: Manchester Univ. Press.

Courtney, Kevin. 2000. "Still on Thyme." *Irish Times,* Nov. 3, 12.

Craig, Patricia. 2007. "A Commitment to Tolerance." *Sunday Tribune,* Sept. 16, "Magazine," 18.

Critchley, Simon. 2002. *On Humour.* London: Routledge.

Cronin, Mike, and Daryl Adair. 2002. *The Wearing of the Green: A History of St. Patrick's Day.* Abingdon: Routledge.

Crosson, Seán. 2008a. "'The Hurley Is the New Chainsaw': Hurling and Horror in Contemporary Irish Cinema." Paper presented at "Home and Elsewhere: The Spaces of Irish Writing," the conference of the International

Association for the Study of Irish Literatures, University of Porto, Portugal, July 28–Aug. 1.

———. 2008b. "'They Can't Wipe Us Out, They Can't Lick Us. We'll Go on Forever Pa, 'Cause We're the People': Misrepresenting Death in Jim Sheridan's *In America* (2003)." *Estudios Irlandeses* 3: 65–71.

Cullingford, Elizabeth Butler. 2001. *Ireland's Others: Gender and Ethnicity in Irish Literature and Popular Culture.* Cork: Cork Univ. Press, 2001.

Davis, Kimberly Chabot. 2004. "Oprah's Book Club and the Politics of Cross-Racial Empathy." *International Journal of Cultural Studies* 7, no. 4: 399–419.

DeMott, Benjamin. 1995. *The Trouble with Friendship: Why Americans Can't Think Straight about Race.* New York: Atlantic Monthly.

Dentith, Simon. 1994. *Bakhtinian Thought: An Introductory Reader.* Florence, KY: Routledge.

Des Bishop: Live at Vicar St. 2005a. DVD. RMG Entertainment.

Des Bishop Live. 2005b. DVD. RTÉ.

The Des Bishop Work Experience. 2004. Produced by Tom Johnson and Aisling Milton. DVD. EMI Music Ireland.

Devlin, Martina. 2007. "Now We All Want to Be Like the Big Spender Himself, Flatley." *Irish Independent,* Aug. 30. http://www.independent.ie/opinion/columnists/martina-devlin/now-we-all-want-to-be-like-the-big-spender-himself-flatley-1068240.html.

Dixon, Stephen, and Deirdre Falvey. 1999. *Gift of the Gag: The Explosion in Irish Comedy.* Belfast: Blackstaff.

Docker, John. 1994. *Postmodernism and Popular Culture: A Cultural History.* Cambridge: Cambridge Univ. Press.

Donoghue, Emma. 2007. *Landing.* Florida: Harcourt.

Douglas, Mary. 1999. *Implicit Meanings: Essays in Anthropology.* London: Routledge.

Douglass, Frederick. 1849. "Gavitt's Original Ethiopian Serenaders." *North Star,* June 29. http://www.iath.virginia.edu/utc/minstrel/miar03at.html.

———. 1979. "American Prejudice Against Color: An Address Delivered in Cork, Ireland, October 23, 1845." In vol. 1 of *The Frederick Douglass Papers: Series One—Speeches, Debates, and Interviews,* edited by John Blassingame et al. New Haven, CT: Yale University Press.

———. 1994. *Autobiographies: Narrative of the Life, My Bondage, and My Freedom, Life, and Times*. Edited by Henry Louis Gates Jr. New York: Library of America.

Downes, John. 2009. "Hurler and Cousin 'Treated Like Terrorists' by US Customs." *Sunday Tribune*, July 19, 5.

Doyle, Laura. 1994. *Bordering on the Body: The Racial Matrix of Modern Fiction and Culture*. New York: Oxford Univ. Press.

Doyle, Roddy. 1987. *The Commitments*. London: Vintage.

———. 1991. *The Snapper*. London: Vintage.

———. 1992. *The Van*. London: Vintage.

———. 2000. *A Star Called Henry*. New York: Penguin.

———. 2004. *Oh, Play That Thing*. London: Jonathan Cape.

———. 2006. "Green Yodel No. 1." In *Re-imagining Ireland*, edited by Andrew Higgins Wyndham, 69–71. Charlottesville: Univ. Press of Virginia.

———. 2007a. *The Deportees*. London: Jonathan Cape.

———. 2007b. *Paula Spencer*. London: Vintage.

———. 2010. *The Dead Republic*. London: Jonathan Cape.

Drew, April. 2008. "In the Name of the Bishop." *Irish Voice*, Jan. 16. http://www.irishabroad.com/news/irishvoice/news/Articles/In-the-Name-of-the-Bishop190108.aspx.

DuBois, W. E .B. 1990. *The Souls of Black Folk*. New York: Library of America.

Dudgeon, W. 2007. "Illegal Niceties." Letters to the editor. *Irish Times*, Mar. 22, 19.

Duggan, Keith. 2006. "Perilous Times of the Black Pearl." *Irish Times*, Nov. 18, "Weekend," 11.

Dunbar, Paul Laurence. 1969. *The Sport of Gods*. New York: Arno.

Dwyer, Ciara. 2003. "A Simple, Superb Story of Life, Love, and Loss." *Sunday Independent*, Oct. 26. http://www.independent.ie/entertainment/film-cinema/a-simple-superb-story-of-life-love-and-loss-496074.html.

Dwyer, Michael. 2004. "Sheridan: 'It Puts the Picture Right Up There Now.'" *Irish Times*, Jan. 28, 16.

Dyer, Richard. 1999. *White: Essays on Race and Culture*. Abingdon: Routledge.

Eagan, Catherine M. 2006. "Still 'Black' and 'Proud': Irish America and the Racial Politics of Hibernophilia." In *The Irish in Us: Irishness,*

Performativity, and Popular Culture, edited by Diane Negra, 20–63. Durham, NC: Duke Univ. Press.

Eagleton, Terry. 1996. *Heathcliff and the Great Hunger: Studies in Irish Culture.* London: Verso.

———. 2003. "Another Country." Review of *Star of the Sea,* by Joseph O'Connor. *Guardian,* Jan. 25. http://books.guardian.co.uk/review/story /0,12084,880838,00.html.

Edwards, Elaine. 2008. "FG Creating 'Resentment' on Immigration— Lenihan." *Irish Times,* Sept. 5. http://www.irishtimes.com/newspaper /breaking/2008/0905/breaking56.html.

Estevez-Saá, José Manuel. 2005. "An Interview with Joseph O'Connor." *Contemporary Literature* 46, no. 2: vi, 161–75.

Faulkner, William. 1993. *Light in August.* London: Picador.

Ferreira, Patricia. 2001. "Frederick Douglass in Ireland: The Dublin Edition of His *Narrative.*" *New Hibernia Review* 5, no. 1: 53–67.

The Field. 1990. Directed by Jim Sheridan. DVD. Cinema Club.

Fincham, Kelly. 2001. "A Darker Shade of Green." *Irish America* (Apr.– May): 22–25.

Fitting In. 2006. Performed by Des Bishop. DVD. Peer Pressure.

Fitz-Simon, Christopher, and Sanford Sternlicht. 1996. Introduction to vol. 1 of *New Plays from the Abbey Theatre, 1993–1995,* edited and introduced by Christopher Fitz-Simon and Sanford Sternlicht, ix–xxiv. Syracuse, NY: Syracuse Univ. Press.

Foner, Philip S., ed. 1975. *The Life and Writings of Frederick Douglass.* Vol. 1. New York: International.

Foner, Philip S., and Yuval Taylor, eds. 1999. *Frederick Douglass: Selected Speeches and Writings.* Chicago: Chicago Review.

Fottrell, Quentin. 2009. "Give Up Your Oul' Sins? Go Ahead, Minister, Make My Day." *Irish Times,* Feb. 21. http://www.irishtimes.com/newspaper /weekend/2009/0221/1224241563372.html.

Foucault, Michel. 1986. "Of Other Spaces." *Diacritics* 16, no. 1: 22–27.

Fraiberg, Allison. 1994. "Between the Laughter: Bridging Feminist Studies Through Women's Stand-Up Comedy." In *Look Who's Laughing: Gender and Comedy,* edited by Gail Finney, 315–34. Langhorne, PA: Gordon and Breach.

Frederick Douglass agus na Negroes Bána. Dir. John J. Doherty. Dublin: Camel Productions.

Freud, Sigmund. 1960. *Jokes and Their Relation to the Unconscious*. Translated by James Strachey. London: Routledge and Kegan Paul.

Friel, Brian. 2005. *The Home Place*. London: Faber and Faber.

Gaffney, Maureen. 2007. "What's the Craic?" *Irish Times*, Aug. 25, "Magazine," 10.

Gangs of New York. 2002. Dir. Martin Scorsese. DVD. Miramax.

Gantz, Jeffrey. 2002. "Alien Nation: Ronan Noone Blows Back In." *Boston Phoenix*, Dec. 12–19. http://www.bostonphoenix.com/boston/arts/theater/documents/02580300.htm.

Garman, Bryan K. 2000. *A Race of Singers: Whitman's Working-Class Hero from Guthrie to Springsteen*. Chapel Hill: Univ. of North Carolina Press.

Garner, Steve. 2004. *Racism in the Irish Experience*. London: Pluto.

———. 2006. "The Uses of Whiteness: What Sociologists Working on Europe Can Draw from US Research on Whiteness." *Sociology* 40, no. 2: 257–75.

———. 2007a. "Babies, Bodies, and Entitlement: Gendered Aspects of Access to Citizenship in the Republic of Ireland." *Parliamentary Affairs* 60, no. 3: 437–51.

———. 2007b. "Ireland and Immigration: Explaining the Absence of the Far Right." *Patterns of Prejudice* 41, no. 2: 109–30.

Gibbons, Luke. 1996. *Transformations in Irish Culture*. Cork: Cork Univ. Press.

———. 2002. "The Global Cure? History, Therapy, and the Celtic Tiger." In *Reinventing Ireland: Culture, Society, and the Global Economy*, edited by Peadar Kirby, Luke Gibbons, and Michael Cronin, 89–106. London: Pluto.

———. 2005a. "Projecting the Nation: Cinema and Culture." In *The Cambridge Companion to Modern Irish Culture*, edited by Joe Cleary and Claire Connolly, 206–24. Cambridge: Cambridge Univ. Press.

———. 2005b. "'We Knew Their Plight Well': Race and Immigration in Some Recent Irish Films." *Third Text* 19, no. 5: 555–66.

———. 2006a. "Beyond the Pale: Race, Ethnicity, and Irish Culture." In *Re-imagining Ireland*, edited by Andrew Higgins Wyndham, 49–68. Charlottesville: Univ. Press of Virginia.

———. 2006b. *The Quiet Man*. Cork: Cork Univ. Press.

Gillespie, Michael Patrick. 2008a. *The Myth of an Irish Cinema: Approaching Irish-Themed Films*. Syracuse, NY: Syracuse Univ. Press.

———. 2008b. "The Odyssey of *Adam and Paul*: A Twenty-First-Century Irish Film." *New Hibernia Review* 12, no. 1: 41–53.

Gilman, Sander. 1994. *Disease and Representation: Images of Illness from Madness to AIDS*. Ithaca: Cornell Univ. Press.

Gilroy, Paul. 1993. *The Black Atlantic: Modernity and Double Consciousness*. London: Verso.

Ging, Debbie. 2002. "Screening the Green: Cinema under the Celtic Tiger." In *Reinventing Ireland: Culture, Society, and the Global Economy*, edited by Peadar Kirby, Luke Gibbons, and Michael Cronin, 177–95. London: Pluto.

———. 2008. "Goldfish Memories? On Seeing and Hearing Marginalised Identities in Contemporary Irish Cinema." In *Facing the Other: Interdisciplinary Studies on Race, Gender, and Social Justice in Ireland*, edited by Borbála Faragó and Moynagh Sullivan, 182–203. Newcastle: Cambridge Scholars.

Ging, Debbie, and Jackie Malcolm. 2004. "Interculturalism and Multiculturalism in Ireland: Textual Strategies at Work in the Media Landscape." In *Resituating Culture*, edited by Gavan Titley, 125–35. Strasbourg: Council of Europe Publishing.

Gleeson, David T. 2010. "'To Live and Die [for] Dixie': Irish Civilians and the Confederate States of America." *Irish Studies Review* 18, no. 2: 139–53.

Goldberg, David Theo. 1997. *Racial Subjects: Writing on Race in America*. New York: Routledge.

Grattan, Thomas Colley. 1859. *Civilized America*. Vol. 2. Carlisle, MA: Applewood.

Gray, Breda. 2003. "Global Modernities and the Gendered Epic of the 'Irish Empire.'" In *Uprootings/Regroundings: Questions of Home and Migration*, edited by Sara Ahmed, Claudia Castañeda, Anne-Marie Fortier, and Mimi Sheller, 157–78. Oxford: Berg.

Grene, Nicholas. 2000. *The Politics of Irish Drama: Plays in Context from Boucicault to Friel*. Cambridge: Cambridge Univ. Press.

Hansson, Heidi. 2005. "From Reformer to Sufferer: The Returning Exile in Rosa Mulholland's Fiction." In *Re-mapping Exile: Realities and*

Metaphors in Irish Literature and History, edited by Michael Boss, Irene Gilsenan Nordin, and Britta Olinder, 89–106. Aarhus: Aarhus Univ. Press.

Haraway, Donna. 1997. *Modest_Witness@Second_Millenium.FemaleMan ©_Meets_OncoMouseTM: Feminism and Technoscience.* New York: Routledge.

Harper, Phillip Brian. 1996. *Are We Not Men? Masculine Anxiety and the Problem of African-American Identity.* New York: Oxford Univ. Press.

Harte, Liam. 2006. "Variations of the Returned Yank." *Irish Times,* Apr. 8, "Weekend Review," 11.

Healy, Alison. 2009. "Texan Backpackers Offered Free Trip from Hotel Group." *Irish Times,* July 10. http://www.irishtimes.com/newspaper /ireland/2009/0710/1224250387958.html.

"Heart of Nation Is Still Booming." 2007. *Sunday Independent,* July 1, 28.

Hogan, Senan. 2008. "O Cuiv Calls for 250,000 Irish Speakers to Save Language." *Irish Independent,* Apr. 4. http://www.independent.ie /national-news/o-cuiv-calls-for-250000-irish-speakers-to-save-language -1337266.html.

hooks, bell. 1994. *Outlaw Culture: Resisting Representations.* Abingdon: Routledge.

———. 1999. *Black Looks: Race and Representation.* Boston: South End.

Howard, Aideen. 1997. "Recurring Modes of Male Representation: The Lads in Irish Theatre." *Theatre Forum* 1, no. 1. http://www.ucd.ie /irthfrm/firstiss.htm#ahoward.

Hutcheon, Linda. 1991. *The Politics of Postmodernism.* Florence, KY: Routledge.

———. 1994. *Irony's Edge: The Theory and Politics of Irony.* Florence, KY: Routledge.

———. 2000. *A Theory of Parody.* Urbana: Univ. of Illinois of Press.

Hutchison, Coleman. 2007. "On the Move Again: Tracking the 'Exploits, Adventures, and Travels of Madame Loreta Janeta Velazquez.'" *Comparative American Studies* 5, no. 4: 423–40.

Ibrahim, Habiba. 2007. "Canary in a Coal Mine: Performing Biracial Difference in *Caucasia*." *LIT: Literature, Interpretation, Theory* 18, no. 2: 155–72.

Ignatiev, Noel. 1995. *How the Irish Became White.* New York: Routledge.

———. 2006. "Gangs of New York." In *Re-imagining Ireland,* edited by Andrew Higgins Wyndham, 79–81. Charlottesville: Univ. Press of Press.

In the Name of the Fada. 2008. Directed by Pat Comer. RTÉ One. Six episodes. Mar. 13–Apr. 17.

"Ireland and America—Our Two Republics." 2008. Address by An Taoiseach, Mr. Bertie Ahern, TD, to a Joint Meeting of the United States Congress, Washington, DC, Apr. 30. http://www.taoiseach.gov.ie/index .asp?locID=582&docID= 3867.

"Ireland Ranked Second Wealthiest, According to Bank of Ireland's 'Wealth of the Nation' Report." 2006. Bank of Ireland press release, July 10. http://applications.boi.com/updates/Article?PR_ID=1388.

"Irish Asylum Statistics: Statistics Report for 2005." 2005. Irish Refugee Council. June 7. http://www.irishrefugeecouncil.ie/stats.html.

"Irish Lobby for Immigration Reform: A Voice for Change." N.d. http:// www.irishlobbyusa.org/.

Jacobson, Matthew Frye. 2006. *Roots Too: Ethnic Revival in Post–Civil Rights America.* Cambridge, MA: Harvard Univ. Press, 2006.

Jen, Gish. 1996. "An Ethnic Trump." *New York Times Magazine,* July 7. http://query.nytimes.com/gst/fullpage.html?res=9807E2D91039F934 A35754C0A960958260.

Jensen, Richard. 2002. "'No Irish Need Apply': A Myth of Victimization." *Journal of Social History* 36, no. 2: 405–29.

Johnson, James Weldon. 1995. *The Autobiography of an Ex-Colored Man.* New York: Dover.

Joyce, James. 1914. *Dubliners.* London: Penguin.

———. 1922. *Ulysses.* Harmondsworth, Penguin.

Kaufman, Will. 2006. *The Civil War in American Culture.* Edinburgh: Edinburgh Univ. Press.

Kekic, Laza. 2004. "The World's Best Country." *Economist,* Nov. 7. http:// www.economist.com/theworldin/international/displayStory.cfm?story _id=3372495.

Kelleher, Margaret. 1997. *The Feminization of Famine: Expressions of the Inexpressible?* Cork: Cork Univ. Press.

Kelly, John. 1998. "Picture of Innocence." *Irish Times,* Jan. 2, 14.

Kennedy, Geraldine. 2009a. "The Changing Face of Migration." *Irish Times,* July 21, 17.

———. 2009b. "Death of Frank McCourt." *Irish Times,* July 21, 17.

Kenny, Kevin. 2003. "Diaspora and Comparison: The Global Irish as a Case Study." *Journal of American History* 90, no. 1: 134–62.

Kenny, Pádraig. 2009. "Éire's Rock, Australia." *Sunday Tribune,* Mar. 1, "Magazine," 10–13.

Kiberd, Declan. 1996. *Inventing Ireland: The Literature of the Modern Nation.* London: Vintage.

———. 2007. "Sites of Endless Ambiguity." *Irish Times,* May 5, "Weekend," 12.

King, Jason. 2003. "Ireland Abroad, Broadening Ireland: From Famine Migrants to Asylum-Applicants." In *Ireland Abroad: Politics and Professions in the Nineteenth Century,* edited by Oonagh Walsh, 202–14. Dublin: Four Courts Press.

———. 2005. "Interculturalism and Irish Theatre: The Portrayal of Immigrants on the Irish Stage." *Irish Review* 33: 23–39.

———. 2007a. "Beyond Ryanga: The Image of Africa in Contemporary Irish Theatre." In *Echoes Down the Corridor: Irish Theatre—Past, Present, and Future,* edited by Patrick Lonergan and Riana O'Dwyer, 153–67. Dublin: Carysfort Press.

———. 2007b. "Remembering and Forgetting Diaspora: Immigrant Voices and Irish Historical Memories of Migration." In *Rethinking Diasporas: Hidden Narratives and Imagined Borders,* edited by Aoileann Ní Éigeartaigh, Kevin Howard, and David Getty, 61–71. Newcastle: Cambridge Scholars.

———. 2009. "Irish Multicultural Fiction: Metaphors of Miscegenation and Interracial Romance." In *Affecting Irishness: Negotiating Cultural Identity Within and Beyond the Nation,* edited by James P. Byrne, Padraig Kirwan, and Michael O'Sullivan, 159–77. Bern: Peter Lang.

Koziski, Stephanie. 1984. "The Standup Comedian as Anthropologist: Intentional Culture Critic." *Journal of Popular Culture* 18, no. 2: 57–76.

Kuti, Elizabeth. 2006. *The Sugar Wife.* London: Nick Hern.

Lacey, Colin. 1997. "Back Home with Pierce Brosnan." *Irish America* (May–June): 24–29.

Lacey, Hester. 2000. "Play the Hurdy Gurdy Man." *Independent,* Feb. 13, "Features," 3.

Lanters, José. 2005. "'Cobwebs on Your Walls': The State of the Debate about Globalisation & Irish Drama." In *Global Ireland: Irish Literatures for the New Millennium,* edited by Ondrej Pilny and Clare Wallace, 33–44. Prague: Litteraria Pragensia.

Larsen, Nella. 1928 and 1929. *Quicksand and Passing.* London: Serpent's Tail.

The Late Late Show. 2005. RTÉ One, Sept. 16. http://www.rte.ie/tv/late late/20050916.html.

Lee, Rachel. 2003. "'Where's My Parade?': On Asian-American Diva-Nation." *Scholar and Feminist Online* 2, no. 1. http://www.barnard .edu/sfonline/ps/lee2.htm.

Lentin, Ronit. 2002. "Anti-racist Responses to the Racialisation of Irishness: Disavowed Multiculturalism and Its Discontents." In *Racism and Anti-racism in Ireland,* edited by Ronit Lentin and Robbie McVeigh, 226–38. Belfast: Beyond the Pale.

———. 2003. "Pregnant Silence: (En)gendering Ireland's Asylum Space." *Patterns of Prejudice* 37, no. 3: 301–22.

———. 2007. "Illegal in Ireland, Irish Illegals: Diaspora Nation as Racial State." *Irish Political Studies* 22, no. 4: 433–53.

Limon, John. 2000. *Stand-up Comedy in Theory; or, Abjection in America.* Durham, NC: Duke Univ. Press.

Linehan, Hugh. 1998. "Fathers, Daughters, Nephews—and Orphans." *Irish Times,* July 17, 13.

Lipsitz, George. 1994. *Dangerous Crossroads: Popular Music, Postmodernism, and the Politics of Place.* London: Verso.

Llewellyn-Jones, Margaret. 2002. *Contemporary Irish Drama and Cultural Identity.* Bristol: Intellect.

Lloyd, David. 1999. *Ireland after History.* Cork: Cork Univ. Press.

Lonergan, Patrick. 2005. "Review of 'The Cambria' by Donal O'Kelly." *Irish Theatre Magazine* 23: 61–63.

———. 2009. *Theatre and Globalization: Irish Drama in the Celtic Tiger Era.* Basingstoke: Palgrave Macmillan.

Longley, Edna, and Declan Kiberd. 2001. *Multi-culturalism: The View from the Two Irelands.* Cork: Cork Univ. Press.

Looby, Claire. 2008. "Hacking to a Happy Ending." Review of *Whose Life Is It Anyway?,* by Sinéad Moriarty. *Irish Times,* Aug. 16, "Weekend Review," 10.

Lott, Eric. 1995. *Love and Theft: Blackface Minstrelsy and the American Working Class.* Oxford: Oxford Univ. Press.

Loyal, Steve. 2003. "Welcome to the Celtic Tiger: Racism, Immigration, and the State." In *End of Irish History?: Critical Approaches to the Celtic Tiger,* edited by Colin Coulter, 74–94. Manchester: Manchester Univ. Press, 2003.

Luibhéid, Eithne. 2004. "Childbearing Against the state? Asylum Seeker Women in the Irish Republic." *Women's Studies International Forum* 27: 334–49.

Lynch, Brian. 2005. Introduction to *Star of the Sea.* London: Paperview.

———. 2007. "Joe O'Connor's American Gothic." *Irish Independent,* Apr. 28, "Review," 18.

Lynch, Donal. 2007. "P.P.S. Please Remember to Find More Irish Actors Next Time . . ." *Sunday Independent,* Dec. 23, "Living," 13.

Mac Cormaic, Ruadhán. 2007a. "Finding a Creative Voice to Break the Stereotypes of Victimhood." *Irish Times,* May 23, 15.

———. 2007b. "Signs of New Vitality in How Film and Drama Treat Immigrants." *Irish Times,* May 23, 15.

MacKinnon, Kenneth. 1992. *The Politics of Popular Representation: Reagan, Thatcher, AIDS, and the Movies.* Rutherford, NJ: Fairleigh Dickinson Univ. Press.

Malouf, Michael. 2006. "Feeling Éire(y): On Irish-Caribbean Popular Culture." In *The Irish in Us: Irishness, Performativity, and Popular Culture,* edited by Diane Negra, 318–53. Durham, NC: Duke Univ. Press.

Marc, David. 2002. *Comic Visions: Television Comedy and American Culture.* Oxford: Blackwell.

Mathews, P. J. 2005. "Joseph O'Connor." In *The UCD Aesthetic: Celebrating 150 Years of UCD Writers,* edited by Anthony Roche, 256–64. Dublin: New Island Books.

McCarthy, Dermot. 2003. *Roddy Doyle: Raining on the Parade.* Dublin: Liffey Press.

McCarthy, Margaret. 2001. *My Eyes Only Look Out: Experiences of Irish People of Mixed Race Parentage.* Dingle: Mount Eagle.

McCourt, Frank. 1996. *Angela's Ashes.* London: Flamingo.

McGlynn, Mary. 2004. "Why Jimmy Wears a Suit: White, Black, and Working Class in *The Commitments.*" *Studies in the Novel* 36, no. 2: 232–50.

———. 2006. "Garth Brooks in Ireland; or, Play That Country Music, Whiteboys." In *The Irish in Us: Irishness, Performativity, and Popular*

Culture, edited by Diane Negra, 196–219. Durham, NC: Duke Univ. Press.

McGonigle, Lisa. 2005. "Rednecks and Southsiders Need Not Apply: Subalternity and Soul in Roddy Doyle's *The Commitments.*" *Irish Studies Review* 13, no. 2: 163–73.

McGreevy, Ronan. 2007. "Tourism Chief Hails St. Patrick as Visitors Top 50,000." *Irish Times,* Mar. 16, 6.

McInerney, Sarah. 2006. "Irish United in States of Anxiety." *Sunday Tribune,* Feb. 26, 9.

McKay, Claude. 1928. *Home to Harlem.* Lebanon, NH: Univ. Press of New England.

McKeon, Belinda. 2009. "Beyond the Soundtrack of the Boom." *Irish Times,* Mar. 14, "Weekend Review," 7.

McLoone, Martin. 2000. *Irish Film: The Emergence of a Contemporary Cinema.* London: BFI.

———. 2008. *Film, Media, and Popular Culture in Ireland: Cityscapes, Landscapes, Soundscapes.* Dublin: Irish Academic Press.

McWilliams, David. 2005. *The Pope's Children: Ireland's New Elite.* Dublin: Gill and Macmillan.

Meaney, Gerardine. 2007. "Race, Sex, and Nation." *Irish Review* 35, no. 1: 46–63.

Melia, Paul, and Senan Hogan. 2007. "Tiger Boom Has Boosted Quality of Life, Says ERSI [*sic*]." *Irish Independent,* June 29, 8.

Merriman, Victor. 2000. "Songs of Possible Worlds: National, Representation, and Citizenship in the Work of Calypso Productions." In *Theatre Stuff: Critical Essays on Contemporary Irish Theatre,* edited by Eamonn Jordan, 280–91. Dublin: Carysfort Press.

Miller, Kerby A. 2006. "Re-imagining Irish Revisionism." In *Re-imagining Ireland,* edited by Andrew Higgins Wyndham, 223–43. Charlottesville: Univ. Press of Virginia.

Mintz, Lawrence E. 1985. "Standup Comedy as Social and Cultural Mediation." *American Quarterly* 37, no. 1: 71–80.

———. 2005. "Stand-Up Comedy." In *Comedy: A Geographic and Historical Guide,* edited by Maurice Charney, 2:575–85. Westport, CT: Praeger.

Mitchell, Margaret. 1936. *Gone with the Wind.* London: Pan.

Monteith, Sharon. 1999. "America's Domestic Aliens: African Americans and the Issue of Citizenship in the Jefferson/Hemings Story in Fiction and Film." In *Alien Identities: Exploring Difference in Fiction and Film,* edited by Deborah Cartmell, I. Q. Hunter, Heidi Kaye, and Imelda Whelehan, 31–48. London: Pluto.

Monteith, Sharon, Jenny Newman, and Pat Wheeler. 2004. *Contemporary British and Irish Fiction: An Introduction Through Interviews.* London: Arnold.

Moriarty, Sinéad. 2008. *Whose Life Is It Anyway?* Dublin: Penguin Ireland.

Morrison, Angeline D. 2004. "Irish and White-ish: Mixed 'Race' Identity and the Scopic Regime of Whiteness." *Women's Studies International Forum* 27, no. 4: 385–96.

Morrison, Toni. 1987. *Beloved.* London: Picador.

Mulcahy, Orna. 2008. "The Long Goodbye." *Irish Times,* Oct. 18, "Magazine," 22–23.

Murphy, Denis. 2007. "'Undocumented' Irish in the US." Letter to the editor. *Irish Times,* Mar. 24, 17.

Murphy, Tom. 2000. *The House.* Introduced by Fintan O'Toole. London: Methuen.

Nash, Catherine. 1994. "Remapping the Body/Land: New Cartographies of Identity, Gender, and Landscape in Ireland." In *Writing Women and Space: Colonial and Postcolonial Geographies,* edited by Alison Blunt and Gillian Rose, 227–50. New York: Guilford.

Negra, Diane. 1996. "The Stakes of Whiteness." *Minnesota Review* 7: 109–14.

———. 2006a. "Irish, Innocence, and American Identity Politics Before and after September 11." In *The Irish in Us: Irishness, Performativity, and Popular Culture,* edited by Diane Negra, 354–72. Durham, NC: Duke Univ. Press.

———. 2006b. "The Irish in Us: Irishness, Performativity, and Popular Culture." In *The Irish in Us: Irishness, Performativity, and Popular Culture,* edited by Diane Negra, 1–19. Durham, NC: Duke Univ. Press.

Neill, Stephen. 2009. "Obama's Moneygall Connection." Letter to the editor. *Irish Times,* Jan. 27. http://www.irishtimes.com/newspaper/letters/2009/0127/1232923367413.html.

The Nephew. 1998. Directed by Eugene Brady. Irish Dreamtime.

Newhall, Beth. 2005. "'Ebony Saint' or 'Demon Black'? Racial Stereotype in Jim Sheridan's *In America*." In *Film History and National Cinema,* edited by John Hill and Kevin Rockett, 143–53. Dublin: Four Courts Press.

Nishime, LeiLani. 2008. "The Matrix Trilogy, Keanu Reeves, and Multiraciality at the End of Time." In *Mixed Race Hollywood,* edited by Mary Beltrán and Camilla Fojas, 290–312. New York: New York Univ. Press.

Noble, Janet. 1990. *Away Alone.* New York: Samuel French.

Noone, Ronan. 2003. *The Lepers of Baile Baiste.* New York: Samuel French.

———. 2006. *The Blowin of Baile Gall.* New York: Dramatists Play Service.

———. 2007. "Being Afraid to Breathe." *Princeton University Library Chronicle* 68, nos. 1–2: 614–19.

O'Brien, Breda. 2007. "Integration That Unravels Like a Garda's Turban." *Irish Times,* Aug. 25, 14.

O'Connor, Áine. 1996. *Leading Hollywood: Gabriel Byrne, Liam Neeson, Aidan Quinn, Stephen Rea, Patrick Bergin, Pierce Brosnan in Conversation with Áine O'Connor.* Dublin: Wolfhound Press.

O'Connor, Joseph. 1991a. *Cowboys and Indians.* London: Flamingo.

———. 1991b. *True Believers.* London: Vintage.

———. 1993a. "Four Green Fields." In *Ireland in Exile: Irish Writers Abroad,* edited by Dermot Bolger, 115–51. Dublin: New Island.

———. 1993b. Introduction to *Ireland in Exile: Irish Writers Abroad,* edited by Dermot Bolger, 11–18. Dublin: New Island Books.

———. 1994a. *Desperadoes.* London: Flamingo.

———. 1994b. *The Secret World of the Irish Male.* London: Minerva.

———. 1995. *Red Roses and Petrol.* London: Methuen.

———. 1996. *Sweet Liberty: Travels in Irish America.* London: Picador.

———. 1998. *The Salesman.* London: Secker and Warburg.

———. 2000. *Inishowen.* London: Secker and Warburg.

———. 2002. *Star of the Sea.* London: Vintage.

———. 2005. "Two Little Clouds." In *New Dubliners,* edited by Oona Frawley, 1–17. Dublin: New Island Books.

———. 2006. "We Happen upon a Street-Statue of the Virgin Mary." *Sunday Independent,* Oct. 22. http://www.unison.ie/irish_independent/stories .php3?ca=42&si=1710581&issue_id=14796.

———. 2007a. Interview with Páraic Breathnach. On *The Eleventh Hour.* RTÉ Radio 1, May 30.

———. 2007b. Interview with Tom McGurk. On *Today with Tom McGurk.* RTÉ Radio 1, June 22.

———. 2007c. Interview with Ryan Tubridy. On *The Tubridy Show.* RTÉ Radio 1, Apr. 30.

———. 2007d. *Redemption Falls.* London: Harvill Secker.

———. 2010. *Ghost Light.* London: Harvill Secker.

O'Doherty, Ian. 2007. "Immigration Is Not All Black and White." *Irish Independent,* Sept. 1, "Review," 18.

O'Donnell, Katherine. 2007. "St. Patrick's Day Expulsions: Race and Homophobia in New York's Parade." In *Irish Postmodernisms and Popular Culture,* edited by Wanda Balzano, Anne Mulhall, and Moynagh Sullivan, 128–40. Basingstoke: Palgrave.

O'Dwyer, Davin. 2007. "How's Your Fada?" *Irish Times,* Aug. 25, "Magazine," 20–21.

O'Hanlon, Ray. 1998. *The New Irish Americans.* Dublin: Roberts Rinehart.

O'Hearn, Denis. 2000. "Globalization, 'New Tigers,' and the End of the Developmental State? The Case of the Celtic Tiger." *Politics and Society* 28, no. 1: 67–92.

O'Kelly, Donal. 1996. *Asylum! Asylum! New Plays from the Abbey Theatre, 1993–1995.* Edited and introduced by Christopher Fitz-Simon and Sanford Sternlicht. Syracuse, NY: Syracuse Univ. Press.

———. 1998. "Strangers in a Strange Land." *Irish Theatre Magazine* 1, no. 1: 10–13.

———. 2005. *"The Cambria": Frederick Douglass' Voyage to Ireland in 1845.* http://www.irishplayography.com.

———. 2009. "Donal O'Kelly in Conversation with Paul Murphy." In *The Dreaming Body: Contemporary Irish Theatre,* edited by Melissa Sihra and Paul Murphy, 199–204. Gerrard's Cross: Colin Smythe.

O'Leary, Philip. 2000. "Yank Outsiders: Irish Americans in Gaelic Fiction and Drama of the Irish Free State, 1922–1939." In *New Perspectives on the Irish Diaspora,* edited by Charles Fanning, 253–65. Carbondale: Southern Illinois Univ. Press.

Once. 2006. Dir. John Carney. Bord Scannán na hÉireann.

O'Neill, Eugene. 1960. *Ah, Wilderness! The Hairy Ape, All God's Chillun Got Wings.* Harmondsworth: Penguin, 1960.

O'Neill, Kevin. 2001. "The Star-Spangled Shamrock: Memory and Meaning in Irish America." In *History and Memory in Modern Ireland*, edited by Ian McBride, 118–38. Cambridge: Cambridge Univ. Press.

O'Neill, Peter D., and David Lloyd. 2009. "The Black and Green Atlantic: An Introduction." In *The Black and Green Atlantic: Cross-Currents of the African and Irish Diasporas*, edited by Peter D. O'Neill and David Lloyd, xv–xx. New York: Palgrave Macmillan.

Onkey, Lauren. 1999. "'A Melee and a Curtain': Black-Irish Relations in Ned Harrigan's *The Mulligan Guard Ball*.'" *Jouvert* 4, no. 1. http://english.chass.ncsu.edu/jouvert/v4i1/onkey.htm.

O'Toole, Fintan. 1990. "Don't Believe a Word: The Life and Death of Phil Lynott." In *A Mass for Jesse James: A Journey Through 1980's Ireland*. Dublin: Raven Arts.

———. 1994. *Black Hole, Green Card: The Disappearance of Ireland*. Dublin: New Island Books.

———. 2001. "Writing the Boom." *Irish Times,* Jan. 25, 12.

———. 2005. "Reviews." *Irish Times,* Mar. 26, "Features," 2.

———. 2006. "Notes from the Notice Box: An Introduction." In *Re-imagining Ireland*, edited by Andrew Higgins Wyndham, 1–15. Charlottesville: Univ. Press of Virginia.

———. 2009. "What the Moneygall Obama Song Really Says about the Irish." *Irish Times,* Jan. 24. http://www.irishtimes.com/newspaper/weekend/2009/0124/1232474677855.html.

Pabst, Naomi. 2003. "Blackness/Mixedness: Contestations over Crossed Signs." *Cultural Critique* 54: 178–212.

Palmer, Caitriona. 2006. "Fear of the Irish 9/11 Heroes." *Irish Independent,* Sept. 2, "Review," 8.

Perkins, Roger. 2007. "How Does a Nation of Emigrants Cope with Immigrants?" *Sunday Telegraph,* Sept. 23, sec. 7, 56.

Phelan, Andrew. 2008. "Abbey in Legal Fight over Its *Playboy* Run." *Evening Herald,* Dec. 22. http://www.herald.ie/national-news/city-news/abbey-in-legal-fight-over-its-playboy-run-1583074.html.

"Plane Wreck at Los Gatos (Deportee)." 2008. *Woody Guthrie: The Official Website,* Apr. 24. http://www.woodyguthrie.org/Lyrics/Plane_Wreck_At_Los_Gatos.htm.

"Population and Migration Estimates." 2004. Dublin: Central Statistics Office, Apr. http://www.cso.ie/statistics/documents/popmig.pdf.

"Population and Migration Estimates." 2008. Dublin: Central Statistics Office, Apr. http://www.cso.ie/releasespublications/documents/population/current/popmig.pdf.

"Population and Migration Estimates." 2010. Dublin: Central Statistics Office, Sept. http://www.cso.ie/eleasespublications/documents/population/current/popmig.pdf.

Pramaggiore, Maria. 2007. *Irish and African American Cinema: Identifying Others and Performing Identities, 1980–2000*. Albany: State Univ. of New York Press.

Questions and Answers. 2007. RTÉ One, Nov. 12. http://www.rte.ie/news/2007/1112/qanda.html.

Quinlan, Kieran. 2005. *Strange Kin: Ireland and the American South*. Baton Rouge: Louisiana State Univ. Press.

Raimon, Eve Allegra. 2004. *The "Tragic Mulatta" Revisited: Race and Nationalism in Nineteenth-Century American Fiction*. New Brunswick, NJ: Rutgers Univ. Press.

Rains, Stephanie. 2006. "Irish Roots: Genealogy and the Performance of Irishness." In *The Irish in Us: Irishness, Performativity, and Popular Culture,* edited by Diane Negra, 130–60. Durham, NC: Duke Univ. Press.

Ramazani, Jahan. 2001. *The Hybrid Muse: Postcolonial Poetry in English*. Chicago: Univ. of Chicago Press.

Reddy, Maureen T. 2007. "Reading and Writing Race in Ireland: Roddy Doyle and *Metro Eireann*." In *Irish Postmodernisms and Popular Culture,* edited by Wanda Balzano, Anne Mulhall, and Moynagh Sullivan, 15–26. Basingstoke: Palgrave.

"Remarks by Tánaiste Mary Harney at a Meeting of the American Bar Association." 2000. Law Society of Ireland, Blackhall Place, Dublin, July 21. http://www.entemp.ie/press/2000/210700.htm.

Rice, Alan J., and Martin Crawford. 1999. "Triumphant Exile: Frederick Douglass in Britain, 1845–1847." In *Liberating Sojourn: Frederick Douglass and Transatlantic Reform,* edited by Alan J. Rice and Martin Crawford, 1–27. Athens: Univ. of Georgia Press.

Richards, Shaun. 2007. "'To Me, Here Is More Like There': Irish Drama and Criticism in the 'Collision Culture.'" *Irish Studies Review* 15, no. 1: 1–15.

"The Richness of Change." 2008. Forum on Migration and Communications. http://www.fomacs.org/project_detail.php?id=51.

Roberts, Diane. 2007. "Loving That Briar Patch: Southern Literature and Politics." *Global South* 1, nos. 1–2: 127–34.

Robinson, Amy. 1996. "Forms of Appearance of Value: Homer Plessy and the Politics of Privacy." In *Performance and Cultural Politics*, edited by Elin Diamond, 237–61. London: Routledge.

Robinson, Mary. 1995. "Cherishing the Irish Diaspora: An Address to the Houses of the Oireachtas, 2 Feb. 1995." http://www.rootsweb.ancestry.com/~irlker/diaspora.html.

Rockett, Kevin, Luke Gibbons, and John Hill. 1987. *Cinema and Ireland*. London: Croon Helm.

Rodgers, Nini. 2007. *Ireland, Slavery, and Anti-Slavery, 1612–1865*. New York: Palgrave.

Roediger, David R. 2003. *Colored White: Transcending the Racial Past*. Berkeley and Los Angeles: Univ. of California Press.

Rolston, Bill, and Michael Shannon. 2002. *Encounters: How Racism Came to Ireland*. Belfast: Beyond the Pale.

"RTÉ Announces a Week of Special Programmes Looking Back over the Last 20 Years of Irish Life." 2006. RTÉ Press Release, May 16. http://www.rte.ie/about/pressreleases/2006/0516//20years.html.

Scally, Robert James. 1995. *The End of Hidden Ireland: Rebellion, Famine, and Emigration*. New York: Oxford Univ. Press.

"Schedule." 2008. TG4, May 18. http://www.tg4.ie/Bearla/Scei/scei.php?date=2008-04-02.

Schreiber, Mark. 2008. "Mirror Up to Tiger: Screening the Margins of Irish Society in the Films of Lenny Abrahamson and Mark O'Halloran." Paper presented at "Home and Elsewhere: The Spaces of Irish Writing," the conference of the International Association for the Study of Irish Literatures, University of Porto, Portugal, July 28–Aug. 1.

Senna, Danzy. 1998. *From Caucasia with Love*. London: Bloomsbury.

Sheridan, Jim. 2003. "Director's Commentary." *In America*. DVD. 20th Century Fox.

Sheridan, Jim, Naomi Sheridan, and Kirsten Sheridan. 2003. *In America: A Portrait of the Film*. Original screenplay. New York: Newmarket.

Shortall, Eithne. 2008. "Designer Costelloe Blasts Rose of Tralee Racists." *Sunday Times,* Aug. 17. http://www.timesonline.co.uk/tol/news/world/ireland/article4548056.ece.

Shouldice, Frank. 2005. "Changes in Ireland." *Irish America* (Oct.–Nov.): 47.

Singleton, Brian. 2001. "Strangers in the House: Reconfiguring the Borders of National and Cultural Identity in Contemporary Irish Theatre." *European Review* 9, no. 3: 293–303.

Smyth, Gerry. 1997. *The Novel and the Nation: Studies in the New Irish Fiction*. London: Pluto.

———. 2005. *Noisy Island: A Short History of Irish Popular Music*. Cork: Cork Univ. Press.

Sollors, Werner. 1986. *Beyond Ethnicity: Consent and Descent in American Culture*. New York: Oxford Univ. Press.

———. N.d. "Americans All: 'Of Plymouth Rock and Jamestown and Ellis Island'; or, Ethnic Literature and Some Redefinitions of 'America.'" Retrieved Feb. 13, 2009. http://www.nyupress.org/americansall /americansall3.html?$string.New York: New York Univ. Press Electronic Titles.

Spain, John. 2007. "The Storyteller." *Irish Independent*, Apr. 28, "Weekend," 6–11.

Spillane, Margaret. 2008. "Fiction in Review." *Yale Review* 96, no. 2: 145–51.

Stop You're Killing Me 2. 2007. RTÉ Two, Dec. 27. Recorded at the Shelbourne Hall, RDS, Dublin, Jan. 14, 2007.

Stott, Andrew. 2005. *Comedy*. New York: Routledge.

Sullivan, Moynagh. 2007. "Boyz to Men: Irish Boy Bands and Mothering the Nation." In *Irish Postmodernisms and Popular Culture*, edited by Wanda Balzano, Anne Mulhall, and Moynagh Sullivan, 184–96. Basingstoke: Palgrave Macmillan.

Sweeney, Fionnghuala. 2008. "Other People's History: Slavery, Refuge, and Irish Citizenship in Donal O'Kelly's 'The Cambria.'" *Slavery and Abolition* 29, no. 2: 279–91.

"Tangled Roots: A Project Exploring the Histories of Americans of Irish Heritage and Americans of African Heritage." Yale University. Gilder Lehrman Center for the Study of Abolition, Resistance and Slavery. http://www.yale.edu/glc/tangledroots/.

Taylor, Charlie. 2009. "New Work Permit Changes Begin." *Irish Times*, June 1. http://www.irishtimes.com/newspaper/breaking/2009/0601 /breaking7.html.

Taylor, Timothy D. 1998. "Living in a Postcolonial World: Class and Soul in *The Commitments.*" *Irish Review* 6, no. 3: 291–302.

This Is My Father. 1998. Directed by Paul Quinn. DVD. Cinema Club.

Thornburg, Aaron. 2008. "St. Patrick's Day Parade, Dublin 2007: 'City Fusion' and Sikhs; or, Whatever Happened to Our Irishness?" Paper presented at the American Conference for Irish Studies Southern Regional Conference, Savannah, GA, Mar. 6–8.

Tölölyan, Khachig. 1991. "The Nation-State and Its Others: In Lieu of a Preface." *Diaspora: A Journal of Transnational Studies* 1, no. 1: 3–7.

Tongues. 2008. Performed by Des Bishop. DVD. Peer Pressure.

Trotter, Mary. 2008. *Modern Irish Theatre.* Cambridge: Polity.

Tubridy Tonight. 2006. RTÉ One, Nov. 4.

Turner, Victor. 1982. *From Ritual to Theater: The Human Seriousness of Play.* New York: PAJ.

Vejvoda, Kathleen. 2007. "The Blood of an Irishwoman: Race and Gender in *The Nephew* and *In America.*" *Irish Studies Review* 15, no. 3: 365–76.

Wald, Gayle. 1998. "Soul's Revival: White Soul, Nostalgia, and the Culturally Constructed Past." In *Soul: Black Power, Politics, and Pleasure,* edited by Monique Guillory and Richard C. Green, 139–58. New York: New York Univ. Press, 1998.

Wall, Eamonn. 1999. *From the Sin-É Café to the Black Hills: Notes on the New Irish.* Madison: Univ. of Wisconsin Press.

Wartenberg, Thomas E. 1999. *Unlikely Couples: Movie Romance as Social Criticism.* Boulder, CO: Westview Press.

Waters, Maureen. 1984. *The Comic Irishman.* Albany: State Univ. of New York Press.

Watkins, S. Craig. 2006. *Hip Hop Matters: Politics, Pop Culture, and the Struggle for the Soul of a Movement.* Boston: Beacon.

Weitz, Eric. 2009. "Who's Laughing Now? Comic Currents for a New Irish Audience." In *Crossroads: Performance Studies and Irish Culture,* edited by Sara Brady and Fintan Walsh, 225–36. Basingstoke: Palgrave Macmillan.

"What Is Afri?" N.d. Afri: Action from Ireland. http://www.afri.ie/.

Whelan, Kevin. 2004. "The Green Atlantic: Radical Reciprocities Between Ireland and America in the Long Eighteenth Century." In *A New Imperial History: Culture, Identity, and Modernity in Britain and the*

Empire, 1660–1840, edited by Kathleen Wilson, 216–38. Cambridge: Cambridge Univ. Press, 2004.

White, Caramine. 2001. *Reading Roddy Doyle.* Syracuse, NY: Syracuse Univ. Press.

Williams, Linda. 2001. *Playing the Race Card: Melodramas of Black and White from Uncle Tom to O. J. Simpson.* Princeton, NJ: Princeton Univ. Press.

Williamson, Joel. 1980. *New People: Miscegenation and Mulattoes in the United States.* New York: Macmillan.

Wilson, Christopher. 1979. *Jokes: Form, Content, Use, and Function.* London: Academic.

Winter, Jessica. 2003. "The Innocence Mission: Starting over in New York City, an Irish Family Discovers All That You Can't Leave Behind." *Village Voice,* Nov. 26–Dec. 2. http://www.villagevoice.com/film/0348,winter,48928,20.html.

"Women Writers in the New Ireland: The Blog and Online Forum of Women Writers in Ireland." N.d. http://wwinc.wordpress.com/2007/06/14/hello-world/ (accessed July 21, 2009).

Zanger, Jules. 1966. "The 'Tragic Octoroon' in Pre–Civil War Fiction." *American Quarterly* 18, no. 1: 63–70.

Index

Sinéad Moynihan grew up in County Wicklow and was educated at the National University of Ireland, Galway, University College Cork, and the University of Nottingham. She is a lecturer in twentieth-century literature at the University of Exeter, United Kingdom.